P9-DTG-980

GREAT MOMENTS IN SCIENCE

GREAT MOMENTS IN SCIENCE

Experiments and Readers Theatre

Kendall Haven

LIBRARIES
U N L I M I T E D
A Member of the Greenwood Publishing Group

Westport, Connecticut • London

L.C.C. SOUTH CAMPUS LIBRARY

This book is dedicated to
those bright and inquisitive minds everywhere
who find real pleasure in asking themselves,
"I wonder what would happen if I . . ."
They are one of our greatest resources and treasures.

Copyright © 1996 Kendall Haven
All Rights Reserved
Printed in the United States of America

No part of this publication may be reproduced, stored in a retrieval system, or transmitted, in any form or by any means, electronic, mechanical, photocopying, recording, or otherwise, without the prior written permission of the publisher. An exception is made for individual library media specialists and teachers who may make copies of activity sheets for classroom use in a single school. Other portions of the book (up to 15 pages) may be copied for in-service programs or other educational programs in a single school. Performances may be videotaped for school or library purposes.

Libraries Unlimited
A member of Greenwood Publishing Group, Inc.
88 Post Road West,
Westport, CT 06881
www.lu.com

Production Editor: Tama Serfoss
Copy Editor: Carol Rossini
Indexer: Nancy Fulton
Layout and Interior Design: Kay Minnis

Q
180.55
.D57
H35
1996

Library of Congress Cataloging-in-Publication Data

Haven, Kendall F.
    Great moments in science : experiments and readers theatre /
Kendall Haven.
    xii, 227 p. 22x28 cm.
    Includes index.
    ISBN 1-56308-355-8
    1. Discoveries in science--History. 2. Science--History.
I. Title.
Q180.55.D57H35   1995
509--dc20   95-42545
                                                 CIP

P

In order to keep this title in print and available to the academic community, this edition was produced using digital reprint technology in a relatively short print run. This would not have been attainable using traditional methods. Although the cover has been changed from its original appearance, the text remains the same and all materials and methods used still conform to the highest book-making standards.

AUG 0 9 2007

Contents

Introduction

Science seems to evoke a strong personal reaction from every student. For some, that reaction is positive. Science seems creative, important, and challenging. It explains what they see in the world around them.

For many students, science is not such a positive experience. For them, science seems an unintelligible jumble of cryptic equations. It seems an endless list of rote memorization, a crushing series of mindless and boring repetitions. It appears a cold and impersonal world of unyielding dictates and seemingly arbitrary absolutes.

While a grain of truth lies buried at the core of each of these reactions, none conveys even a hint of the majesty and wonder of the world of science.

Recently, a re-energized trend has spread across the world of science teaching. Make science interesting. Make science fun. Make it real. Make it relevant. The response has been to infuse science classes with as many student experiments as possible, both to cut up the dry, rote book learning of classic science with hands-on activities and to demonstrate science concepts and make them real for students through active participation in the learning process.

It is certainly true that experiments make abstract concepts seem real, tangible, and much more interesting. Both research and teacher experience confirm this. But more can be done. Experiments demonstrate the application of a concept. However, experiments do not create context, perspective, and relevance for those concepts and theorems. Experiments alone cannot connect abstract concepts with the flow of human drama and history and with human science development.

Stories do that.

Stories, in their many forms, are the sparks that fire the imagination into eager, motivated learning. Stories are the anchors that keep science fact and information from drifting free and unattached in our minds, that lock them into an overall conceptual framework, and that give them relevance.

Turn students loose on a science experiment or research project after they have been armed with an effective story about the development and significance of that particular science, and you will have focused, enthusiastic, motivated learners. What they learn will be grounded in a context of relevant people and events. Isolated information is no longer abstract. Learning is more rapid and more usable. Both research and teacher experience confirm this.

This book combines these two powerful and effective tools for the teaching of science: stories to create context and relevance, and experiments to make it real and tangible. Both are presented in total "hands-on" format to make science interesting and immediate. The book, then, is a series of stories presented in readers theatre script format so that students may benefit from participation in the telling of the story as well as from its content. Each story is linked with hands-on student experiments to amplify, demonstrate, and clarify the story's science concepts.

I selected 12 moments in the development of Western science from the 50 science stories in the book *Marvels of Science: 50 Fascinating 5-Minute Reads* and have created readers theatre scripts for each. Following the scripts are step-by-step instructions to re-create, or at least simulate, the experiments the original scientists performed. Finally, I have included two sections at the end of each of the 12 stories and experiments designed as springboards to facilitate further student research on either the scientists or major topics. One of these is a brief bibliography of solid references. The other, called "Bridges to Books," supplies students with key words and concepts to act as pathways for entering a library's resources to continue the investigation of each set of scientists and concepts.

My selection of the scientists and stories for this book was based on a cumulative evaluation of three criteria: 1) Is the science and scientist important and relevant to classroom teaching? 2) Is this an interesting story and will it work well in readers theatre form? and 3) Are the related experiments affordable, do-able, and interesting for fourth- through ninth-grade students in a public school classroom? From those fulfilling these criteria, I selected the final dozen to include a wide mix of disciplines and achieve a representative gender balance. Each of the scientists represented here is a dynamic, fascinating individual who has significantly advanced our understanding of the natural world.

Readers Theatre Scripts

Readers theatre scripts are designed to be read aloud by students, using expressive language and phrasing. They are not designed to be play scripts, which are memorized and acted out by the performers. Readers may want to practice reading the scripts so that they can do so smoothly and with characterization and emotion, but they shouldn't attempt to memorize their lines.

Each readers theatre script provides four to six roles. Directorial suggestions on how best to deliver many of the lines are included in italics. However, once students are familiar with the roles, they may choose to vary the method of their readings.

At the beginning of each script I have included a staging diagram that will place student readers so their script conversations will flow most naturally, and where audience focus can most easily be maintained on the lead characters. I find that standing helps student readers project and stay focused on the lead characters. But certainly there are no firm rules against having them sit on stools or even chairs.

Movements on stage add little to the readers theatre presentation and will almost always distract the audience's attention away from their visualization of the story scenes. Look at readers theatre as live radio drama, and let the actions take place in the imagination of your audience.

I also find that props and costumes are neither necessary nor, in most cases, beneficial to a readers theatre production. Readers often need both hands to keep track of their script, and handling props and costumes gets in their way and distracts them from their real mission: effective vocal delivery of their lines. Similarly, props and costumes tend to pull the audience out of the story being presented. If props seem to be called for by the action of the script, I recommend that students simply *pretend* to hold and use reports, sextants, pumps, and other equipment. This will keep everyone focused on the story rather than on the individual antics of the readers.

If you have period scientific equipment or costumes and feel student exposure to them would enhance your production, I recommend that students be allowed to see, touch, and handle those props before you begin the readers theatre.

Your students should act out the readers theatre script before they tackle the experiments. The story will create context and relevance for their learning during the experiment and give it increased meaning and significance.

Experiments

There are three main purposes for science experiments in the classroom. The first is to entertain and impress: a goal that should not be either ignored or overrated. I have heard teachers call this the "Wow!" or the "Yuck!" factor. In recent years, the "Yuck!" factor seems to be more sought after and laudable than the "Wow!" factor. Both, however, use an experiment to impress and entertain, which an experiment should do, but not exclusively.

The second goal of an experiment is to reinforce and extend learning, to demonstrate a science concept or principle, and to show its application. This is usually the purpose used to justify taking class time to conduct an experiment in the first place. Certainly any experiment worth its salt will be designed to have a high probability of achieving this goal.

The final goal is to demonstrate the actual process of conducting scientific investigation. Every real experiment is a painstaking search for possible error; misinterpretation; and for factors, forces, or reactions that were not anticipated, controlled, and accounted for. Part of showing that changes in A cause changes in B is showing that nothing else is affecting B other than changes in A.

Science is, in part, a perpetual repetition of the questions, "What haven't I considered? What haven't I accounted for? What could have gone wrong?" Once students understand that these questions are not hindrances on the path of science but are really a cornerstone of that process, they are much more willing to incorporate them into their experiments.

A science experiment, like an intriguing Sherlock Holmes mystery case, is a search for clues about what is really going on and why the elements of an experiment act as they do. Each clue leads to a new design of the experiment to eliminate or control another unwanted factor. The end goal of an experiment is not to say, "I have seen that changes in A cause changes in B." Rather, it is to say, "My experiments have shown me that B is affected by many things, including these factors I have identified and tried to control: A, C, D, E, F, and G. After adjusting my experiment to control all other factors, I have seen that a change in A of amount *a* produces a change in B of amount *b*." That kind of understanding comes from a rigorous use of the scientific process, or from the perpetual search for why what's actually happening isn't what you originally thought was supposed to happen.

While straightforward and simple to direct and perform, the experiments in this book have been specifically constructed to allow students numerous opportunities to investigate the sources of error and misinterpretation that invariably creep into their work and to then revise the design, conduct, and materials of the experiment to improve their results. I am convinced this is a valuable and vital element in any science teaching.

Of course, all experiments should be supervised by the teacher, and safety guidelines and precautions should be addressed before any experiment is begun.

Above all, infuse your class's use of this material with joy and curiosity. There can be no greater tools for successful exploration of science. Also remember that these are not the only 12 scientists and concepts worthy of this type of treatment. Adapt, modify, augment, and improve these experiments. Create your own scripts and experiments for other researchers. Share them with colleagues. Remember always that science is a world of understanding and passion. Understanding comes from guided experimentation. Passion comes from stories.

I owe particular thanks for the successful completion of this work to Dr. Nelson Kellogg, Sonoma State University Hutchins School of Liberal Studies. He has become a valued friend and an invaluable guide to proven, practical information for many of the chosen experiments. This book would not exist without his generous help, guidance, and fertile imagination.

Enjoy and good luck!

Teetering at the Beginning of Knowledge

Archimedes' discovery of the lever principle in 259 B.C.

Scientific Background

Can you lift 1,000 pounds? No? Actually you can. Lifting isn't a matter of strength. It is a matter of understanding.

Today we might think of the problem of how to lift a 1,000-pound weight as an interesting scientific and engineering challenge. However, in the earliest days of scientific development, it would not have been considered a science problem at all. Early man studied stars as his first scientific endeavor. By 300 B.C. the study of geometry had been added as a second, legitimate scientific field, mostly because of the work of Euclid. Geometry consisted of a study of shapes and their relationships to each other. Science, however, was still very separate from engineering, agriculture, medicine, architecture, and daily life. No one tried to link science with engineering. No one either saw, or was looking for, the connection.

Then Archimedes sat on a hillside ignoring his teacher's lecture and watched four boys playing on the beach. In the mind of this brilliant man, suddenly the connection was made, and our world of science was able to advance.

Readers Theatre

Characters

Narrator

Archimedes. Archimedes is 26 years old. He's thoughtful, inquisitive, and serious. He's a student of Conon.

Conon. Conon is a famous teacher and scientist. At 42 years old, he's short-tempered and demanding.

Palomenes. Palomenes is a 19-year-old, good-natured man who loves to laugh. He is also a student of Conon, but he is not nearly as serious as Archimedes.

Child 1. Nine or 10 years old, playing on the beach.

Child 2. Nine or 10 years old, playing on the beach.

Sonyah. Archimedes' six-year-old niece.

Staging

Figure 1.1. Suggested placement of readers for *Teetering at the Beginning of Knowledge*.

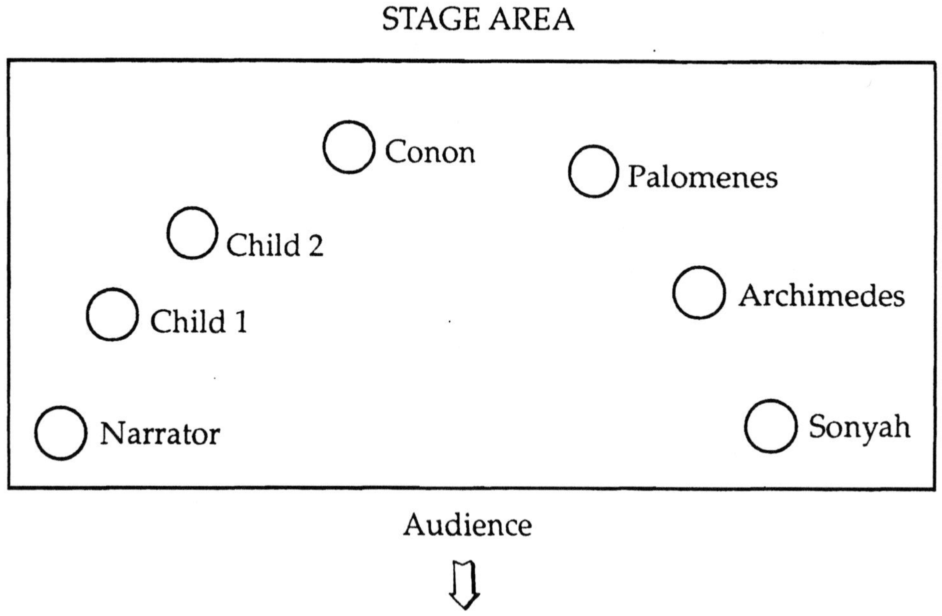

STAGE AREA

◯ Conon   ◯ Palomenes

◯ Child 2

◯ Child 1   ◯ Archimedes

◯ Narrator   ◯ Sonyah

Audience

From *Great Moments in Science: Experiments and Readers Theatre*. © 1996. Teacher Ideas Press. (800) 237-6124.

Teetering at the Beginning of Knowledge

NARRATOR:

Gentle waves rolled across the Mediterranean Sea and ran up a sandy Sicilian shore. A fierce summer sun poured heat onto the proud island nation of Sicily. Hiero II was king. Syracuse, the largest city, was a bustling center of commerce. By our reckoning, it was 259 B.C.

CONON:

Earth, the Sun, and the great multitude of stars beyond: these are the bodies that inhabit the universe.

NARRATOR:

Four men sat on a small knoll overlooking the sea and the south end of Syracuse Harbor. One of the men, Conon, was a famous science teacher. The other three were his students. All four squatted under scrub olive trees for shade.

PALOMENES: (*Complaining softly to Archimedes*)

It's too hot to study, Archimedes. Tell Conon it's a better day for a swim.

ARCHIMEDES: (*Startled*)

What? (*Louder and faster*) The stars all rotate across the sky in fixed relation . . . to . . . each . . .

CONON: (*Angry and sarcastic*)

Yes, Archimedes? Is there something you wanted to say?

ARCHIMEDES: (*Embarrassed*)

I . . . No. Sorry, Conon.

PALOMENES: (*Softly*)

You're supposed to say it's too hot to study.

CONON:

If any of you hope to lift yourselves up from ignorant fools, you must study *every* day—especially you, Palomenes.

ARCHIMEDES:

But the stars are all so far away. Besides, during the day I see no stars to study. (*Softer and just to Palomenes*) On a day like this day, astronomy is boring.

(*PALOMENES laughs. CONON raises his eyebrows and glares at his red-faced students.*)

From *Great Moments in Science: Experiments and Readers Theatre.* © 1996. Teacher Ideas Press. (800) 237-6124.

CONON:

Archimedes, you are a nephew of the King and are here to study the only two worthwhile sciences: astronomy and geometry.

ARCHIMEDES:

Yes, Conon.

NARRATOR:

But Archimedes couldn't concentrate on his teacher's words of astronomy. In the middle of a blisteringly hot day, it didn't seem real. As Archimedes wiped the sweat from his face, what *did* seem both real and fascinating was a group of four boys playing on the beach below.

CHILD 1: (*Excited*)

Look! A decking plank from some old ship to play with.

CHILD 2: (*Excited*)

Drag it over to that rock.

NARRATOR:

Laughing and dashing along the soft white beach, kicking up sprays of sand on each sharp turn, the boys dragged the board to a waist-high rock.

CHILD 1:

Balance it on the rock.

CHILD 2:

I'll get on. You three bounce me!

NARRATOR:

They slid their board across that rock until it exactly balanced, teetering gently up and down in the onshore breeze. As sea gulls circled overhead, one child straddled one end of the board.

CHILD 1:

Here we come. One, two, three. Go!

CHILD 2:

YAHOO!

NARRATOR:

The child's three friends jumped hard onto the other end. The lone child was tossed into the air, crashing down to the sand with a soft thud and a cheer.

CHILDREN:

YEAH!

From *Great Moments in Science: Experiments and Readers Theatre.* © 1996. Teacher Ideas Press. (800) 237-6124.

CHILD 1:
Now it's my turn. Slide the board way off-center. Then I'll lift all three of you.

NARRATOR:
The children slid the board along their balancing rock so that only one quarter of it remained on the short side. The longer, heavier side dropped to the sand with a dull thud. Giggling, three of the children climbed up the slick, inclined board to sit on the short, top end.

CHILD 2:
Wooah!

NARRATOR:
With the weight of three children, the plank's short end swung slowly down to the beach.

CHILD 1:
Here I come!

NARRATOR:
At the last moment the fourth child bounded onto the rising long end, crashing it back to the sand, and catapulting his three friends into the sky. All three squealed with glee. Two laughed so hard they fell off.

CHILDREN:
YEAH!

ARCHIMEDES: (*To himself*)
Fascinating! The first time it took three children to lift one. But now one easily lifts three.

NARRATOR:
The children saw an old, weather-beaten board to play with. Archimedes thought he saw Euclid's mathematics at work.

ARCHIMEDES: (*Thoughtfully to himself*)
But how? How does an old plank of wood give one child the strength to lift three? This seems far more real to me than stars I can't see. I must understand what just happened on the beach.

CONON:
Archimedes! Are my classes so boring that you can't pay attention? Maybe you'd rather play on the beach like a child!

PALOMENES: (*Laughing*)
Now you've done it, Archimedes.

From *Great Moments in Science: Experiments and Readers Theatre.* © 1996. Teacher Ideas Press. (800) 237-6124.

ARCHIMEDES: (*Embarrassed*)

I'm sorry, Conon.

PALOMENES: (*Still laughing*)

You were supposed to say it's too hot to study.

CONON: (*Sternly*)

Do not waste your time on the games of children, Archimedes. The King expects you to learn the worthwhile sciences.

ARCHIMEDES:

But Conon, isn't it worthwhile science to ask how one ordinary child is able to lift a weight greater than himself?

CONON:

No! Lifting is for servants, and has nothing to do with science. Now pay attention to your classes!

NARRATOR:

But Archimedes couldn't concentrate on astronomy.

ARCHIMEDES: (*To himself*)

I must understand how that board gave one child such strength.

NARRATOR:

Walking slowly home, head bowed, hands clasped behind his back, Archimedes was lost deep in thought.

ARCHIMEDES:

Euclid studied ratios and proportions. The answer lies there, somehow. But how do I find it?

NARRATOR:

Suddenly the eager student brightened.

ARCHIMEDES: (*Excited*)

I'll experiment! That's what Euclid did.

NARRATOR:

Archimedes rushed to the sprawling family home.

ARCHIMEDES:

But what can I use for my experiment?

From *Great Moments in Science: Experiments and Readers Theatre*. © 1996. Teacher Ideas Press. (800) 237-6124.

NARRATOR:
Archimedes rummaged frantically through the house until he reached the room of his six-year-old niece.

ARCHIMEDES:
Ah! Sonyah's play blocks will be perfect!

NARRATOR:
Archimedes clawed through Sonyah's wide box of blocks, gathering ones he liked in his lap, tossing the others over his shoulder onto the floor.

ARCHIMEDES:
Good one . . . Too small . . . Too big . . . Wrong shape . . . Perfect . . . Too long . . .

NARRATOR:
He now held five blocks in his hands—two small cubes and one larger, one rectangular block about the same size as all three cubes combined, and one triangular-shaped prism to act as the balancing point.

ARCHIMEDES:
And now to find my board to balance them on.

NARRATOR:
Behind the house he found a thin strip of wood about 15 inches long to act as his lever. Archimedes called his balancing board a "lever," from the Latin word meaning "to lift."

ARCHIMEDES: (*Excitedly*)
Now the experiment. And from the experiment will come understanding.

NARRATOR: (*In hushed, fascinated tones*)
He placed the prism on a table and carefully balanced his lever across it. His curling brown beard touched the table top as he picked up the two small cubes, one in each strong hand, and leaned close to watch.

SONYAH: (*Loudly*)
What are you doing playing with my blocks?

NARRATOR:
Surprised and embarrassed, Archimedes snapped straight up, knocking his lever to the floor.

ARCHIMEDES:
I'm not playing. This is a science experiment.

From *Great Moments in Science: Experiments and Readers Theatre.* © 1996. Teacher Ideas Press. (800) 237-6124.

SONYAH:
Looks like you're playing.

ARCHIMEDES:
When you play very carefully, it's an experiment.

SONYAH:
Can I play, too?

ARCHIMEDES:
I'm *not* playing. And, no, you're too young to help.

SONYAH: (*Growing angry*)
They're *my* blocks.

ARCHIMEDES: (*Sighing*)
All right, Sonyah. You can be my assistant.

SONYAH:
Yea! What are we playing?

ARCHIMEDES: (*Exploding in frustration*)
We're NOT playing! This is science. First pick up that piece of wood.

NARRATOR:
Again, Archimedes placed the middle of his lever on the point of his niece's triangular prism. It balanced. On each end of this board he placed one of the small cubes. The whole thing balanced like two children on a teeter-totter, rocking slightly up and down.

ARCHIMEDES: (*Thoughtfully*)
Now what does this teach me?

SONYAH: (*Hopefully*)
That this is a boring game so far?

NARRATOR:
Archimedes stared at his balancing cubes, thoughtfully stroking his beard.

ARCHIMEDES: (*Growing excited*)
It teaches me that equal weights pushing down on equal lengths of board balance each other. Good. What did the boys do next? Ah, yes. Three on one side; one on the other.

From *Great Moments in Science: Experiments and Readers Theatre.* © 1996. Teacher Ideas Press. (800) 237-6124.

NARRATOR:

Archimedes picked up the large cube to represent the weight of the extra two boys. He held it over one of the balanced cubes.

SONYAH: (*Grumbling*)

When are we going to play something fun?

ARCHIMEDES:

Shhh, Sonyah! This is an important experiment, and it *is* fun.

SONYAH: (*Whining*)

No, it's not.

NARRATOR:

Archimedes dropped the large cube. It crashed down onto the lever smashing that end to the table. The other end shot up. The small cube on it flew into the air. Archimedes' niece giggled.

SONYAH: (*Laughing*)

That was fun. Let's do that part again.

NARRATOR:

Archimedes ignored his niece and thoughtfully stroked his beard.

ARCHIMEDES:

What does *that* teach me? That when unequal weights push down on equal-length boards, the heavier weight goes down, and the lighter one rises.

NARRATOR:

Archimedes smiled and clapped his hands.

ARCHIMEDES:

Learning is such a wonderful thing! Now, I wonder if I could balance the big cube with just one of the small cubes. . . .

SONYAH:

Flip them into the air again. I like that part.

NARRATOR:

Archimedes held the large cube on one end of his lever and a small cube on the other. Slowly he slid the board across the point of his triangular block until the two sides exactly balanced. The end with the small cube was much longer than the end with the big cube.

SONYAH:

It's getting boring again.

From *Great Moments in Science: Experiments and Readers Theatre.* © 1996. Teacher Ideas Press. (800) 237-6124.

ARCHIMEDES:

Shhhh. This is an important part of our experiment.

SONYAH:

Doesn't *look* important.

NARRATOR:

Archimedes carefully measured the length of board sticking out on each side of the balance point.

ARCHIMEDES: (*Triumphantly*)

Ah, ha! The side with the small weight is exactly twice as long as the side with the big weight.

NARRATOR:

He compared the two weights. The big cube was exactly twice as heavy as the small one.

ARCHIMEDES:

What does *this* teach me?

NARRATOR:

Archimedes thought for a long moment.

ARCHIMEDES: (*In excited understanding*)

To balance twice the weight, I need only half as much board. And half the weight needs twice as much board. I wonder . . .

NARRATOR:

He stacked one small cube, the big cube, and the large rectangular block all on one side. The other side held only one of the small cubes. Archimedes guessed that the heavy side weighed five times that of the one small cube. Now he tried to balance the board again.

ARCHIMEDES:

Ha! It balances!

NARRATOR:

The stacked heavy side was almost on top of Archimedes' balance point. The end with one small cube seemed to hang way out in space, wobbling up and down. It reminded Archimedes of the three boys sitting on the short end of their board at the beach.

SONYAH: (*Giggling*)

I like this one. It looks funny.

From *Great Moments in Science: Experiments and Readers Theatre.* © 1996. Teacher Ideas Press. (800) 237-6124.

NARRATOR:

Archimedes measured the length of each side of his board. The side with the one small cube was five times as long as the side with the stacked weights.

ARCHIMEDES:

To balance one-fifth the weight, I need five times as much board.

NARRATOR:

Like a beacon slicing through the foggy mist of his mind, Archimedes saw one of Euclid's proportions.

ARCHIMEDES:

So that's how the board made one child so strong! Simple proportions.

NARRATOR:

The force pushing down on one side was proportional to the lengths of board on each side of the balance point. One child could lift a stone 40 times his or her own weight if he or she understood proportions. All that was needed was a long board with the child's side 40 times as long as the side wedged under the stone.

ARCHIMEDES:

That's it! I understand!

SONYAH: (*Sadly shaking head*)

Experiments aren't nearly as much fun as play.

ARCHIMEDES: (*Laughing*)

You might be right, Sonyah. But think how much more we learn from experiments. In one afternoon I have learned how a lever lets people lift heavy weights, and that Euclid's mathematics really describe exactly how our everyday world works.

SONYAH:

Maybe tomorrow you can learn something more fun.

NARRATOR:

No human had tried to use science and mathematics to understand a simple physical occurrence in the world before. But curious Archimedes did, thereby launching us on the path of scientific discovery. Springing from Archimedes' work were the many fields of applied science and engineering. But that is another story.

From *Great Moments in Science: Experiments and Readers Theatre.* © 1996. Teacher Ideas Press. (800) 237-6124.

Related Experiments

Here is a series of simple experiments you can use to recreate the steps that led Archimedes to his discoveries. These experiments will help you understand both the work of Archimedes and the scientific concepts involved.

Necessary Equipment

For the first two experiments, each small group will need:

- A small (8- to 12-inch), light board to use as a lever

- Some sturdy, pointed object to use as a fulcrum

- A series of small, uniform weights

- Two good rulers for measuring distances

Each group should gather their own supplies, as the different choices each group makes will affect the accuracy of results and the ease with which these experiments are performed. Groups may then compare to see what works well and what doesn't.

Wooden paint stirring sticks (free at most paint stores) will do nicely for levers; Legos® building blocks or small batteries (9 volt, AA, AAA, or AAAA) work well as weights. Each group should evaluate their choice of materials.

For the class as a whole:

- One board for a lever. It should be between a 2 x 6 and a 2 x 10 and 8 to 12 feet long. Preferably, get a *very* imperfect board with lots of knots, gouges, and poorly milled ends. But avoid warped boards.

- A dozen large cinder blocks

- Several rounded, large metal angle irons

- One tape measure (at least as long as your board)

- One level (optional)

- About 30 Legos®, or similar building blocks

From *Great Moments in Science: Experiments and Readers Theatre.* © 1996. Teacher Ideas Press. (800) 237-6124.

➤ *Getting a Balanced View of Levers* (Done in small groups)

What You'll Investigate: In this experiment you will explore how a lever works and how it creates mechanical advantage.

The Setup: In small groups balance your board over your fulcrum on a sturdy table. Think of a teeter-totter if you're having trouble envisioning what a lever looks like. Have a supply of equal-sized weights handy.

What to Do: The following steps will answer the question: If you change the weight on either end of a lever, how must the position of the fulcrum change in order to keep the lever balanced?

1. Place equal weights on each end of your lever. Slowly slide the board over your fulcrum until it exactly balances (rests horizontally).

2. Carefully measure the length of the beam on each side of the fulcrum. First, as a group, agree on where you'll measure from and to: from the fulcrum to the near edge of your weight? to the middle of the weight? to the end of the lever? Are both weights right at the end of the beam? For best results, you'll probably want to measure to the middle of each weight. Can you think of why this position gives you the best measurement of where that weight pushes down on your beam?

   How accurately can you make this measurement? to $\frac{1}{8}$ of an inch? to $\frac{1}{64}$ of an inch? Why are more accurate measurements better?

3. On a piece of paper create a two-column chart. On the first line in the first column enter the ratio of the weights you placed on each end of your beam for this first test. Since you place an equal weight on each end, write "1 to 1," or "1:1."

   In the second column enter the ratio of the length of the balance beam on each side of the fulcrum. For example, "$3\frac{5}{8}$ inches to $5\frac{1}{4}$ inches." If both sides were the same length for this first test, you could write "$4\frac{1}{2}$ to $4\frac{1}{2}$," or simply "1:1," since they are the same. Be careful to keep the measurements in this column for the left and right sides of your lever in the same order as those in the first column.

4. Now add a second weight to one end of the lever and re-balance. Again carefully measure the length on each arm of the lever and record the ratios of both weights and lengths on the second line of your chart.

   Add a third weight to the heavy end and repeat the test. Now add a fourth weight.

   Keep adding weights, re-balancing, measuring, and recording your measurements until you have used all of your weights, or until one side of the lever is so short you can no longer make accurate measurements.

5. Finally, make a graph that shows the data in your chart. On one axis list the ratio of weights. On the other list the ratio of lengths of the lever arms. Plot a point on this graph for each individual test. Your teacher can help if you are unfamiliar with creating graphs. Now connect the data points with a line.

From *Great Moments in Science: Experiments and Readers Theatre.* © 1996. Teacher Ideas Press. (800) 237-6124.

What's Going On?—Sources of Error: Did the length ratios on your chart come out in neat whole number ratios like the weight ratios? Is the line connecting the points on your graph perfectly straight? Probably not. Most likely your measurements were close to whole number ratios, but were off a little bit. Most likely the line on your graph is a little crooked.

So what's going on? How could errors sneak into such a simple experiment? See how many potential sources of error you can find. Compare your results with those of other groups.

Some likely errors include:

- Not measuring to exactly the center of the total weight every time. This error probably increases as you pile more and more weights on the heavy side of your lever.

- Errors in the weights. Were all your weights exactly the same weight? If not, they will create a similar error in your length measurement.

- Flaws in the board used as a lever. One end may be a little thicker and heavier than the other. This is like placing an extra weight on one end—a weight you didn't include in your calculations.

- Errors in your actual length measurement. Because all distances are short in this experiment, an error of little more than the width of a pencil line could create a noticeable error in your results.

Now try to find ways to reduce the problems that might have created errors in your results. See if the weights, beams, or procedures other groups used worked better than yours. Redo these tests with your improved setup and see if your results are better.

What to Observe: Look for a pattern to emerge on your chart and graph. You should see a regular relationship between weight (force) and length of the lever arm. Look at the way these two values change. Does it look like simple ratios?

Notice how a small weight, or force, can balance a large weight, or force, if it has a longer lever to push down on. On a teeter-totter could you balance five people your same size? Where would you have to place them?

Questions to Ask Yourself: Does there seem to be a simple relationship between the amount of weight you place on each side of a lever and the length of beam each needs to stay balanced with the other side? Could you guess about where to place the fulcrum so a very heavy object would balance with a much lighter one?

If you wanted to balance a 50-pound weight and a 5-pound weight on a 12-foot board, could you figure out exactly where to place the fulcrum so the two sides would balance? Would your chart and graph help?

Could you create a simple equation that shows the relationship between weight and length on each side of a lever? Would that equation look like a ratio?

From *Great Moments in Science: Experiments and Readers Theatre.* © 1996. Teacher Ideas Press. (800) 237-6124.

➤ *How Does a Lever Work?* (Done in small groups)

What You'll Investigate: Levers create mechanical advantage and let us lift objects much heavier than we could lift without the lever. We've just learned that if you place the fulcrum closer to a heavy object, you won't have to push down nearly as hard on the other end of the lever to lift that weight. (A small force with a long lever arm balances a large force with a short lever arm.) Does this mean you can do less *work* as you raise the weight by moving the fulcrum closer and closer to the heavy weight? What determines how much *work* you do when you lift a heavy object?

The Setup: In small groups place a weight on one end of your lever with the fulcrum near the middle.

What to Do: So far you have looked at the relation between weight, or force, and length of lever arm. Now we add in the concept of work, or getting something done. You will look at how levers make work seem easier first qualitatively (by deciding when it feels easier), and then with some quantitative measurements.

But first, a quick review of "work." Work is the application of a force over some distance to accomplish something (force x distance = work). If you carried a 500-pound rock 1 step, you would accomplish the same amount of work as if you carried a 1-pound rock for 500 steps. You might choose to carry the 1-pound weight because it seems easier, but you have to carry it much farther to accomplish the same amount of work. A lever gives us this same choice. Here's what you'll do.

1. Place a weight near one end of your lever. Place the fulcrum near the empty end of the beam so that the length of the lever on that side is exactly 1 inch, and so that the distance from fulcrum to weight is exactly 7 inches. Slowly push the empty end of the lever down to the table and try to "feel" how hard the weight is to lift.

2. Now slide the fulcrum and weight so that the fulcrum is 2 inches from the empty end of your lever and so that the weight is still 7 inches from the fulcrum. Again slowly push the empty end of the lever down to the table and raise the weight. Did it feel easier? Did it feel twice as easy? Because the lever arm on your side was twice as long the second time, you only had to push down half as hard to lift the weight.

3. Slide the weight so that it is only 1 inch from the fulcrum and the empty side of the lever arm is 7 inches long. Again push down on the empty side and lift the weight. Was it almost effortless this time? Does that mean you did less work?

4. Now add in some measurement. Repeat each of the length combinations in 1, 2, and 3 above. But this time have two other students in the group hold a ruler vertically next to each end of your lever. Initially the weight will be near the table. Have a student record its height. Have the student at your end record the height of your end of the lever. Now push your end down to the table. Record the height of both the weight and of your end of the lever.

Compare the distance moved by each end of your lever with the length of its lever arm.

From *Great Moments in Science: Experiments and Readers Theatre.* © 1996. Teacher Ideas Press. (800) 237-6124.

What's Going On?—Sources of Error: There are few possible sources of error in this experiment. There are, however, many ways in which the experiment is difficult to measure. Weights tend to roll and fall as the beam is raised. It is often harder to measure vertical distance. See how many other minor errors or measurement problems you can find and eliminate.

What to Observe: In the first setup, you had to apply a relatively great force over a short vertical distance to lift the weight over a much larger distance. You accomplished a lot of work. In the last setup, you applied a very small force over a much greater distance, but only lifted the weight a very short distance. You accomplished more work the first time. That is, you lifted the weight higher.

To accomplish the same amount of work the last time (lift the weight the same total distance), you would have had to lift it seven times! You would then have accomplished the same amount of work. It would have still *felt* easier, even though it would have taken longer, because you would have had to apply only a small force at any given time.

This principle is called "conservation of energy." Levers don't create energy, or reduce the amount of work you have to do. They allow you to accomplish that work in a variety of ways (a small force acting over a long distance, or a large force acting over a short distance) to make the work easier for you.

Questions to Ask Yourself: What is the difference between "work" and "force"?

If a weight is a force, what determines how much work that force can do?

If you want to lift a 1,000-pound weight 3 feet, it will take the same amount of work to lift it whether you muscle it straight up in your arms, whether you use a lever with five times the length on your end, or whether you use a lever with twenty times the length on your end. What's the advantage of the longer lever, then? How do levers let you do things you couldn't do otherwise?

► *The Big Picture (Done outside as a whole class activity)*

What You'll Investigate: Some of the errors that could have affected your results in the first two exercises resulted from the small size of your beam and weights. Now we'll repeat the experiment using a much longer board and bigger weights.

The Setup: The class should stand in a circle. Several students should place angle irons on the ground as a fulcrum, and then lift and place the board over this fulcrum. Divide the cinder blocks into two piles with two blocks near one end and 10 near the other. Remember that cinder blocks are heavy and rough and safety should be stressed at all times during this experiment.

What to Do: Repeat the steps in the first two experiments: "Getting a Balanced View of Levers," and "How Does a Lever Work?" See if the larger scale makes the experiments easier to do and makes your results more accurate.

What's Going On?—Sources of Error: Are your measurements better on this bigger scale? Are your errors smaller? Why or why not? See if you can find where errors still creep into your experiment.

From *Great Moments in Science: Experiments and Readers Theatre.* © 1996. Teacher Ideas Press. (800) 237-6124.

What to Observe: See if your results confirm the simple ratio relationship between length and force on a lever. Because the scale is larger, your measurements will most likely be better.

Questions to Ask Yourself: Do you understand how levers give you a mechanical advantage when you use them to lift? Do you see how you have to do the same amount of work to lift something, but levers allow you to "spread out" your effort by using a smaller force over a greater distance to get the same work done?

Do you see how the function of levers can be represented by simple mathematical ratios?

➤ *Let's Investigate the Beam (Done outside as a whole class activity)*

What You'll Investigate: In each of the last three experiments you have assumed that the board serving as the lever is perfectly uniform over its entire length. Let's see how true that is, and then see if the size of the beam itself can affect our results when we try to balance weights on it.

The Setup: The same outside setup as for the last experiment.

What to Do: The following steps will help you determine the effect the lever itself has on the experiments.

1. Find the exact balance point for the wood plank beam. The beam is balanced over the fulcrum when it lies still and is completely horizontal. Use a level if you want to find the exact balance point faster. Otherwise, eyeball it, until the whole class agrees that this 8- to 10-foot board is really horizontal.

2. One student should mark where the fulcrum touches the board.

3. Remove the board and carefully measure the length of each side of this balance beam. You should measure along both edges of the board and average these lengths as milling cuts may not be exact and the board's ends might not be square.

4. Replace the board over the fulcrum on its exact balance point. Now if you add a weight onto one end, that end should crash to the ground, right? Place 20 or 25 Legos® on one end. What happens? Why?

What's Going On?—Sources of Error: Why weren't the two sides exactly the same length? Could it be that your board isn't completely uniform over its whole length? Could that be one source of errors in the previous experiments?

When you placed a weight on one end of the board, why didn't it fall to the ground? What held the board up?

What to Observe: Small, unnoticed variations in any of the materials of an experiment can create significant errors in your results. This is why scientists must be so careful with each step and aspect of an experiment. It is also why experiments must be repeated with different pieces of equipment to make sure it's the scientific concept and not the specific equipment that's creating the results.

Also notice that the weight you added this time was very small compared to the overall weight of your board. This final test is designed to point out several additional sources of potential error you might not have considered. Tiny amounts of drag, or friction, resist any movement by the lever. Although this force is always there, it only shows up when the weight you place on your lever is small compared to the size and weight of the lever itself.

Questions to Ask Yourself: Can you think of ways to design a better balance beam, one with fewer possibilities for error, one that would be much more accurate? How would you test your new design to determine if it is better than the ones you have already used?

From *Great Moments in Science: Experiments and Readers Theatre.* © 1996. Teacher Ideas Press. (800) 237-6124.

Bridges to Books

This story deals with one aspect of our understanding of the physical world around us. You can learn much more about these concepts in your library. The following list gives you key words, concepts, and questions to begin your exploration in a school or public library.

Archimedes and **Euclid** were two giants of early Western science. What is Euclid most famous for? What are the fields of study he helped to found? Besides linking science and engineering and developing the principle of levers, what other contributions did Archimedes make to our knowledge? See what your library has on these two remarkable scientists.

Archimedes' work described in this script deals with **levers**. Can you find examples of how this **simple machine** is used today? Can you find descriptions of levers and of their mathematical properties in your library?

The engineering concepts associated with levers include **mechanical advantage, conservation of energy**, and **work**. Search your library using these as key words for information on how these concepts contribute to our modern world.

Archimedes also relied on the mathematical concept of **proportions**. Can you define a proportion? Have you used proportions in the past week? You probably have. Research proportions in your library and then observe how they enter into your normal daily life.

References for Further Reading

The following references deal with the major characters, concepts, and scientific processes in this chapter.

Allen, Pamela. *Mr. Archimedes.* Bath, NY: Lothrop, 1980.

Bendick, Jeanne. *Archimedes and the Door to Science.* New York: Franklin Watts, 1972.

Clagett, Marshall. *Great Science in Antiquity.* New York: Abeland-Schuman, 1965.

Dijkslerhuis, E. J. *Archimedes.* Princeton, NJ: Princeton University Press, 1987.

Gardner, Martin. *Archimedes, Mathematician and Inventor.* New York: Macmillan, 1965.

Harvey, Ted. *The Quest of Archimedes.* New York: Doubleday, 1972.

Hellman, Hal. *The Lever and the Pulley.* New York: Evans, 1971.

Ipsen, D. C. *Archimedes, Greatest Scientist of the Ancient World.* Hillside, NJ: Enslow, 1988.

Jonas, Arthur. *Archimedes and His Wonderful Discoveries.* Englewood Cliffs, NJ: Prentice-Hall, 1973.

Lafferty, Peter. *Archimedes.* New York: Bookwright, 1991.

Lampton, Christopher. *Seesaws, Nut Crackers, and Brooms.* Brookfield, CT: Millbrook Press, 1991.

Lexan, Joan. *Archimedes Takes a Bath.* New York: Thomas Y. Crowell, 1969.

Sellers, Mick. *Wheels, Pulleys, and Levers.* Boston: Gloucester Press, 1993.

Wade, Harlan. *The Lever.* New York: Raintree, 1977.

Consult your librarian for additional titles.

The Fall of Galileo

Galileo Galilei's discovery of the law of falling objects in 1598

Scientific Background

Hold a ball at eye level. What will happen if you let it go? It falls, right? We all know that. We also know that gravity is the force that pulls it down to earth. Mathematical equations let us calculate how fast the ball will travel as it falls. But for the thousands of years before those forces and equations were discovered, humankind wondered. Why do objects fall? How do they fall? How fast do they fall? Do heavier objects (a house, for example) fall faster than smaller objects (like a paper clip)? Does an object fall at the same speed everywhere? On top of Mt. Everest? Even on the moon?

Such questions puzzled scientists for centuries. Then Aristotle, the famed Greek mathematician and philosopher, said that heavy objects fall faster than light ones because their attraction to earth is greater.

For nearly two millenia everyone believed him. Do you?

In 1596 a young Italian mathematician, Galileo Galilei, began experimenting with pendulums. He watched them swing down faster and faster, slicing through the bottom of their arc and racing back up the other side, until after slowing to a stop, they began swinging back the other way.

Galileo watched until he realized pendulums didn't swing around a circle. They fell. Their chains and metal bars made them curve through an arc. But always they simply fell from the top of their arc to restart their motion. Over and over again they fell.

Heavier pendulums should swing back and forth faster, then. Right? Aristotle said heavier objects fell faster. So Galileo observed massive, heavy pendulums held up by thick metal beams and heavy chains. He watched tiny pendulums dangling from nearly invisible threads. He compared their motions.

Something was wrong. They all fell at the same speed. But Aristotle said heavier objects fall faster. All European scientists believed him. What Galileo saw didn't match what Aristotle said. Something was very wrong.

Readers Theatre

Characters

Narrator

Galileo Galilei. Twenty-five-year-old mathematics professor at the University of Pisa. Bold, confident, cocky.

Enricci. Sixteen-year-old student of Galileo, eager but cautious. Sponsored by the Church, as were most students. As many students do, he often whispers side comments to his fellow student, Felip.

Felip. Felip is a 16-year-old student of Galileo.

Ostillo Ricci. Ostillo is a traditional-thinking mathematics professor at the university, now in his mid-thirties. He is wary of challenging Church teachings and power and is skeptical of bold, revolutionary theories. His friend, Galileo, gives him great cause for concern.

Cardinal Bezanti. The cardinal is in his early fifties and is an established member of the Church hierarchy. He is loyal and conservative in his views.

Staging

Figure 2.1. Suggested placement of readers for *The Fall of Galileo*.

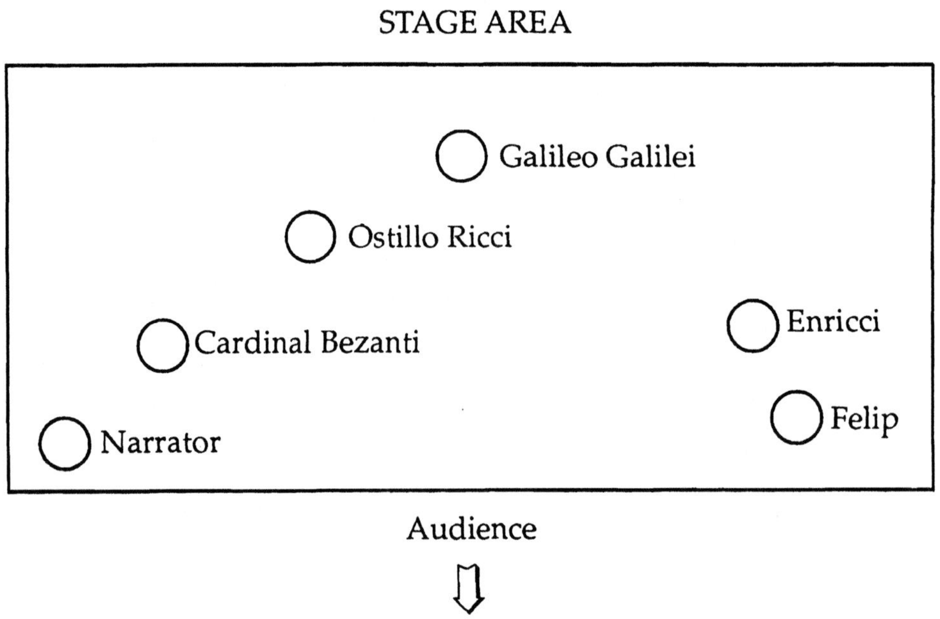

STAGE AREA

Audience

From *Great Moments in Science: Experiments and Readers Theatre*. © 1996. Teacher Ideas Press. (800) 237-6124.

The Fall of Galileo

NARRATOR:

A cocky 25-year-old mathematics professor, Galileo Galilei, stood before his students at the University of Pisa, Italy, on a cloudy afternoon in the spring of 1598. He held out two bricks for them to see—one in each hand as if weighing and comparing them.

GALILEO:

Aristotle is wrong!

ENRICCI: (*Shocked*)

Aristotle?!

FELIP:

Wrong?!

GALILEO:

Gentlemen, I have been watching pendulums swing back and forth. I have watched them very carefully. And I have come to a conclusion. Aristotle is wrong.

ENRICCI:

But how can Aristotle be wrong?

FELIP: (*Softly*)

Enricci, isn't Aristotle always supposed to be right?

NARRATOR:

In the late 1500s, the first fact every schoolboy learned in beginning science was that Aristotle was right. The writings of the ancient Greek philosopher, Aristotle, were the very foundation of known science at that time.

ENRICCI: (*Whispering*)

Felip, I think Professor Galileo is just joking, or maybe he's testing us.

FELIP:

I think he's lost his mind!

GALILEO: (*Very confident*)

I am prepared to prove what I say. Observe.

NARRATOR:

Galileo climbed onto the edge of his desk and again held out the two ordinary bricks at eye level.

From *Great Moments in Science: Experiments and Readers Theatre.* © 1996. Teacher Ideas Press. (800) 237-6124.

GALILEO:

Observe carefully, gentlemen. Time their fall.

NARRATOR:

Galileo released both bricks. Thud! They crashed to the floor in the center of a knot of eager students.

FELIP:

Wow! Look at those dents!

GALILEO:

Did you get a good reading?

ENRICCI: (*Softly, hopefully*)

Felip, did *you* get a good timed reading?

FELIP:

Me? I thought *you* would . . .

ENRICCI:

But . . . how can Aristotle be wrong?

FELIP:

But look at Galileo. He seems so sure of himself.

GALILEO:

Now class, what did Aristotle say about falling objects?

ENRICCI: (*Raising his hand*)

I know! I know! Aristotle said heavier objects fall faster because they weigh more. More weight means greater attraction to the earth.

FELIP: (*Whispering*)

Show-off!

GALILEO:

Very good, Enricci. But Aristotle is wrong. Observe and time this fall very carefully.

NARRATOR:

Galileo picked up two bricks that he had cemented together. This new brick thus weighed more than twice as much as a single brick.

GALILEO:

If Aristotle were right, this heavier brick would fall faster.

From *Great Moments in Science: Experiments and Readers Theatre.* © 1996. Teacher Ideas Press. (800) 237-6124.

NARRATOR:

The ring of students actually held their breath in anticipation as Galileo held the heavier, double brick at eye level. All eyes were glued to the brick.

FELIP: (*To Enricci*)

Move over. I can't see!

ENRICCI:

No! Then *I* won't be able to see. And shhh!

NARRATOR:

The room grew graveyard quiet. Galileo released the brick. Smash! The blow to the floor echoed around the classroom.

GALILEO:

Did the heavier brick fall faster than the single bricks I dropped last time?

ENRICCI: (*Whispering to Felip*)

Didn't the double brick fall faster? Didn't it sound faster? Isn't it *supposed* to fall faster?

FELIP: (*Shrugging and whispering back*)

I don't know what to think. I timed all the bricks at just over two heartbeats. But you're probably right. (*Raising his hand and louder to Galileo*) I think the bigger one fell faster. . . . Didn't it? . . . I hope . . .

GALILEO:

Are you guessing, or did your measurements tell you that?

FELIP: (*Nervously*)

Well . . . I think I'm guessing that my measurement said that? Isn't it supposed to be faster?

GALILEO:

NO! Really look, observe this time! Hand all the bricks back up to me.

ENRICCI: (*Whispering*)

Ha, ha. You sure messed up that time, Felip.

FELIP: (*Angrily*)

You told me to say it!

NARRATOR:

Galileo held out a single brick in one hand and the double brick in the other. He let them fall. Smash! The bricks gouged the worn wooden floor.

FELIP: (*Whispering*)

Boy, he's gonna get in trouble for all those dents.

GALILEO: (*Demanding*)

Did the heavier brick fall faster?

ENRICCI: (*Timidly*)

I think they landed together.

FELIP: (*To Enricci*)

Show-off!

GALILEO:

Observe again! Hand me the bricks.

NARRATOR:

His students stood transfixed as Galileo again dropped the single and double bricks.

GALILEO:

Did the heavier brick fall faster?

FELIP: (*Hissing to Enricci*)

Get your hand down. It's my turn. (*Louder to Galileo*) No! They landed at exactly the same time.

GALILEO:

You see? Aristotle is wrong. They landed together. The heavier brick did not fall faster.

ENRICCI:

Wow! Aristotle *is* wrong!

FELIP: (*Confused*)

Then why has everyone always told us that Aristotle was right?

NARRATOR:

That evening a friend and fellow mathematician, Ostillo Ricci, found Galileo still testing, comparing the fall of his bricks.

OSTILLO: (*Shocked*)

What? Aristotle? Wrong?!

GALILEO: (*Sighing*)

Observe. The truth speaks for itself. If I show you the evidence, you will have to believe.

From *Great Moments in Science: Experiments and Readers Theatre.* © 1996. Teacher Ideas Press. (800) 237-6124.

OSTILLO: (*Stammering in disbelief*)

But, Galileo . . . You're only 25. How can you hope to prove Aristotle wrong?

GALILEO:

Because he *is* wrong.

OSTILLO:

But he's Aristotle.

GALILEO: (*Angrily*)

Whom will you believe? Someone 2,000 years dead or your own eyes?

NARRATOR:

Galileo leapt onto his desk and held out a single brick in one hand, his double brick in the other.

GALILEO:

Watch their fall carefully, Ostillo.

NARRATOR:

The bricks plummeted to the floor. Crash!

GALILEO: (*Demanding*)

Did the heavier brick fall faster as Aristotle said it would? Yes or no?

OSTILLO: (*Sheepishly*)

Well . . . maybe. It might have. . . . It all happened so fast. How can I not believe Aristotle?

GALILEO:

Use your eyes, man! Believe only what you can see. Hand me the bricks again.

NARRATOR:

Again Galileo dropped the bricks. And again. And again until the floor around his desk was ringed with gouges and dents.

OSTILLO:

Enough! Stop! I am convinced. That is, in *this* demonstration, Galileo, I admit that you are right. *This* double brick falls at the same rate as *this* single brick. Still, I cannot believe so easily that Aristotle is wholly wrong. You have not shown that the same will happen in all cases. Search for another explanation, my friend. The world will not be eager to hear what you want to tell.

GALILEO: (*Sighing*)

I give up. It seems I will need a much more dramatic demonstration to convince you. And how can I convince a skeptical world if I cannot convince my good friend?

From *Great Moments in Science: Experiments and Readers Theatre.* © 1996. Teacher Ideas Press. (800) 237-6124.

OSTILLO:
Maybe if the drop were longer to be sure one wasn't a trifle faster . . .

GALILEO: (*Growing excited*)
You mean drop them from some place higher?

OSTILLO:
Yes, higher. Much higher.

GALILEO:
Yes. "Much higher" would be much more dramatic. But where is there such a place?

NARRATOR: (*After a pause*)
Powerful Cardinal Bezanti stopped Galileo on the university grounds the next afternoon. He was a respected scientist and teacher as well as an influential clergyman.

BEZANTI: (*Authoritative, contemptuous*)
Galileo, there is a rumor in the air that you are trying to get yourself in trouble.

GALILEO:
The truth can never create trouble. Truth creates only knowledge.

BEZANTI:
But lies that discredit the Church and all the world's scientists will get you in very grave trouble.

GALILEO:
Then I will be sure that my experiments do not lie.

BEZANTI: (*Growing angry*)
Experiments can *appear* to prove something they do not. Be careful, Galileo. You are young and impulsive. All scientists in the known world say Aristotle is correct. The Church has decreed it. You will not be allowed to prove him wrong.

GALILEO: (*Stunned*)
It is not a question of right and wrong. Mine is only a search for the truth.

BEZANTI:
I have told you the "truth" Galileo. Heed it well.

NARRATOR:
Galileo's search for a dramatic demonstration of the truth of his discovery led him to the famed Leaning Tower of Pisa. On the day announced for his demonstration, Galileo approached the tower carrying two cannonballs: one roughly 10 pounds, the other about 1 pound. His friend, Ostillo, rushed to intercept him.

OSTILLO:

Don't do this, Galileo. Cardinal Bezanti has gathered a large group of Church scholars.

GALILEO:

Good. They will all see the truth of my experiment with their own eyes.

OSTILLO: (*Very worried*)

No, Galileo. They will see the world and all you do through the Church's eyes. I fear they are only here to discredit you.

BEZANTI:

I warned you, Galileo. Do not challenge Aristotle!

GALILEO:

These cannonballs know nothing of Aristotle or of me, Cardinal Bezanti. They only know and speak the truth. Do you dare to listen?

ENRICCI: (*Whispering*)

Felip! There's Professor Galileo. He's starting up the tower. He's really going to do it!

FELIP:

And with such a big crowd here to watch . . .

NARRATOR:

A crowd of students, onlookers, and skeptical professors and priests formed a thick circle below the tower. As he held the cannonballs over the edge of the tower Galileo called down.

GALILEO:

This demonstration will be the final test of whether Aristotle's or my "Theory of Falling Objects" is correct. From such a great height there can be no miscalculation, no mistake, no doubt.

FELIP:

This is so exciting, Enricci. We're watching scientific history being made.

OSTILLO: (*Sadly*)

I fear this experiment will destroy a gifted teacher and friend.

BEZANTI: (*Vengefully*)

No matter what happens, Galileo must be discredited. This experiment must fail!

From *Great Moments in Science: Experiments and Readers Theatre.* © 1996. Teacher Ideas Press. (800) 237-6124.

NARRATOR:

Galileo dropped the balls. The crowd stood hushed and riveted as they fell. Down, down they whistled. Thud—thud! The two balls smashed into the ground 191 feet below at almost the same instant. Aristotle was wrong. The cannonballs had spoken. The evidence was clear.

ENRICCI:

He did it! *Our* teacher just proved Aristotle wrong!

FELIP:

Wow! Look at the dents he made in the plaza!

NARRATOR:

But the world in 1598 was neither ready nor willing to hear the truth Galileo's cannonballs spoke as they plummeted from the Leaning Tower of Pisa. Galileo was fired from his teaching job at the university. His experiment was discredited as faulty and error-filled. It was ignored for a hundred years.

Still, Galileo's work on falling objects, and the truth of his discovery, became the foundation from which another well-known scientist, Sir Isaac Newton, was able to reach his own famous discoveries. But that is another story.

From *Great Moments in Science: Experiments and Readers Theatre.* © 1996. Teacher Ideas Press. (800) 237-6124.

Related Experiments

Here is a series of simple experiments you can use to recreate the steps that led Galileo to his discoveries. These experiments will help you understand both the work of Galileo and the scientific concepts involved.

Necessary Equipment

Each group of students will need:

- Either a sturdy table a student can stand on or a ladder
- 2 softballs (or similarly sized rocks)
- 2 golf balls (or similarly sized rocks)
- 2 marbles (or similarly sized rocks)
- 1 feather
- 1 piece of cardboard ($8\frac{1}{2}$ x 11 is ideal)
- 2 pieces of string, each about 10 feet long
- 1 tape measure at least 10 feet long

➤ *Getting into the Swing of a Pendulum* (*Done in small groups*)

What You'll Investigate: Have you ever watched a clock pendulum? They don't swing very wide, do they? In fact, you will rarely find a pendulum that swings through an arc of more than 10 degrees on either side of dead center. As a pendulum's arc increases, its period (the time to complete one cycle) changes. Wind resistance increases. The regular, predictable qualities of a pendulum's swing are lost.

Do all pendulums swing through their full arcs in the same amount of time? Do they all travel at the same speed? (Speed equals the distance an object travels divided by the time required to get there.) What determines how fast a pendulum will travel, its weight or the length of its pendulum arm? This is the first question you will investigate, for it is here that Galileo first suspected that Aristotle was wrong.

The Setup: Tie a softball on the end of one of your strings and a golf ball on one end of the other string. From each ball measure back 5 inches, 30 inches, and 90 inches, marking each spot on both strings.

One student holds one string. A second holds the other. These two "holders" stand facing each other, holding their strings at the 30-inch mark with their hands next to each other at about eye level. A third student is the "dropper" and stands on one side of the holders. Others in the group are "observers." They will stand on the other side of the two holders and measure and record the results.

From *Great Moments in Science: Experiments and Readers Theatre.* © 1996. Teacher Ideas Press. (800) 237-6124.

What to Do:

1. Dropper pulls each ball about 10 degrees (5 inches) back from dead center and releases both balls at exactly the same instant. Observers watch to see if the heavier ball travels faster and to determine which ball completes its arc to the top of its swing first. Then they record the results. Do this experiment at least three times to be sure your results are consistent.

    Did the heavier ball travel faster? Did they both reach the top of their arc at the same time? How long did it take for each ball to swing through one arc?

    Repeat the experiment holding both strings at the 5-inch marks. Do the balls now travel at the same speed as before? Do they complete one arc in the same amount of time? That is, do they still swing with the same period?

2. Holders climb onto either a table or ladder (make sure they have a spotter to stabilize the table or ladder and make sure they don't fall) and hold their strings at the 90-inch mark. Dropper again pulls both balls back about 10 degrees off dead center (now about 15 inches) and simultaneously releases both balls. Observers time both balls through one arc and record the results.

    Did the heavier softball travel faster than the golf ball this time? Did they both travel faster than on 30-inch strings? Did it take more or less time for each ball to complete one arc?

3. Now repeat the experiment two more times: first with the softball on a 30-inch string and the golf ball on a 90-inch string, and second with the softball at 90 inches and the golf ball at 30. Dropper must make sure both balls start off right next to each other and that the ball on the short string is pulled back 5 inches while the ball on the 90-inch string is pulled back 15 inches before releasing them simultaneously.

    Observers compare and record speed and time for these two sets of arcs to confirm the findings from the first two experiments.

What's Going On?—Sources of Error: If your results did not always come out the same, or if the results of your group differ from those of another group, it must be because an error crept into one or both experiments. What could go wrong with such a simple experiment?

Did either holder move or jiggle his or her hand? Did the dropper release one ball slightly before the other? Is it possible that, at the moment of release, the dropper accidentally pushed or impeded one or both balls? As observers, how did you decide when a ball actually reached the exact top of its arc? Was it easier to time the swings on 90-inch strings than on the 30-inch strings?

See if you can find other ways errors might have crept into your tests. Then see if you can redesign and improve the experiment to preclude as many of these errors as possible.

What to Observe: You must decide if a pendulum does, or does not, drop faster because its weight (ball) is heavier. Aristotle said it would. Galileo said it would not. It is very hard to directly measure speed. It is easier to measure time and distance. On each drop observe which ball reaches the bottom of its arc first, and which reaches the top first.

From *Great Moments in Science: Experiments and Readers Theatre.* © 1996. Teacher Ideas Press. (800) 237-6124.

You must also decide if the length of a pendulum's string affects its speed and the time it takes to swing through one arc. Watch and time each drop to decide for yourself what determines how fast a pendulum weight will travel.

Questions to Ask Yourself: What determines how fast a pendulum ball will travel as it swings through its arc? Is it weight or length of pendulum string? Does your answer make sense to you? Do you agree with Aristotle or with Galileo?

➤ *The Drop Test* (Done in small groups)

What You'll Investigate: In this experiment you will look at two separate concepts: how fast different weights fall, and how hard it was to measure time in Galileo's day when there were no digital stopwatches or second hands on clocks.

The Setup: One student is the "dropper" and stands on a sturdy table or halfway up a ladder (make sure the dropper has a "spotter" to make sure the ladder is steady and to help prevent a fall). The dropper should have the softball, golf ball, marble, feather, and piece of cardboard. All other members of the group act as observers and form a semicircle below the dropper.

What to Do:

1. Dropper holds the softball and golf ball at eye level and simultaneously releases both balls. Half the observers simply watch to see which ball lands first (which traveled faster).

   The other half must try to measure the time it takes for each ball to fall without using a watch or clock that has a second hand or any other measuring device that was not available in Galileo's day. How will you time each ball's fall? Discuss it in the group before you try this test. See if you can create several different timing schemes to test and compare.

   After each drop decide which ball landed first and how long each ball took to fall. Record your results. Repeat this experiment at least three times to be sure your results are consistent.

2. Now repeat the experiment using the softball and the marble. Then with the marble and the golf ball. Do you think changing balls will change your results? Record your results.

3. Finally, the dropper should try dropping the softball and the feather. Record your results. Which falls faster? Why? Try the golf ball and the piece of cardboard. Did they both fall together as the differently sized balls did? If all objects fall at the same rate regardless of weight, why did the feather and cardboard take longer to fall?

What's Going On?—Sources of Error: Could any of the same errors discussed in the previous experiment have crept into this experiment? Did you take steps to eliminate them? How would you redesign this experiment to make it as error-free as possible?

From *Great Moments in Science: Experiments and Readers Theatre.* © 1996. Teacher Ideas Press. (800) 237-6124.

Were you able to time any of the falls? What made timing so difficult? How could you reduce this error?

What to Observe: During each drop be sure to see which ball lands first. Did you consistently find that one landed first, or did they touch down virtually simultaneously? If one ball landed first, are you sure it wasn't also dropped first? How long did it take for each ball to reach the floor?

Questions to Ask Yourself: Do your results support Galileo, who said all objects fall at the same rate, or Aristotle, who said heavier objects fall faster? Based on your results, do heavier objects fall faster?

What about the feather and piece of cardboard? What force slowed their fall? Does that same force affect the balls when they fall? Why was the effect more pronounced on the feather and cardboard? Would the balls fall faster in a vacuum? Would the feather? Would the feather fall as fast as the softball in a vacuum?

► *Doing It Digitally (Done in small groups)*

What You'll Investigate: You will repeat the Drop Test, above, using a digital watch or stopwatch to see if more accurate timing of each fall improves your results or the amount of information you can gain from the experiment.

The Setup: Same as previous experiment (see "The Setup" on page 33).

What to Do:

1. Repeat each step of the previous experiment, timing each fall with more than one digital watch or stopwatch.

2. You have probably noticed that all the balls gain speed, or accelerate, as they fall. The longer the fall, the faster the balls are traveling as they hit the floor. But how much faster? Is there a pattern to how objects speed up as they fall?

    To find out, drop one of the balls five times, each time from a different height. Use a tape measure to carefully measure heights of 2 feet, 4 feet, 6 feet, 8 feet, and 10 feet for these five drops. Time each drop with at least three watches. Average their readings to get a time for each fall. Record your results.

    Make a graph of your results. On one axis plot the height of the fall. On the other plot the time. Do the dots form a straight line? If they did, it would mean that your ball always fell at the same speed: during the first second, the last second, and all seconds in between.

    Can you draw a smooth curved line that passes through all the points? Any wiggle in this line is the result of errors either in how you dropped the ball or in your time measurements. The curve, or changing slope of this line represents the acceleration of your ball due to the constant pull of the force of gravity.

From *Great Moments in Science: Experiments and Readers Theatre.* © 1996. Teacher Ideas Press. (800) 237-6124.

What's Going On?—Sources of Error: Does the use of digital watches or stopwatches introduce new opportunities for error? Are you sure you started and stopped each reading exactly as the ball was released and as it hit the floor? How can you minimize the effect of this timing error?

What to Observe: Did more accurate measurements of the time of each fall improve your results? Did it change your conclusions?

Questions to Ask Yourself: Did having a better timing device make it easier for you to obtain good, consistent results? Did better time measurement change your overall conclusions? Did you really need a better timing device? Can you think of a way to get a more accurate measure of the time of a ball's fall? What equipment would you need?

Did your experiment show you that objects continue to accelerate as they fall? Are you able to "see" that acceleration by the curve of the line on your graph? That is, can you see how the ball requires less and less extra time to fall each additional two feet?

➤ *The Big Picture (Done in small groups)*

What You'll Investigate: Most people still have trouble accurately timing a ball's fall when it happens in the few seconds it takes for the ball to drop 6 feet. It's hard to tell if one ball's landing a small fraction of a second sooner is significant or just an error. Certainly Galileo's class and friend had trouble convincing themselves of their measurements at this height.

It would be good to try this basic drop experiment one more time over a much greater height.

The Setup: Have a teacher, administrator, or custodian climb onto the school roof or other high place (at least 20 feet high). The class stands in a semicircle below (standing well away from the base of the building, so that no one is in danger of being hit by a dropped object) to act as timers and observers.

What to Do: The teacher holds two balls of different weight at eye level and simultaneously releases both. Students below carefully observe to see if the balls land at the same time or if one lands significantly sooner and record their results.

Try drops using each of the possible combinations of balls you have used in earlier experiments. Record your results.

What's Going On?—Sources of Error: Are there any new possible sources of error from conducting this experiment outside? Can you minimize or eliminate them?

What to Observe: Again carefully watch to see if the balls land at approximately the same instant, or if the heavier ball always lands first. This is a final test to be sure Aristotle was really wrong.

Questions to Ask Yourself: Did the balls all fall at the same rate? Is Galileo right and Aristotle wrong? Do these experiments give you a good feel for how objects move and speed up as gravity pulls them toward earth? Will objects continue to speed up, or accelerate, as long as they fall? What forces could act to slow them down? See if there are books in your library that hold these answers.

From *Great Moments in Science: Experiments and Readers Theatre.* © 1996. Teacher Ideas Press. (800) 237-6124.

Bridges to Books

This story deals with one aspect of our understanding of the physical world around us. You can learn much more about these concepts in your library. The following paragraphs will give you key words, concepts, and questions to begin your exploration in a school or public library.

Galileo and **Aristotle** are among the most creative, inventive scientific minds in the history of mankind. Both men made vast and wide-ranging contributions to our body of knowledge. See if you can find a dozen other discoveries, theories, and inventions by these two giants of history.

Galileo's work contributed to our early understanding of the force we now call **gravity**. In watching how objects fell, Galileo noticed that, while all objects fell at the same rate, they all continued to **accelerate** (fall faster) the longer they were allowed to fall. See if you can find out exactly what gravity is. Why does it pull objects toward earth and make them fall? Why does it make them accelerate the farther they fall? What determines how hard gravity pulls an object toward earth?

Pendulums have been used for 500 years to control the ticking of clocks and to keep them ticking at a constant rate. Why do pendulums swing at such a steady rate? See what information you can find in the library about how and why pendulums work the way they do.

References for Further Reading

The following references deal with the major characters, concepts, and scientific processes in this chapter.

Barley, George. *Galileo's Children*. New York: Arcade, 1990.

Bernkoph, Michael. *The Sciences of Galileo*. New York: Regents, 1983.

Bixby, M. *The Universe of Galileo and Newton*. New York: American Heritage Books, 1964.

Branley, Franklin. *Gravity Is a Mystery*. New York: Thomas Y. Crowell, 1986.

Cavelin, Maurice. *The Natural Philosophy of Galileo*. Cambridge, MA: MIT Press, 1974.

Drake, Stillman. *Galileo*. New York: Hill and Wang, 1980.

———. *Galileo at Work*. Chicago: University of Chicago Press, 1978.

Fermi, Lauri. *Galileo and the Scientific Revolution*. New York: Basic Books, 1981.

Finocchiaro, Maurice. *Galileo and the Art of Reason*. Boston: D. Reidel, 1980.

Fisher, Leonard. *Galileo*. New York: Macmillan, 1992.

Haines, Gail. *Which Way Is Up?* New York: Atheneum, 1987.

Hitzeroth, Deborah. *Galileo Galilei.* San Diego, CA: Lucent Books, 1992.

Hummel, Charles. *The Galileo Connection.* Downers Grove, IL: Inter-Varsity Press, 1986.

Marcus, Rebecca. *Galileo and Experimental Science.* New York: Franklin Watts, 1961.

McTavish, Douglas. *Galileo.* New York: Bookwright Press, 1991.

Parker, Steve. *Galileo and the Universe.* New York: HarperCollins, 1992.

Reston, James. *Galileo: A Life.* New York: HarperCollins, 1994.

Ronan, Colin. *Galileo.* New York: Putnam, 1974.

Suggett, Martin. *Galileo and the Birth of Modern Science.* Hove, England: Wayland, 1981.

Consult your librarian for additional titles.

A Weighty Matter

*Evangelista Torricelli's discovery
of air pressure in 1642*

Scientific Background

Scoop up a double handful of air. Can you see it? Smell it? Feel it? Can you feel the weight of that air pressing down into your palms? Now close your hands into a ball and slowly squeeze them together until your palms touch. Did your hands run into this air as they closed together? Did you feel the air at all? How do you know it was really there?

Today, in the late twentieth century we can rely on chemical analysis and photos taken from space to convince ourselves that there is matter (substance) in air. But what if you had to rely just on your own senses? Can you think of any way your own senses can detect the existence of air?

Back in the seventeenth century, when science was just beginning to unravel and understand the workings of the physical world, little thought had been given to the real nature of air. That changed in the town of Florence, Italy, when Galileo tried to see how high he could raise water with a vacuum pump. But neither he nor his coworkers could understand the results of these experiments.

Four years later, Evangelista Torricelli, a student of Galileo's, took up the problem again. Through one of those flashes of brilliance peppered across the history of science, Torricelli uncovered the real nature of air, of wind, and of vacuums—all in one genius stroke. He also discovered atmospheric, or barometric pressure, and began the scientific study of weather.

Readers Theatre

Characters

Narrator

Galileo Galilei. Famed astronomer and physicist. Now more than 60 years old and under house arrest by the Church, Galileo is still an active and dedicated researcher.

Evangelista Torricelli. Galileo's 32-year-old pupil, an impulsive and intuitive scientist.

Giovanni Baliani. Cautious, thoughtful 41-year-old scientist. Orthodox in his views, Giovanni is skeptical of all new ideas.

Madam Baliani. Giovanni's 35-year-old wife. She has a keen eye and intellect, as well as a good sense of humor. But in Italy in the early seventeenth century, women had few rights and could not directly participate in science.

Staging

Figure 3.1. Suggested placement of readers for *A Weighty Matter*.

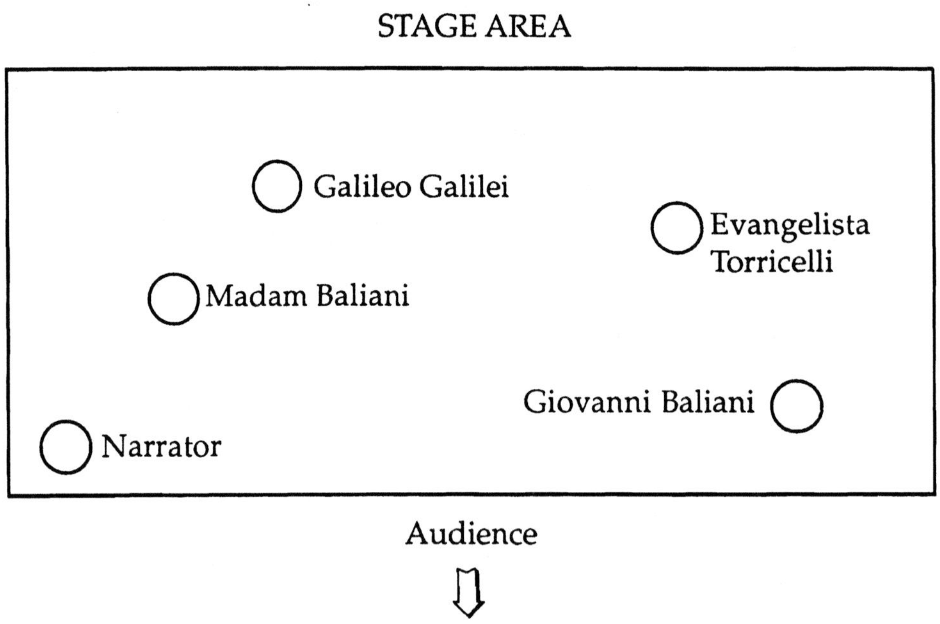

STAGE AREA

○ Galileo Galilei

○ Evangelista Torricelli

○ Madam Baliani

○ Narrator

Giovanni Baliani ○

Audience

⇩

From *Great Moments in Science: Experiments and Readers Theatre.* © 1996. Teacher Ideas Press. (800) 237-6124.

A Weighty Matter

GALILEO: (*Excited*)

Quickly, Evangelista! Set the pump down next to this well.

TORRICELLI: (*Out of breath*)

Coming, Galileo. But this pump is heavy.

NARRATOR:

Thirty-two-year-old Evangelista Torricelli dragged a cumbersome two-man wooden pump into the public square of Florence, Italy, on a blustery October day in 1640.

GALILEO:

Giovanni, bring the tube! I'll lower one end to the water while you connect the other to the pump.

NARRATOR:

Giovanni Baliani, a well-known local physicist, struggled under the long, flexible tube coiled over his shoulder and back.

MADAM BALIANI:

Galileo, what experiment could you possibly conduct at a public well in this market plaza?

GALILEO:

Ah, Madam Baliani. It is a pleasure to have you with us to observe.

MADAM BALIANI:

I watch all my husband's experiments. (*Laughs*) But so far today he looks more like a pack mule than a noble scientist.

NARRATOR:

The fashionably dressed foursome huddled around a public well as Galileo lowered one end of his long tube into the murky water, eight meters below the lip of the well's waist-high stone wall.

GALILEO:

Quickly, please. Attach the pump. I don't have a pass to be out today.

NARRATOR:

Galileo had been under house arrest by the all-powerful Church Inquisition Board since 1632, when he refused to recant his astronomical finding that the sun, rather than the earth, was the center of the universe. Being caught away from his house without a pass meant punishment and possibly imprisonment.

From *Great Moments in Science: Experiments and Readers Theatre.* © 1996. Teacher Ideas Press. (800) 237-6124.

MADAM BALIANI:
I ask again, Galileo. What do you hope to discover with a tube, a pump, and a well?

GALILEO: (*Thoughtfully stroking his shoulder-length white beard*)
Evangelista and I have noticed a curious phenomenon in several previous tests. We can suck air out of our tube with a pump and thereby draw water up into the tube.

MADAM BALIANI:
You mean you create a vacuum in the tube.

GALILEO:
Exactly. And that vacuum pulls water into the tube. (*Louder and to Torricelli*) Drape the tube over the well's cross beam to get sufficient height.

NARRATOR:
Galileo pointed to a wooden cross beam suspended some two meters above the well's stone rim.

GALILEO:
I'm sorry, Madam Baliani. Where was I? Ahh, we can thus suck water into the tube. . . .

MADAM BALIANI: (*Interrupting*)
Everyone knows that, Galileo. That's what vacuums do.

GALILEO: (*Sternly*)
But, we find we can only draw water into the tube to one certain height, and never any higher.

MADAM BALIANI:
I see. And you want to find out why you can't draw water all the way to the top.

GALILEO:
Exactly! We must discover what stops us.

MADAM BALIANI:
And the red stripes. What are they for?

NARRATOR:
Galileo had painted thin red lines across the tube at half-meter intervals like zebra stripes rising up the tube. The 10-meter line rested just below the raised wooden cross beam high above.

GALILEO:
They mark height above the water so we can record our progress.

From *Great Moments in Science: Experiments and Readers Theatre.* © 1996. Teacher Ideas Press. (800) 237-6124.

EVANGELISTA:
The tube is ready, Galileo.

BALIANI:
So is the pump.

GALILEO:
Excellent! If you please, gentlemen, let us begin.

NARRATOR:
Torricelli and Baliani took their places, standing side by side, both gripping the one wide wooden handle bar of the pump.

TORRICELLI: (*With a sigh and a groan*)
I hate this part.

BALIANI:
Couldn't he hire servants to do the pumping?

GALILEO:
Save your breath for pumping, gentlemen.

BALIANI:
On my mark, Evangelista. Ready . . . and begin!

NARRATOR:
With a nod of Baliani's head to coordinate their efforts, the two men began to pump the handle bar up and down, slowly sucking air out of Galileo's tube.

MADAM BALIANI: (*With a skeptical laugh*)
This is science? It looks more like forced labor.

GALILEO: (*Chuckling*)
There are times when there is little difference between the two. (*Louder to the two men*) Good work, gentlemen. Water is rising.

NARRATOR:
A small crowd of curious onlookers gathered around the well. With grunts and grimaces Torricelli and Baliani pumped harder and harder.

TORRICELLI: (*Panting*)
How are we doing?

NARRATOR:
Air steadily hissed from the tube. Water steadily crept higher and higher into it. Galileo called out the water levels to his two friends.

From *Great Moments in Science: Experiments and Readers Theatre.* © 1996. Teacher Ideas Press. (800) 237-6124.

GALILEO:
Five meters . . . 6 meters . . . 7 meters . . .

NARRATOR:
Sweat poured down the pumpers' faces. The crowd cheered as well water inched toward the 8-, and then 8½-meter marks.

GALILEO:
Nine meters! Keep pumping!

BALIANI: (*Gasping*)
My arms . . . are too tired. . . . I can't . . . go on.

TORRICELLI:
Keep pumping!

NARRATOR:
Torricelli clenched his teeth as he redoubled his weary efforts to keep the pump going. He and Giovanni pumped until the tube began to flatten in on itself. Galileo pounded his fist on the well's stone wall.

GALILEO: (*With frustration and wonder*)
Nine and seven-tenths meters again! Why always to 9.7 meters and no higher? (*Louder and to the men*) The tube's collapsing. You can stop now.

NARRATOR:
Both men collapsed, panting, to the smooth stones of the plaza. Air hissed as it rushed back into Galileo's tube. Water quickly sank back to its natural level in the well. The crowd wandered off.

MADAM BALIANI:
And you have no idea why the water will only rise to that one height?

GALILEO: (*Sadly*)
None . . .

MADAM BALIANI:
Very curious. Surely *something* must cause it to happen.

GALILEO:
But what?

TORRICELLI: (*Still panting*)
I'm exhausted. Science is too much work.

GALILEO:
The real work, Evangelista, will be in thinking about what our experiment means.

BALIANI: (*Also still panting*)
Could I have a drink of water, please?

MADAM BALIANI: (*Laughing*)
You should have thought of that when you had pumped the water up to the 9.7-meter mark. Now you'll have to drag a bucket up from the bottom of the well.

GALILEO:
Come. We'll talk more at my house. I should be getting back.

NARRATOR: (*After a momentary pause*)
Seated on Galileo's terrace, the four sipped tea to ward off the cool wind that swirled across them.

GALILEO:
We know there is some . . . some force in a vacuum that pulls things in.

TORRICELLI:
But what is that force?

MADAM BALIANI:
And why doesn't it continue to pull water in, instead of stopping at that one height?

GALILEO:
These are the questions we are here to answer. I can't help but feel that our experiment has shown us all we need to know. But I can't see the answer.

TORRICELLI:
How can we hope to understand how water is affected by a vacuum if we don't even know why this wind blows?

BALIANI:
You'll never understand, Galileo. It is simply an act of nature. Just accept the way it is.

GALILEO: (*Angered*)
No! Science cannot "just accept." We must struggle to understand. It is our duty.

BALIANI: (*Laughing*)
But Galileo, how can you hope to understand the works of God?

NARRATOR:
Evangelista studied the leaves swirling in the wind.

From *Great Moments in Science: Experiments and Readers Theatre.* © 1996. Teacher Ideas Press. (800) 237-6124.

TORRICELLI:

A vacuum is a space with no air in it. I think the key is something about the air itself. But . . . but what?

NARRATOR: (*After a momentary pause*)

Other projects pulled the men's minds away from vacuums until after Galileo's death in 1642. Torricelli again took up the problem. But this time with a fresh idea. Would a vacuum treat other liquids the same way it treated water?

TORRICELLI:

Ah, Giovanni. I'm so glad you are able to help me with these tests.

NARRATOR:

They repeated Galileo's experiment using progressively heavier and heavier liquids.

BALIANI:

The heavier our liquid grows, the shorter the height to which a vacuum will raise it.

TORRICELLI:

Next we'll try the heaviest liquid of all: liquid mercury.

NARRATOR:

No matter how hard they pumped on a vacuum pump, the mercury would only rise 0.77 meters in their test tube. As the air hissed back into his short tube, Torricelli brightened.

TORRICELLI:

The height always seems to be proportional to the weight, or density, of the liquid. The weight. Perhaps a vacuum always sucks up the same *weight* of liquid.

MADAM BALIANI:

Sounds plausible. Could that be the long-missing key?

TORRICELLI:

The weight . . . But what does the weight of the liquid have to do with a vacuum only pulling it in to a height of 0.77 meters?

NARRATOR:

The next day, as a fierce storm rumbled into Florence, Evangelista and Giovanni repeated their experiment with liquid mercury. However, no matter how hard they pumped, the mercury rose only 0.75 meters into the tube.

MADAM BALIANI:

Why only 0.75 meters today?

From *Great Moments in Science: Experiments and Readers Theatre.* © 1996. Teacher Ideas Press. (800) 237-6124.

BALIANI:

What is different today that a vacuum can't raise the same weight of mercury it did yesterday?

TORRICELLI: (*Unsure*)

The storm? That's the only difference.

BALIANI:

But what has the storm got to do with anything?

MADAM BALIANI:

How can a storm affect either a vacuum or the weight of liquid mercury?

NARRATOR:

Staring at the wind-whipped trees, suddenly Torricelli's mind latched onto a revolutionary new idea.

TORRICELLI:

Maybe we're only wrong in the way we think about a vacuum. What if the air all around us has weight, substance?

BALIANI: (*Disbelieving*)

Air? Have weight?

TORRICELLI:

Yes, weight. What if a vacuum has no force of its own? A vacuum is just the absence of air. What if a vacuum only allows the weight of air outside a tube to push down on mercury in a bowl and force it up into the tube?

MADAM BALIANI:

But what does that have to do with this storm?

TORRICELLI: (*Thinking aloud*)

We know weights exert pressure. What if this pressure of the air were different at one spot than at another, and from one time to another? The higher pressure would push air toward the lower pressure. "Pushing air" is wind. Wind—the wind of this storm—is caused by differences in air pressure and air weight.

MADAM BALIANI:

Then, Evangelista, you're saying that Galileo's vacuum force is really just the weight of the air outside the vacuum *pushing* liquid up into the vacuum?

TORRICELLI: (*Excited*)

Exactly!

MADAM BALIANI:

And normally the weight of air pushes liquid mercury 0.77 meters up into a vacuum tube? Is that a measure of how much the air above us weighs?

TORRICELLI:

Yes. It *must* be so!

BALIANI:

Then why only 0.75 meters today when before you measured 0.77 meters?

TORRICELLI:

The storm. Somehow the storm lowered the air weight. It lowered the pressure that the air pressure is exerting down. That must be why we have such strong winds today. That's also why the mercury only rose 0.75 meters. Less air pressure.

MADAM BALIANI:

I think you're right, Evangelista!

BALIANI:

How can this be? A brick has weight. If I hold a brick, I feel its weight. Why can't I feel this weight of air?

MADAM BALIANI:

You're too skeptical, Giovanni. If you had always held that brick you would no longer feel its weight. Because you have always borne the weight of air, you are no longer aware of the feel of its pressure.

NARRATOR:

Baliani opened his mouth to argue more, but could think of nothing to say. Could young Evangelista be right with such a wild idea?

Air had weight. It exerted a pressure on every surface on earth. Its weight could change from day to day, and those changes caused the winds to blow. This was such a magnificent set of discoveries to have come tumbling into one person's head all at once! But how Torricelli's work led to the development of our modern barometer, and how his work so greatly improved our understanding of how earth's atmosphere and its weather systems function, is another story.

From *Great Moments in Science: Experiments and Readers Theatre.* © 1996. Teacher Ideas Press. (800) 237-6124.

Related Experiments

Here is a series of simple experiments you can use to recreate the experimental steps that led Evangelista Torricelli to his discoveries. These experiments will help your students understand both the work of Torricelli and the scientific concepts involved.

Necessary Equipment

For each group:

- A glass of water

- Six or eight straws

- A small graduated cylinder or test tube to measure water volume and weight

- One tin can

- One balloon

- Scissors, duct tape, and cellophane tape

For the whole class:

- A 40-foot section of clear tube (1-inch diameter works best)

- A large tub full of water

- A hand vacuum pump (camping stores stock these) or vacuum cleaner to which you can attach your clear tube

- A room thermometer or air thermometer

- A ladder

➤ *Getting Pumped Up About Vacuums (Done in small groups)*

What You'll Investigate: The search that led Evangelista Torricelli to a realization that air had mass and weight and exerted pressure began with a simple water pump and a vacuum. Galileo assumed that a vacuum, itself, exerted the force that pulled water into it. He was thus amazed to find that his vacuum would only pull water up to a specific height. He overlooked the existence of air pressure. No one had ever considered that air had weight because no one can sense the pressure it exerts on the body even though that weight and pressure have always been there.

In this first experiment you will discover how high you can pump water with a vacuum and see how much force is created by the air weighing down on you.

The Setup: Divide into small groups. Each group should fill a glass with water and have three or four straws, a sharp pencil, and a small glass measuring cylinder handy.

From *Great Moments in Science: Experiments and Readers Theatre.* © 1996. Teacher Ideas Press. (800) 237-6124.

What to Do: One student in each group dips a straw to the bottom of the glass of water, being careful to hold the straw vertically. Using a sharp, soft pencil, a second student should mark the straw exactly at the waterline, being careful not to puncture the straw.

The student holding the straw should now clamp one finger over the top of the straw, sealing it tightly, and then lift it completely out of the water. A second student carefully marks the straw at the waterline inside the straw.

Completely drain the straw into a graduated cylinder and measure the volume of water held in the straw. Your teacher can help you convert this volume of water into the weight of water your partial vacuum supported.

What to Observe: We know that water will not fall out of a close-ended straw because the suction of a partial vacuum inside holds the water in. The downward force pulling the water out of the straw equals the weight of the water, which you have calculated. The partial vacuum of the reduced air pressure inside the straw must exactly equal that force or the water would either rise or fall.

But how is a partial vacuum being created? The weight of the water pulls it down. As it does, the air inside the straw expands, creating a partial vacuum. Notice how small an expansion is needed (see the two lines you marked on the straw) to create a powerful partial vacuum.

Questions to Ask Yourself: What is the relationship between air weight and air pressure? Why is air pressure reduced as air expands?

► The Strength of Air Pressure

What You'll Investigate: Now try the same sort of experiment on a much larger scale. You have seen that a slight partial vacuum can hold water in a straw. You also know that a stronger partial vacuum (that is, less air per unit volume) can suck water up even a long straw.

You do it all the time when you drink through a straw. When you breathe, your muscles expand your lungs, creating a partial vacuum. The outside air pressure pushes air (or liquid if you are sucking on a straw) into that partial vacuum. The more you expand your lungs, the larger and faster will be that flow of air or liquid.

Now see how strong a partial vacuum your lungs can create.

The Setup: Cut your 40-foot tube into 10-foot and 30-foot sections. Fill a large tub with water and place it on the floor. One student climbs a ladder holding one end of the 10-foot tube.

What to Do: Insert the bottom end of the 10-foot tube into the tub and mark where the waterline hits the tube. The student on top of the ladder now tries to suck water as high as he or she can into the tube, covering the top of the tube in between breaths to prevent air from leaking in.

If possible, attach a pressure gauge near the top of the tube. One student monitors this gauge and reports the falling pressure levels.

When the student conducting this test can suck water no higher into the tube, mark the height (h) of the water raised with the lung vacuum pump. Also have a student record the vacuum pressure from a pressure gauge if you are using one.

Let a second and third student test their lung power. Be sure to begin each time with the tub water level at the same mark on the tube.

From *Great Moments in Science: Experiments and Readers Theatre.* © 1996. Teacher Ideas Press. (800) 237-6124.

What to Observe: How high did you raise water in this tube? The more the students were able to use chest muscles to force open their lungs, the stronger a partial vacuum they created and the higher they were able to raise the water.

How much water was raised into the tube by the strongest-lunged student? Measure the inside diameter of the tube. Divide this in half to find the radius (r), and use the formula

$$V = \pi r^2 h$$

to find the volume of the water raised. From that number calculate the weight of water lifted. This weight equals the upward force of the partial vacuum that was created.

Questions to Ask Yourself: Why and how is water lifted into a partial vacuum? How close did you come to achieving a total vacuum? How much water could a total vacuum lift? How high would it lift water in your tube? Are there any other forces (like friction) that will affect how high water is drawn into your tube? How can you minimize the effect of such unwanted forces?

➤ *Mega-Pump*

What You'll Investigate: You have seen that the human lung is not capable of creating a very strong vacuum. Now see if simple mechanical devices can do better.

The Setup: Attach the 30-foot section of tube to a hand pump or vacuum cleaner. Find a place (inside or outside) where the pump can be 10 or 15 feet above the water tub. The top of a flight of stairs is a good spot.

What to Do: Mark the waterline where the bottom of this tube falls into the water tub. Several students go to the top of the stairs to operate the pump. They see how high they can pump water until either the tube collapses, or the pump simply won't lift any further.

If possible, attach a pressure gauge to the clear tube high enough so that it will always stay above the waterline. One student monitors this gauge and reports the vacuum pressure levels as they fall.

What to Observe: See if you can gain a feel for the relationship between the strength of a partial vacuum and the amount of water it will lift. Also try to gain a sense of how hard it is to create a strong partial vacuum.

Questions to Ask Yourself: Why is it so hard to create a vacuum? What force makes it so hard? If you had to pump water 100 feet up, how would you do it? What equipment would you need?

➤ *Building a Better Barometer*

What You'll Investigate: Torricelli's work led to an understanding of air pressure and to the development of modern barometers. Some barometers use a sealed vacuum chamber. Others rely on a chamber of trapped air that either expands or contracts depending on the outside barometric pressure. You can build a simple barometer that uses this same concept.

The Setup: Each group of students needs one tin can, one balloon, one straight straw, heavy duct tape, and a little cellophane tape.

Figure 3.2. A simple tin-can barometer.

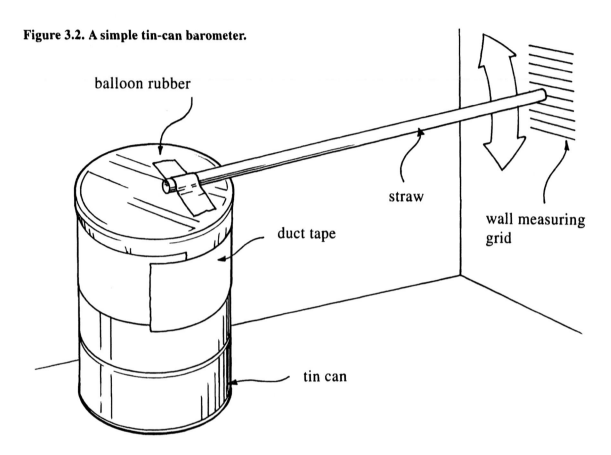

What to Do: Cut open the balloon and stretch it tight across the open end of your tin can. The tighter you stretch your balloon, the better. If it tears as you stretch it, use another balloon.

Tape the balloon all around to the sides of the tin can with heavy duct tape. Be sure to tape all around the sides, but do not tape across the top of the can. Finally, lay your straw across the top of the can as a pointer from near the center out along a radius line so that it extends well beyond the edge of your can and points straight out from the center.

Position the can near a wall so that the straw almost touches, and is aimed at, the wall.

Tape a piece of paper to the wall and mark the spot on the paper at which the straw now points. Find the current barometric pressure from a weather station or service and write that pressure next to the mark.

For the next several days periodically repeat this process: mark the paper and record actual barometric pressure next to it. Do you find that soon you can predict the pressure by looking at where your barometer straw points?

From *Great Moments in Science: Experiments and Readers Theatre.* © 1996. Teacher Ideas Press. (800) 237-6124.

What's Going On?—Sources of Error: For most of you the answer is probably "no." Why? Are there any factors you ignored that affect your barometer?

The biggest of these factors is certainly temperature. Your barometer is sensitive to temperature changes just as it is to air pressure changes.

Move your barometer to a room where you can easily control the temperature and repeat the steps above using a new piece of paper. However, this time check and adjust the room temperature before you check your barometer so that the temperature will always be the same when you record a barometric mark.

Did this work better? Did you find that your straw pointer swung up and down with changes in the atmospheric pressure?

Additional errors in your barometer's ability to track and predict actual atmospheric pressure changes are probably due to either tiny holes in the rubber or to leaks around the tape.

What to Observe: Your barometer works because a fixed mass (amount) of air is trapped inside a cylinder with one flexible side. When atmospheric pressure changes outside the can, the air inside will adjust its pressure to match. It does this by expanding its volume as atmospheric pressure decreases or by contracting its volume as pressure increases. These expansions and contractions are possible because the rubber top of your can barometer easily flexes. Your straw pointer rises and falls as the rubber bulges and contracts with these pressure changes.

Questions to Ask Yourself: Should the tip of your pointer rise or fall as barometric pressure increases? Why? Why does barometric, or atmospheric pressure change? What changes it?

Where is the air that weighs as much as 30 inches of mercury? Why does temperature also affect your barometer? How could you design a barometer to sense pressure changes but not temperature changes?

From *Great Moments in Science: Experiments and Readers Theatre.* © 1996. Teacher Ideas Press. (800) 237-6124.

Bridges to Books

This story deals with one aspect of our understanding of the physical world around us. You can learn much more about these concepts in your library. The following list gives you key words, concepts, and questions to begin your exploration in a school or public library.

Evangelista Torricelli is not nearly as well known now as his teacher and mentor, **Galileo Galilei**. Still, in his day, Torricelli was a famous scientist. Does your library have any information about the rest of Torricelli's life? Did he make any other important discoveries? How long did he live?

This story deals with **vacuums, air pressure, air density, barometric pressure,** and **air weight.** Can you find listings for all of these key words in your library's index? What is the difference among air density, air weight, and air pressure? Is air pressure high or low in a vacuum? Why? What's the difference between barometric pressure and air pressure? The answers are in the library.

We often describe **weather** in terms of its air pressure. **Meteorologists,** who study **atmospheric sciences,** talk about **low pressure systems** and **high pressure systems** or about troughs of cold, high-density air. Try looking under "weather" and "atmospheric sciences" to find additional information about the weather phenomena Torricelli discovered.

References for Further Reading

The following references deal with the major characters, concepts, and processes in this chapter.

Battan, Louis. *Fundamentals of Meteorology.* Englewood Cliffs, NJ: Prentice-Hall, 1984.

Berger, Melvin. *How's the Weather?* New York: Ideal Children's Books, 1993.

Catherall, Ed. *Exploring Weather.* Boulder, CO: Steck-Vaughn Publishers, 1991.

Donn, William. *Meteorology.* New York: McGraw-Hill, 1975.

Macus, Rebecca. *Galileo and Experimental Science.* New York: Franklin Watts, 1971.

McKenzie, A. E. *The Major Achievements of Science.* New York: Simon & Schuster, 1960.

Middleton, W. E. *The History of the Barometer.* Baltimore, MD: Johns Hopkins University Press, 1974.

———. *Invention of the Meteorological Instruments.* Baltimore, MD: Johns Hopkins University Press, 1979.

Simon, Seymore. *Weather.* New York: Morrow Junior Books, 1993.

Consult your librarian for additional titles.

Apples, Moons, and Questions

Isaac Newton's discovery of the principle of gravity in 1666

Scientific Background

People have always taken for granted that rain falls down to earth and that their feet will come down to the ground again after they lift them into the air while walking. But do these things just happen, or is there something that *makes* them happen?

It's easy for us to imagine a world without any gravity because astronauts have shown us weightlessness in space, and because we have all experienced the seemingly weightless free fall of a big roller coaster. But would you be able to imagine what a weightless world (that is, a world without gravity) would be like without those experiences to draw on? What would happen to rain without gravity? Without gravity to pull it down, what would happen to your foot when you lift it as you run?

Now put yourself in the place of seventeenth-century Europeans. Copernicus and Galileo had correctly unraveled the structure of the solar system. Galileo had unveiled our first glimpses into the laws governing motion with his efforts to describe the motion of falling bodies. Scientists knew that objects fell and were busy investigating *how* they fell. But no one could step far enough outside everyday life on earth to ask the most basic question of all: *Why* do objects fall?

But, then, why *should* anyone have bothered to ask such a question? There had never been a time, place, or circumstance when all objects had not fallen to earth. How could someone think about a time when they would not? To see past this veil of ordinary experiences takes real genius.

That all changed when a brilliant English scientist at Cambridge University, barely into his twenties, formed this most important question: *Why* do things fall? His name was Isaac Newton.

But just as he uncovered this most basic of all questions to study, the bubonic plague struck urban centers throughout Europe. Cambridge was closed. England's great scholars were scattered to country estates to wait out this terrible black death. Twenty-three-year-old Isaac Newton found himself isolated on a spacious country manor burdened by this critical question, and with no one there to help him grapple with it, study it, or answer it.

Readers Theatre

Characters

Narrator

Brenda Marsh. The 24-year-old cousin of Isaac Newton. Considers science a waste of time and a bore.

Isaac Newton. An arrogant and brilliant 23-year-old scholar and philosopher.

Joshua Marsh. Brenda's seven-year-old, inquisitive, precocious son.

Staging

Figure 4.1. Suggested placement of readers for *Apples, Moons, and Questions*.

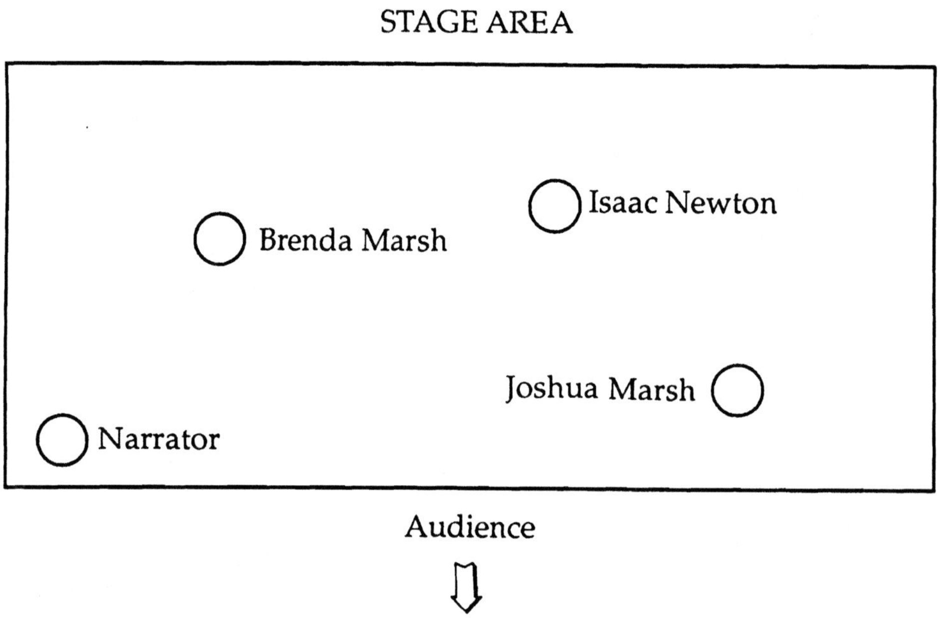

STAGE AREA

Audience

From *Great Moments in Science: Experiments and Readers Theatre*. © 1996. Teacher Ideas Press. (800) 237-6124.

Apples, Moons, and Questions

BRENDA:
Where are you going, Cousin Isaac?

ISAAC: (*Sullen and annoyed*)
To the orchard, Brenda, where I can find some quiet to think.

BRENDA:
Why go way out there when we're all about to play a fun game in here?

ISAAC:
I don't want to play. I want to think.

BRENDA: (*With a laugh*)
What ever about? You're far too serious, Isaac. You're only 23. Life in the country is glorious. Stay and laugh and play with us.

ISAAC: (*To himself*)
Why has nature so cruelly devised to hide me in this intellectual void during the very years when I should be surrounded by the best minds in Cambridge? (*To Brenda*) Thank you. But, no, Brenda. I shall be in the orchard.

NARRATOR:
Unseen bees contentedly buzzed from tree to tree and bush to bush. Butterflies flitted above rolling grassy lawns. It was a lovely country estate garden where the world seemed happily at peace—except for Isaac Newton, who sat glumly brooding on top of the garden's one small hill, his back against a thick apple tree. It was as if his own private rain cloud hovered darkly over his head.

JOSHUA:
Uncle Isaac . . . Uncle Isaac . . .

NARRATOR:
Brenda's seven-year-old son, Joshua Marsh, a buzzing bundle of thick brown hair and questions, darted out through a patchwork of wildflowers. He called Isaac "Uncle," as children often referred to older male relatives by that term.

JOSHUA:
What are you doing, sitting way out here all alone when everyone else is talking and playing in the house?

ISAAC: (*Chuckling*)
Complaining to the heavens, Joshua, and thinking.

JOSHUA:

What cha' thinking 'bout?

ISAAC:

How unfair it is I am stuck out here all alone when there are so many important answers to learn.

NARRATOR:

This was England in the year 1666. In London the bubonic plague ravaged a terrified population. Universities were closed, and students and teachers, like Isaac Newton, had to bide their time in safe country estates waiting for the plague to loosen its death grip on the cities.

JOSHUA:

You're *not* alone, Uncle Isaac. I'm here.

ISAAC: (*Laughing*)

You're absolutely right. All right, Josh, help me think about that moon up there.

JOSHUA: (*Excited*)

I like the moon. Is there really a man living in it?

ISAAC:

The real question, Josh, is why doesn't it fall down to earth?

JOSHUA:

That's easy. It doesn't want to. Why would it want to sit in an apple orchard when it can ride across the sky and see everything?

ISAAC: (*Laughing*)

That's as good as any of my answers. For that matter, if the earth rotates around the sun as Copernicus and Galileo have shown that it does, why doesn't the earth fall down to the sun?

JOSHUA:

That's silly! The sun is *up*. We can't fall *down* to something that's *up*!

ISAAC: (*Sighing*)

Why, oh why, do I have to be stuck way out here with no one to work with?

JOSHUA:

You're living here because of the play. Remember?

ISAAC:

Not play, Josh. It's the pla*gue*, the bubonic *plague*.

From *Great Moments in Science: Experiments and Readers Theatre*. © 1996. Teacher Ideas Press. (800) 237-6124.

JOSHUA:

Oh, yeah . . .

ISAAC:

(*With another sigh*) So here I sit, able to do little but *wonder* about the motion of the moon. What makes the moon move? Every motion needs some mover, some force, to create it. . . .

JOSHUA:

Why?

ISAAC:

Because without a force pushing on an object there is nothing to make it move. If an object is at rest, it will stay at rest until some force acts on it.

JOSHUA: (*Proudly*)

I'm seven. Mother doesn't make me take afternoon rests anymore.

ISAAC:

This kind of rest is different, Josh.

JOSHUA:

Is your kind of resting more fun, Uncle Isaac? Is that what you do?

ISAAC:

No. I am a scientist. I discover questions. It often seems that's all I can do, discover more questions.

NARRATOR:

They both heard the familiar "thunk" of an apple falling to the soft ground, and turned in time to see a second apple fall from an overhanging branch and bounce once before settling gently into the grass. It was certainly not the first apple Isaac Newton had seen fall to the ground, nor was there anything at all unusual about its short journey. All that was different were the specific questions in Isaac's mind, which the falling apple interrupted.

ISAAC:

The apple falls to earth while the moon doesn't. What's the difference between the apple and the moon?

JOSHUA:

That's easy. The moon's big and yellow. The apple is small and red.

NARRATOR:

But like a nasty winter cold, the question wouldn't leave Isaac's mind and lingered into the evening.

From *Great Moments in Science: Experiments and Readers Theatre.* © 1996. Teacher Ideas Press. (800) 237-6124.

ISAAC:

What's the difference between the moon and an apple? The apple fell. So some force must have pushed it, or pulled it, down to earth. Why doesn't that happen to the moon?

BRENDA:

Is this some sort of game, Isaac? Are we supposed to guess?

JOSHUA:

I don't think he wants you to play, mother.

BRENDA:

Quiet, everyone. Isaac has a new game for us to play. Ask your question again, Isaac.

ISAAC:

It's not a game, Brenda. I feel it's a most serious and basic question of the universe. What force pulls an apple to earth but doesn't pull the moon down to earth?

BRENDA: (*After a pause*)

That's it? That's your game, Isaac? *That* is just silly. (*To the group*) Someone pick out a board game. (*To Isaac*) You really need to learn how to have fun, Isaac.

ISAAC: (*Sighing*)

Questions, questions, questions.

NARRATOR:

Isaac's runaway mind wouldn't let him sleep that night. As thick clouds boiled in to block the stars, Isaac paced back and forth in front of the fireplace. It began to rain, a steady, windless rain. Suddenly Isaac stopped and stared wide-eyed out the window.

ISAAC:

The rain is falling.

BRENDA:

Of course it is. This is England. It rains all the time.

ISAAC:

No. I mean the rain is *falling*. It's falling to earth, just like the apple.

BRENDA:

Are you still on your apple and moon question?

ISAAC:

What force makes the rain fall? The same force that made the apple fall this afternoon?

From *Great Moments in Science: Experiments and Readers Theatre.* © 1996. Teacher Ideas Press. (800) 237-6124.

BRENDA:

Call it "nature," or "God," Isaac. That's just the way things are.

ISAAC:

Things always are the way they are for a reason, Brenda. If only I could find the right question.

NARRATOR:

Then, in that dark, gloomy night the first glimmer of an answer crept into his mind.

ISAAC:

The rain, the apple, the rocks, they always fall *straight* to the earth's surface. They fall that way here in England. They do in China and South America. Everywhere on earth objects fall straight down as if pulled by an invisible string straight toward the very center of the earth.

BRENDA: (*Laughing but confused*)

Dear Isaac, how would you have things fall? Sideways? We'd have an awful mess if everything fell sideways, wouldn't we?

NARRATOR:

Again, Isaac paced and thought before answering.

ISAAC:

Maybe there is a force that attracts every object to the earth.... But why should they only be drawn to the earth? Maybe it is a more basic force that attracts every object to every other object—some universal attractive force—and things fall to earth instead of each other because the earth is so much larger! This force, then, must be proportional to the size, or mass, of each object. The bigger the object, the greater the pull.

BRENDA: (*Bewildered*)

Dear cousin, *whatever* are you talking about?

ISAAC: (*Excited*)

Yes! A universal attractive force pulls every object toward every other object. The strength of that force depends on the size of the two objects being attracted.

BRENDA:

But, Isaac, the moon and earth are both large. Then why aren't they crashing into each other?

NARRATOR:

Newton collapsed sourly into a chair. His private dark rain cloud reformed overhead.

From *Great Moments in Science: Experiments and Readers Theatre.* © 1996. Teacher Ideas Press. (800) 237-6124.

ISAAC:

You're right, Brenda. Why doesn't the moon fall down to earth? Why doesn't earth fall down to the sun? Why doesn't this universal force apply to planets? (*Sighing*) Questions, questions, questions, and no answers.

NARRATOR:

Next morning, under a clearing sky, Joshua was out early, playing with a ball just behind the house.

ISAAC:

What's he up to so early?

NARRATOR:

The boy's ball was tied to a string Joshua held tight in his fist. He swung the ball, slowly at first, and then faster and faster until it stretched straight out on its string.

ISAAC:

Ahh, a silly game. . . . But it reminds me of . . . something.

NARRATOR:

Still faster Joshua spun the ball, now whistling over his head, as the two family dogs barked and leapt after it.

ISAAC:

His game shows me something . . . but what?

NARRATOR:

From his window, Isaac was thunderstruck at the simplicity of this obvious answer when it finally hit him.

ISAAC: (*Amazed*)

A string holds the ball in. But its motion makes it want to fly off, to escape. There are *two* forces pulling on the ball, just as there must be two forces pulling on the moon. And it doesn't fall because those two forces just balance each other!

NARRATOR:

Isaac dashed downstairs.

ISAAC:

A ball on a string is just like a moon circling the earth!

NARRATOR:

Isaac burst out the back door.

ISAAC: (*Excited*)

Josh, I need your ball for an experiment!

From *Great Moments in Science: Experiments and Readers Theatre.* © 1996. Teacher Ideas Press. (800) 237-6124.

JOSHUA:

Hey! I'm playing with that!

ISAAC:

I'll give it right back, Josh. I just need it a second.

NARRATOR:

Newton spun the string. The faster the ball spun, the harder it pulled out on the string. Newton released the string. Joshua's ball soared across the lawn and landed in thick blackberry bushes.

JOSHUA:

Hey! You lost it!

ISAAC:

No, Josh. It escaped. And without the universal attractive force holding *it* in, the moon would escape into space.

JOSHUA:

That's not the moon. That's my ball, and I'm telling!

BRENDA:

Telling what?

JOSHUA:

Uncle Isaac escaped my ball into the blackberry bush.

ISAAC:

Josh, Brenda, don't you see? I've answered my question!

BRENDA: (*Confused*)

Is this part of your game?

ISAAC: (*Laughing with the joy of discovery*)

The spinning ball wanted to fly off. But the pull of the string wouldn't let it. The spinning moon also wants to fly off into space. But, just like a string, the pull of the universal attractive force won't let it!

JOSHUA:

Is there really a string attached to the moon?

ISAAC:

An invisible one, Josh. The moon *is* just like an apple. They are both pulled down to earth, but the moon's motion keeps it from falling. There are two forces pulling on the moon, just like there were two forces pulling on the ball, and we just discovered what they are.

From *Great Moments in Science: Experiments and Readers Theatre.* © 1996. Teacher Ideas Press. (800) 237-6124.

JOSHUA:

We did? Now can we discover my ball?

ISAAC:

First come with me.

BRENDA:

This still isn't much of a game, Isaac.

NARRATOR:

Newton ran to his study and began to scribble complex mathematical equations in his journal.

JOSHUA:

What's that?

ISAAC:

An answer this time instead of more questions, Josh.

JOSHUA:

Looks like scribbles.

ISAAC:

Your ball, the apple, the rain, each of them held the answer. But I couldn't see it because I was asking the wrong question. I wondered why the moon doesn't fall. Wrong question. The moon *does* fall toward earth.

JOSHUA:

No, it doesn't, Uncle Isaac. It's still way up there.

ISAAC:

But its *motion*, its speed, also tries to make it fly off into space, just like your ball. The two forces compromise, and instead of doing either, the moon falls *around* the earth, just like the ball fell around my hand until I let it go. In the same way, the earth is falling around the sun!

JOSHUA:

The *earth* is falling?!

ISAAC:

I think this force should be called "gravitation." It's from the Latin. As I recall it means "to come together," more or less. Yes. Gravitation, the universal force that pulls all objects together, the one force that will explain how and why the moon and planets act as they do.

NARRATOR:

Joshua pointed at Isaac's journal.

JOSHUA:

Is that gravitation?

ISAAC:

No, Josh, this is mathematics. Mathematics will describe the existence and nature of gravitation. Your ball and the apple demonstrated it. My job was to discover the right questions.

JOSHUA: (*Pouting*)

I hope your next job is to get my ball back. . . .

NARRATOR:

But, of course, that will be another story.

From *Great Moments in Science: Experiments and Readers Theatre.* © 1996. Teacher Ideas Press. (800) 237-6124.

Related Experiments

Here is a series of simple experiments you can use to recreate the steps that led Sir Isaac Newton to his discoveries. These experiments will help you understand both the work of Newton and the scientific concepts involved.

Necessary Equipment

Each group will need:

- A large smooth surface at least 4 feet in diameter. Finished, well-sanded plywood will do, but a surface coated with a thick polyurethane sealer will do better. A hard plastic or formica or a smooth steel table surface will do better yet.

- One small metal ring or washer. The metal ring around the middle of many ballpoint pens is about the right size and thickness.

- One ball or smooth disc from 1 to 4 inches in diameter to act as the moon. Wood or steel balls will do very well. Rubber will suffice if steel balls are not available.

- One weight to act as gravity. Ideally, this weight should be the same mass as your moon ball.

- One string or thread to connect moon and weight. After connecting this string to ball and weight, it should still be 4 or 5 inches longer than the distance from the center to the edge of your board.

- Tape or staples to attach string to moon and weight balls.

- One stopwatch or digital watch.

➤ *Making the Moon Fall*

What You'll Investigate: Isaac Newton discovered that two forces act on the moon. Gravity pulls the moon straight toward the earth. The motion of the moon pulls it out into space. The net effect of these two balanced and opposing forces (one pulling the moon toward the earth; one pulling the moon away from the earth) is to make the moon forever fall *around* the earth, instead of either toward or away from it.

Newton was able to identify those two forces and develop the mathematical expressions to describe the way in which they acted on the earth, moon, and on all other masses. You will now build a model of the gravitational pull between the earth and the moon and explore how the moon moves through space around the earth as it really does.

From *Great Moments in Science: Experiments and Readers Theatre.* © 1996. Teacher Ideas Press. (800) 237-6124.

The Setup: Drill a hole in the exact center of your large board, which will represent the earth. This hole should be just big enough for you to wedge the metal ring snugly into the hole (it will reduce friction between string and the rough edge of the hole). Drape the string through this hole. Staple or tape the weight (gravity) on the end below the hole. Staple or tape the moon ball to the end on top of your board.

Mark the string in several places. First, with your moon extended either to the edge of the board or almost to the end of the string (1 inch from the end is an adequate amount), mark the string where it emerges at the top edge of the hole. You will start all experiments with string and moon in this position. Next mark the string ¼ of the way, ½ of the way, and ¾ of the way out to your moon ball.

Finally, place your board level and high enough so that the weight will not reach the floor even when your moon has been pulled all the way to the center of the board.

What to Do:

1. Time the fall of the moon. With the string and moon ball in their starting positions, release the moon and start your watch. Stop the watch just as your moon reaches the hole in the center of the board, which represents the earth. This is how long it takes your moon to fall to your earth when it is not moving through space at all. Repeat this experiment several times to ensure your measured time does not vary from one test to the next.

   Watch your moon carefully as it "falls" toward the earth. Does it roll smoothly, or do you see evidence of it bouncing, scraping, snagging, or otherwise being hindered by friction? If you do, smooth and refinish your board. Friction will distort all the tests you run.

2. Return the moon and string to their starting positions. This time, as you release the ball, roll it slowly in a direction perpendicular to the string that connects your moon to the earth. Again, time the moon's fall to the earth and watch the pattern it inscribes as it falls. Did the moon take longer to fall this time? Did it fall in a slow spiral toward the earth?

3. Repeat this experiment. But this time roll the moon ball a little harder (faster) as you let it go. Again time its fall and watch the spiraling fall of the ball. You will not be able to record the initial velocity, or speed, you gave to the moon on each test. But you can record how long it took for it to spiral down and crash to earth, and you will have a good sense of how hard you rolled the ball.

   Also, watch the marks you made on the string to see if your moon falls faster during the beginning or end of its fall. Does it take longer for the first quarter of the string (from starting mark to ¼ mark) to disappear down the hole, or for the last quarter (from ¾ mark to the moon ball)? Is the moon's velocity constant, or does it speed up, or accelerate?

From *Great Moments in Science: Experiments and Readers Theatre.* © 1996. Teacher Ideas Press. (800) 237-6124.

4. Continue to repeat this test, slowly increasing the initial speed of your moon ball. Eventually you will reach an initial speed that overcomes the pull of gravity and pulls the ball outward toward escape off the board.

Having found out how hard you have to roll the ball to overcome gravity, see if you can find the speed that just balances the pull of your gravity ball. When you have found this speed, your moon will roll around the board, with the starting mark on your string always staying right at the lip of the hole.

When you can come close to this speed, time how long it takes your moon ball to complete one-half of a circle, or orbit, around your board. You will use this time later in figuring out how fast your moon ball travels.

What's Going On?—Sources of Error: You will never be able to find a starting speed for your moon ball that lets it roll continuously around your earth as does the real moon. Your ball will always slow and roll to the center. Why? What slows your ball down that does not slow down the real moon?

There are three significant forces that slow your ball. (Remember, Newton proved that nothing changes velocity or direction without some force acting on it.) These forces include friction between your moon ball and the board, air resistance or drag, and resistance created by the string curling and twisting. See if you can find ways to redesign your experiment and reduce or eliminate these forces.

What to Observe: If your moon travels too fast, it tries to escape off the board. If it travels too slowly, your gravity weight pulls it in a spiral descent toward the earth. Our real moon does neither. It travels through space at just the right velocity to balance the pull of gravity. If it sped around the earth any faster, it would spin off into space. If it meandered any slower, it would crash in an earth-shattering collision. How fast does the moon travel around the earth? How fast does your moon ball have to travel to just balance the pull of your gravity ball? Can you calculate those two speeds?

First, what is speed, or velocity? It is a measure of the distance traveled in some amount of time (as in 20 miles per hour, or 10 feet per second). How far does the moon travel when it makes one circle around the earth? The moon is roughly 240,000 miles from the earth, and the formula for the circumference of a circle is

$$C = \pi r$$

How long does it take the Moon to travel once around this orbit? Exactly 28 days, a lunar month. If speed equals distance divided by time, divide the distance the moon travels by 28, and you'll find the speed of the moon measured in miles per day. Can you think of factors you haven't included in this calculation or approximations that will keep your result from being an exact measure of the velocity of the moon?

Now repeat this process for your model of the moon. Earlier you timed one-half of a circle when your moon rolled at a speed that kept it from either flying off the board or falling in toward the center. If you double that time, you will know how long your moon would take to complete one orbit. Can you calculate how far it travels during one orbit? Can you then calculate its velocity? This speed will be measured either in feet per second or in inches per second. Convert the units so that the units for your calculation of the real moon's and your moon's speed will be the same.

From *Great Moments in Science: Experiments and Readers Theatre.* © 1996. Teacher Ideas Press. (800) 237-6124.

Questions to Ask Yourself: You have just set up and tested a model that demonstrates Newton's first law of motion. What does this experiment show you about the movement of the earth around the sun? About the motion of our sun as part of the Milky Way galaxy? About the motion of a ball you throw as far and hard as you can? Do the same forces and principles apply to each of these moving objects?

If an apple falls toward the earth, does the earth also fall toward the apple? If so, why can't you detect that motion? In the same way, does the earth fall toward the moon? Does the sun fall toward the earth? Can and have these motions been detected and measured? See if your library has information on this motion, which is often called "stellar wobble."

From *Great Moments in Science: Experiments and Readers Theatre.* © 1996. Teacher Ideas Press. (800) 237-6124.

Bridges to Books

This story deals with one aspect of our understanding of the physical world around us. You can learn much more about these concepts in your library. The following list gives you key words, concepts, and questions to begin your exploration in a school or public library.

Sir Isaac Newton is considered to be one of the world's greatest physicists. What jobs did he hold? What other discoveries did he make? Until **Albert Einstein** formulated the laws of relativity, **Newtonian physics** were thought to describe all the physical phenomena in the universe. Did Newton receive any honors and recognition while he was alive?

This story centers around **gravity**. What is gravity? Gravity pulls an apple toward the earth. Does it also pull the earth toward that apple? Does it pull two apples toward each other? Does gravity apply to any two objects or just for large bodies such as planets and stars? See if you can find a good explanation of the force we call gravity in your library.

The cornerstone of Newton's work was his three **Laws of Motion**. Can you find out what these laws are about? Can you find descriptions of them? Can you find examples of each working in your daily life?

References for Further Reading

The following references deal with the major characters, concepts, and scientific processes in this story.

Bixby, William. *The Universe of Galileo and Newton.* New York: American Heritage, 1974.

Branley, Franklin. *Gravity Is a Mystery.* New York: Thomas Y. Crowell, 1986.

Christeanson, Gale. *In the Presence of the Creator: Isaac Newton and His Times.* New York: Collier Macmillan, 1984.

Fauvel, John, ed. *Let Newton Be!* New York: Oxford University Press, 1988.

Haines, Gail. *Which Way Is Up?* New York: Atheneum, 1987.

Hall, A. Rupert. *Isaac Newton: Adventurer in Thought.* New York: Blackwell, 1992.

———. *Giants of Science.* New York: M. Cavendish, 1991.

Ipsen, D. C. *Isaac Newton, Reluctant Genius.* Hillside, NJ: Enslow, 1985.

Land, Barbara, and Myrick Land. *The Quest of Isaac Newton.* Garden City, NY: Garden City Books, 1960.

Lerner, Aaron. *Einstein and Newton.* New York: Franklin Watts, 1973.

Maury, Jean-Pierre. *Newton: The Father of Modern Astronomy.* New York: Harry Abrams, 1992.

McTavish, Douglas. *Isaac Newton*. New York: Bookwright Press, 1990.

Narlikar, Jayant. *The Lighter Side of Gravity*. San Francisco: W. H. Freeman, 1982.

Rattansi, M. *Isaac Newton and Gravity*. London: Priory Press, 1974.

Rocard, Jean Michelle. *Newton Versus Relativity*. New York: Vantage Press, 1992.

Sitweitka, Albert. *Physics: From Newton to the Big Bang*. New York: Franklin Watts, 1986.

Skurzynski, Gloria. *Zero Gravity*. New York: Bradbury Press, 1994.

Van Cleave, Janice. *Gravity*. New York: John Wiley, 1993.

Westfall, Richard. *Never at Rest*. Cambridge, England: Cambridge University Press, 1980.

Consult your librarian for additional titles.

From *Great Moments in Science: Experiments and Readers Theatre*. © 1996. Teacher Ideas Press. (800) 237-6124.

A Spark of Genius

Benjamin Franklin's discovery of the nature of electricity in 1750

Scientific Background

Imagine a world with no electric outlets, no hair dryers, no refrigerators, no batteries, no electric lights, no garage door openers, no radios, no televisions, no power plants, no power lines. What kind of electricity would exist in such a world? What would you do with it? Is there any "natural" electricity, or is all electricity artificially created in a generator or power plant?

Electric utilities have only existed for the past 100 years. Utility power lines first snaked across the American landscape during the early part of this century. Many parts of the United States didn't have regular electrical service until the 1930s and 1940s. Much of the world still doesn't have it.

Until the 1800s virtually nothing was known about electricity. No one needed it or used it. No one thought about it with more than mild curiosity. And why should they? No one could envision that electricity could be useful, that it could perform such a great variety of work. No one even knew what electricity was. Some thought it was a liquid. Some thought it was fire. It wasn't even called "electricity." Playful static electricity was called "static." The jagged, deadly bolts that crashed from stormy skies were called "lightning." No one suspected they were really the same.

Benjamin Franklin was first to seriously investigate these two forms of electricity to see how similar or dissimilar their natures were. His interest in electricity began with the growing popularity of Leyden jars. Invented in Europe in the early 1700s, Leyden jars (actually the first electrical capacitors, or storage devices) were popular as party games by Franklin's time. Servants or slaves would charge the jars with handcranks for hours. Then party guests would touch the jar and be shot back across the room by a very amusing and satisfying shock.

The European inventor of Leyden jars believed static was an invisible fluid and so could only be trapped in some vessel, such as a jar or bowl. He never imagined that electricity was actually trapped in the thin sheets of metal foil that lined the jar. Neither did Franklin set out to discover the real nature of electricity. As an inventor, he set out to invent a better Leyden jar—one that would store and deliver more power. This engineering work led him to his famous kite experiment, which defined the real nature of electricity and opened the door to the electric era of the world.

Readers Theatre

Characters

Narrator

Benjamin Franklin. A 44-year-old enthusiastic, energetic scientist, inventor, publisher, and statesman.

William Mercer. Franklin's 38-year-old friend, an enthusiastic and trusting fan.

Joseph Blakely. Franklin's 48-year-old neighbor. He's very skeptical and prone to sarcastic humor.

Jeffrey. Franklin's 14-year-old son. He's cautious and unsure.

Staging

Figure 5.1. Suggested placement of readers for *A Spark of Genius*.

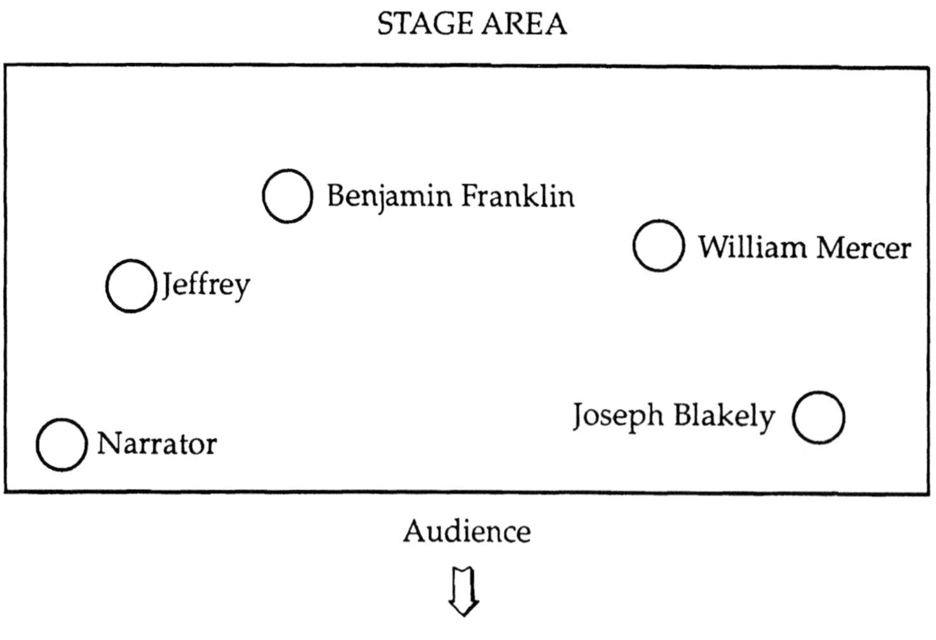

STAGE AREA

Audience

A Spark of Genius

FRANKLIN:
Welcome! Welcome. Both of you please come in.

MERCER:
Thank you, Benjamin. It's so good of you to invite us for dinner.

BLAKELY: (*Irritated*)
Move *all* the way in, William Mercer, and let me inside, too. It's cold out here! . . . Evening, Franklin. . . . (*Sniffs the air*) I thought you invited us for a turkey dinner. But I don't smell any turkey cooking.

FRANKLIN: (*Chuckling to himself*)
But you will, Joseph. You will.

NARRATOR:
It started with an invitation to a turkey dinner two days before Christmas at the home of Mr. Benjamin Franklin, for two of his friends and neighbors. Franklin, the 44-year-old statesman, publisher, and inventor, greeted his guests with the sly giggles and the mischievous twinkle in his eye that always said some gimmick, some new invention, was afoot.

MERCER: (*Shivering*)
Why, I think this is the coldest December I can remember. My feet almost froze just walking from next door.

FRANKLIN: (*Eagerly*)
Enough chit-chat, gentlemen. Come, come. Follow me into the kitchen.

BLAKELY: (*Sarcastic aside*)
Where, I suppose, we'll have to cook our own dinner.

NARRATOR:
Franklin whisked his guests into the spacious kitchen of his Philadelphia home.

FRANKLIN:
Let me take your coats. Warm yourselves by the fire and shed winter's chill.

MERCER: (*Rubbing his hands at the fire*)
Ahh. This is more like it.

BLAKELY: (*Suspiciously*)
No, it isn't. Where's our wintry feast, Franklin? I see no turkey dinner.

From *Great Moments in Science: Experiments and Readers Theatre.* © 1996. Teacher Ideas Press. (800) 237-6124.

NARRATOR:

On Franklin's kitchen table sat not the makings of a splendid feast, but only two large Leyden jars.

MERCER:

Ahh, Leyden jars. Some party games before we eat?

BLAKELY: (*Sourly*)

I didn't trudge over here for mindless games with static electricity. I came for dinner!

FRANKLIN:

I see you've found my new Leyden jars.

BLAKELY: (*Sarcastically*)

They're the only things here to find. Where's our dinner?

FRANKLIN:

All in good time, my skeptical friend. But first a demonstration of my new—and improved—Leyden jars.

NARRATOR:

In the 1750s everyone was familiar with Leyden jars. They were a "must" for every fashionable party. Static electricity was a very popular plaything in America. People would shuffle across a rug and reach out for a metal doorknob to get a spark, a sharp "pop!" and the thrill of a quick jolt running through a finger while everyone else laughed and applauded.

Leyden jars gave the same effect, only better. Invented just four years earlier, they quickly became the rage in Europe and spread to the colonies as a favorite toy.

FRANKLIN:

As you know, Leyden jars are just large glass jars, partially filled with water and wrapped with a tin foil around the outside. A rod extends through an insulating cork out the top of the jar to a knob. When a Leyden jar is charged, static electricity flows down into the water. Then anyone who grabs the knob while touching the tinfoil, or other metal, get a resounding—and, I might add, somewhat disconcerting—shock.

MERCER:

But Benjamin, these Leyden jars look different than the others I've seen.

FRANKLIN: (*Pleased and proud*)

Very observant, William. I *have* made a few modifications.

MERCER:

It looks like they're coated both outside *and* inside with tinfoil. And they're far bigger than the ones I've seen at parties.

From *Great Moments in Science: Experiments and Readers Theatre.* © 1996. Teacher Ideas Press. (800) 237-6124.

BLAKELY: (*Still suspicious*)

And your jars are connected by this wire. (*Now irritated*) And I suppose you want us to grab the rod and receive a shock that will curl both hair and toes before you feed us. Very well, then. Let's get it over with.

FRANKLIN:

No, no! Don't touch!

NARRATOR:

Benjamin leapt in front of his friends as if to protect them from some great danger.

BLAKELY:

Don't be melodramatic, Franklin. They're only Leyden jars.

FRANKLIN: (*Seriously*)

I have found a way to pack more electricity in these jars—much more. (*Now back to his normal jolly self*) Oh, it's all basic experimental physics really. But these now carry a sizable punch, as you shall see. Don't move!

NARRATOR:

Franklin disappeared out a side door. Moments later he burst back in, a large and very live turkey wedged under one arm.

MERCER:

What does a turkey have to do with your Leyden jars?

BLAKELY:

It appears our turkey dinner is a very long way from ready.

FRANKLIN: (*Apologetically*)

I couldn't start without you. You see, the turkey is part of my demonstration.

MERCER:

How can a turkey demonstrate a Leyden jar?

FRANKLIN:

By my calculations these Leyden jars pack enough wallop to kill this turkey and still have enough static energy left over to spark the fire that cooks it.

BLAKELY:

Impossible! I've never seen a Leyden jar produce enough spark to ignite dry tinder, much less kill even the smallest game.

FRANKLIN:

But you're about to! That's why I invited you here tonight. First I should describe my modifications and my recent experiments with this amazing electricity.

From *Great Moments in Science: Experiments and Readers Theatre.* © 1996. Teacher Ideas Press. (800) 237-6124.

BLAKELY:

I could listen far better if I had already enjoyed my turkey dinner.

NARRATOR:

With the squabbling, fluttering turkey held tightly under one arm, Franklin began to enthusiastically describe and point out his modifications to standard Leyden jar design.

FRANKLIN:

Finally, I have connected the jars with this copper wire because I have found that electricity will flow down a wire just as water flows down a streambed.

MERCER:

Amazing, Franklin!

FRANKLIN:

Exactly, my friends! That is what we shall do!

NARRATOR:

Getting carried away by his own enthusiasm, Benjamin reached out one hand, and laid it on the nearest Leyden jar.

MERCER:

Careful, Benjamin!

BLAKELY:

Look out!

NARRATOR:

There was a sharp crack, and a sizzling blue arc leapt from the jar to Franklin's fingers. He shot back half a dozen feet and crashed to the floor. The turkey squawked wildly as it dashed about the room.

MERCER:

Benjamin, are you all right?

BLAKELY:

First things first, man. Catch that turkey. I'm hungry.

NARRATOR:

Dazed, Franklin slowly sat up, rubbed his eyes to clear them, and adjusted his spectacles. Then his face lit with the glow of discovery.

FRANKLIN: (*Murmured*)

That was exactly like a lightning bolt.

MERCER:
Benjamin, do you need a doctor?

FRANKLIN:
That was exactly like a lightning bolt!

BLAKELY:
Hand me an axe. I'll see to the turkey myself!

NARRATOR:
With a far-off glow in his eye, Franklin kept repeating,

FRANKLIN:
That was *exactly* like a lightning bolt. . . .

NARRATOR:
In 1750 everyone believed there were two kinds of electricity: playful static and the fiery electricity that leapt from clouds as lightning. Sitting dazed on his kitchen floor, Benjamin was the first to think that they might be the same.

FRANKLIN:
Would you two see to the turkey? I have to think.

BLAKELY:
I was afraid something like this would happen. I should know better than to accept invitations to a scientist's house.

NARRATOR:
All through dinner's preparation and consumption, Franklin was lost deep in thought about this new discovery.

BLAKELY:
Come, come, Franklin. Stop grousing because your turkey-and-the-Leyden-jar experiment flopped. The meat is delicious.

FRANKLIN:
Don't you see? We have stumbled onto a great discovery.

BLAKELY:
What discovery? That if a host stalls long enough the guests will cook dinner?

FRANKLIN:
No! It seems that static and lightning are the same—that all electricity is the same! I'm thinking about the design of an experiment to prove it.

From *Great Moments in Science: Experiments and Readers Theatre*. © 1996. Teacher Ideas Press. (800) 237-6124.

MERCER:

But how could you prove that? No one can collect and control fierce lightning bolts.

BLAKELY:

Maybe if you held out a turkey, a lightning bolt would kill it and start the fire to cook it.

FRANKLIN:

I must create a huge Leyden-jar-like electric circuit to let electricity flow from the clouds just as it does from a jar.

MERCER:

But how?

BLAKELY:

Line a lake with tinfoil, perhaps?

FRANKLIN:

I need to think. What sort of circuit could collect electricity from the clouds and hold it like a Leyden jar?

NARRATOR:

Franklin was still brooding about the experiment he wanted to conduct when the dinner ended and his guests departed.

Less than a week later Benjamin Franklin knocked on the door of his neighbor, William Mercer.

FRANKLIN:

William Mercer, are you home?

MERCER:

Franklin? Is that you?

FRANKLIN:

Come see. I've completed my electrical circuit, my "Leyden jar for the clouds."

MERCER:

I don't mean to be as skeptical as Joseph Blakely. But that's just an ordinary kite.

FRANKLIN:

Not an ordinary kite at all, William. Look more closely.

NARRATOR:

A sharp metal wire rose from the top of the kite and connected to a ball of thick twine kite string. The string ended at a large iron key tied to a ribbon that Franklin held.

From *Great Moments in Science: Experiments and Readers Theatre.* © 1996. Teacher Ideas Press. (800) 237-6124.

FRANKLIN:
I am beginning to understand how electricity works. Rather than being a kind of fire, I see it more as a fluid: able to flow down wire or cord from place to place, and able to build up in appropriate storage devices like water builds in a lake.

MERCER:
But, Benjamin, how will the kite work?

FRANKLIN:
Electricity will flow from a cloud down the wire, trickle down the twine, and collect in this metal key. But it won't flow beyond the key because my ribbon won't conduct electrical current. Then we'll see if a spark will jump from the key, just as it does from a Leyden jar.

MERCER:
But what will that prove?

FRANKLIN: (*Exasperated*)
That lightning is the same as common static, of course! That there is only one kind of electricity. . . . What I need now is a good thunderstorm.

NARRATOR:
When an afternoon storm brewed up dark and threatening a few weeks later, Franklin rushed to launch his kite.

FRANKLIN: (*Shouting*)
William, help my son, Jeffrey, hold the kite.

MERCER:
In this storm? The winds are too fierce.

NARRATOR:
The wind howled, and the clouds boiled above them. A cold rain pounded down about their upturned collars.

JEFFREY:
I can't hold the kite any longer, father!

FRANKLIN:
Very well. Launch it now.

MERCER:
Are you daft? We'll all be swept away!

From *Great Moments in Science: Experiments and Readers Theatre.* © 1996. Teacher Ideas Press. (800) 237-6124.

FRANKLIN:

I'll hold the ribbon once the ball of twine has played out.

NARRATOR:

Twice William Mercer and Jeffrey had to help brace Franklin as savage gusts grabbed hold of the kite and tried to rip the twine from his hand. The kite twisted and tore at the air like a rampaging bull.

FRANKLIN:

There! Look! It's happening!

JEFFREY:

What's happening? Where?

FRANKLIN:

Look at the twine. Look at the wire!

MERCER:

My heavens! The wire is glowing a faint blue!

FRANKLIN: (*Excited*)

See how the fibers of twine rise up, bristling straight out? That's electricity.

JEFFREY:

I can almost *see* the electricity trickling down the twine!

NARRATOR:

No, a lightning bolt did not strike the kite as has often been reported. And a good thing, too. A French scientist was killed a few months later by a lightning strike when he tried to repeat Franklin's experiment.

FRANKLIN:

Now that we've proved cloud electricity flows like static, let's see if it sparks like static as well.

MERCER:

How do we test that?

FRANKLIN:

Hold your hand near the key. That's where electricity is stored.

MERCER:

Me?

From *Great Moments in Science: Experiments and Readers Theatre.* © 1996. Teacher Ideas Press. (800) 237-6124.

FRANKLIN:
Then you give it a try, Jeffrey.

JEFFREY:
After you, father.

FRANKLIN: (*With a sigh*)
Very well. I'll do it myself. Help steady the kite.

NARRATOR:
Franklin reached out a cautious hand closer and closer to the key. Pop! A spark leapt to his knuckle and shocked him—just like a Leyden jar.

FRANKLIN:
Splendid! Your turn, Jeffrey.

NARRATOR:
Franklin's son timidly stretched out one finger. A blue arc sizzled from key to knuckle. It made him cry out with fright and leap back behind his father.

FRANKLIN:
Well done, Jeffrey.

JEFFREY:
That was fun. Let me try it again!

FRANKLIN:
No, that's enough for one day. Reel in the kite. I'm ready for hot cider.

NARRATOR:
William Mercer hauled in the now tattered kite, and all hurried inside for congratulations, hot cider, and a careful review and discussion of the experiment. And that is how the serious study of electricity was launched. Of course, it would take men like Michael Faraday of England and Samuel Morse of America another 50 years to fully understand the nature and flow of electricity. But that, of course, is another story.

From *Great Moments in Science: Experiments and Readers Theatre*. © 1996. Teacher Ideas Press. (800) 237-6124.

Related Experiments

Here is a series of simple experiments you can use to recreate the steps that led Benjamin Franklin to his discoveries. These experiments will help your students understand both the work of Franklin and the scientific concepts involved.

Necessary Equipment

For the experiment on static electricity:

- A variety of shoes and sandals. Have each member of the class bring in a pair.

- Several common objects to test for static buildup. These can include a balloon, a sweater, a washcloth, and a hand-sized block of wood.

- A variety of floor surfaces. Many schools have carpet squares for young children to sit on. Search these for different kinds and lengths of fibers. Use linoleum, hard wood, short shag, long shag, wool, nylon, and indoor-outdoor flooring coverings.

For each group for the construction of a capacitor:

- Two long (up to 30-inch) sheets of wide aluminum foil.

- Two sheets of paper a little larger than the foil. Try several different kinds of paper—newspaper, art paper, tracing paper, and so on, in different groups to compare the results.

- One wooden dowel ($\frac{1}{2}$ inch to 1 inch in diameter), a little longer than the aluminum foil is wide.

- Two alligator clips.

- Two lengths of wire (about 3 feet each).

- An amber rod and a piece of fur to charge the capacitor. You will need only one set for the entire class.

▶ *Getting a Charge Out of Static (Done as a whole class project)*

What You'll Investigate: Everyone has built up a static charge shuffling across a rug and felt a small spark when it is discharged from a finger to a metal door knob. Everyone has heard the snap of static sparks when pulling off a sweater on a dry day. Many have done this in the dark and have seen the sparks.

Did you know that those brief flashes of sweater sparks often hold as much as 20,000 volts of electric potential? While they have such a high voltage, or potential, they also have only tiny electric currents. This keeps them from being dangerous. Compare that to household current, which is only 110 to 120 volts, but has a much larger current flow and is very dangerous.

First, you'll investigate different types of surfaces to see which build stronger static charges.

From *Great Moments in Science: Experiments and Readers Theatre.* © 1996. Teacher Ideas Press. (800) 237-6124.

The Setup: Choose one metal object about waist height, preferably grounded, to act as the discharge point for your human static charge. Line up the various flooring materials near it.

What to Do: The following steps help you achieve a qualitative, or comparative, sense of which types of surfaces and combinations of surfaces lend themselves to the process of stripping free electrons, otherwise known as the buildup of static electricity. Repeat each test several times to ensure you always get the same results. Your results will be subjective; you will compare whether the spark generated in each test was "big" or "small," whether it was "strong" or "weak," and whether it jumped a "long" distance or a "short" distance.

Differences between tests will often be subtle. None of the sparks you generate, for example, will jump much over one-quarter of an inch. Still, you should be able to detect some differences.

1. Which type of floor covering makes the best sparks? For this test pick four different types of shoes, sandals, or bare feet, and test all four of them on each floor covering. Shuffle across each floor sample the same way and for exactly the same length of time. This way any differences you detect will be attributable to differences in the various floor coverings.

   Don't step off the floor covering you are testing when you reach out to discharge your static spark. Slowly ease your finger closer to a metal object (a doorknob, for example). Go very slowly so you can pinpoint the exact moment of discharge.

   Have several students watching very closely to assess whether the spark was "big," "medium," or "small" and whether it jumped a "small" distance (around $\frac{1}{64}$ of an inch), a "medium" distance (around $\frac{1}{8}$ of an inch), or a "large" distance (around $\frac{1}{4}$ of an inch). The person who carried the spark will have to decide how "strong" or "weak" it felt.

   Record the kind of shoe, type of floor covering, and results for each test. Did patterns emerge? Did certain types of floor covering or foot covering produce consistently stronger or weaker sparks? Why?

2. How does the length of the shuffle affect charge buildup? For this step, use only the two floor coverings and the two types of foot covering that produced the best sparks during your first experiment. Now re-test these combinations to see what effect the length of time you build up a static charge has on the apparent size of the resulting spark.

   Being sure to shuffle back and forth in exactly the same way each time, vary the length of time you shuffle your feet to build up a static charge. Try 5, 10, 20, 40, and 90 seconds. Repeat each several times and record your results. Did the spark grow stronger as shuffle time increased? Did the charge seem to reach a peak level after some length of shuffling, so that more shuffling didn't produce additional static buildup?

3. What type of shoes or other contact surface works best? Use the three floor coverings that produced the best sparks. Select the shortest length of shuffle time that produced a big, strong spark. Now test every kind of shoe your students brought, along with bare feet. Add in whatever miscellaneous objects you have (balloons, sweaters, etc.) by rubbing them across the floor coverings. Repeat each test several times and record your results.

4. All of the above tests were conducted on one day with one certain level of humidity. Wait for another day with a different humidity level and repeat these experiments. Try to run the experiment on one very humid day, at least one intermediate day, and on one very dry day. Which produces the best static charges? Why? See if you can find answers in your library.

What's Going On?—Sources of Error: What makes this experiment most difficult is that often every spark looks like every other spark. You have to be very careful to detect the differences between them. Are there any other sources of error that might affect your results? What about differences in weight between one person and another and the resulting differences in frictional pressure on the carpet as they shuffle? What about differences in skin characteristics from person to person (oiliness, moisture, sweat, etc.) that might affect how conductive their skin is? Also note that experiments where you record only subjective readings make it much harder to repeat the experiment and be sure you get the same results each time.

What to Observe: During this experiment search for patterns and trends. Did you find groups of surfaces that generate better or poorer static charges? Did you find that static electric charges build up better on conductive or nonconductive surfaces? Why? Find reference books in the library that will answer this question.

Can you "feel" a static or electrical charge as it builds up in your body? Why not? As anyone who has been accidentally shocked by household current knows, you feel the flow of electrons (current) rather than the voltage (potential) of those electrons. Static electricity has an extremely high voltage, but minuscule current.

Questions to Ask Yourself: What creates static electric charges? How are electrons tripped from one material and lodged in another to create an electrical charge? Did your experiments uncover any patterns in the buildup of static, or do all surfaces react about the same?

► A Leyden Jar Without the Jar *(Done in small groups)*

What You'll Investigate: You have learned that Leyden jars were early electrical capacitors, or electrical storage devices. They were shaped as jars because their inventor thought that electricity was a fluid and so could only be contained in a jar. We now know that the electrical charge was actually stored in the tin foil sheets that lined the inside and outside of the jar. Now try to build your own simple capacitor.

The Setup: Layer your paper and aluminum foil: paper, foil, paper, foil. Make sure that the two sheets of aluminum foil do not touch each other. It's all right if the papers touch.

What to Do:

1. Tape one end of your paper–aluminum foil sandwich onto the wooden dowel. Then carefully roll your four-layer capacitor around the dowel, making sure that the two pieces of foil never touch.

2. Fold one corner of each piece of foil to triple the thickness and fasten an alligator clip to this thicker portion. Make sure that the two alligator clips do not touch.

3. Attach a wire to one of the clips. Attach the other end of this wire to a metal, grounded object in the room. A radiator works, but find a spot where you can wrap the wire around an unpainted part of the metal.

4. Attach a wire to the other clip. This wire will be the wire you use to charge your capacitor.

5. Rub an amber rod with a piece of fur five or six times. It works best if you always rub in the same direction. Now touch this charged amber rod to your capacitor charging wire. Repeat this step a number of times to build up a bigger charge in your capacitor. Experiment to see if more charging creates a bigger spark when you discharge your capacitor. Make sure your charging wire doesn't touch anything except the amber rod, or it may discharge your capacitor into whatever else it touches.

6. Now test your capacitor. You won't get a lightning bolt or a spark that leaps across the room. You'll only get a spark similar to your static sparks, but it should be a visible spark. Slowly bring the end of the charging wire closer and closer to a metal object in the room (like a doorknob or a radiator post) until a small electric spark jumps from the wire.

7. Compare results using different kinds of paper (dielectric) and different sizes of foil sheets.

What's Going On?—Sources of Error: Did you get a spark from your capacitor? If not, what do you think happened to your charge? Did the two sheets of foil touch somewhere? Did the two alligator clips touch? Did your charging wire touch something else before you touched it to the metal object where you wanted to discharge your spark? Did you get a good connection between the amber rod and charging wire?

What to Observe: A capacitor is a simple electrical energy storage device. It's like a reservoir where energy can flow in, be stored, and then flow back out as needed. Its charge is held between two parallel metal plates. What do you think determines how much energy a capacitor can hold? The type of metal? The distance between metal plates? The type of paper (called a dielectric) that separates the two plates? The size of those plates?

Questions to Ask Yourself: Compare your static electric spark and the spark from your capacitor to lightning. They are really the same thing. Clouds and earth form a big capacitor. A static charge builds up high enough to cause a spark (lightning bolt) to jump between the two. Can you imagine how much bigger the static charge in a cloud must be to get its spark to jump thousands of feet when you can only build up a spark that jumps a small fraction of an inch?

How would you change the design of your capacitor to build a capacitor that could store more electrical energy? What did Benjamin Franklin do to improve his Leyden jar design?

From *Great Moments in Science: Experiments and Readers Theatre.* © 1996. Teacher Ideas Press. (800) 237-6124.

Bridges to Books

This story deals with one aspect of our understanding of the physical world around us. You can learn much more about these concepts in your library. The following list gives you key words, concepts, and questions to begin your exploration in a school or public library.

Benjamin Franklin was one of America's greatest treasures, a fascinating, multitalented man. He has received worldwide recognition as a scientist, engineer, diplomat, and inventor. Did you know that he invented swim fins, or that he opened the first lending library? See how many of his inventions you can find mentioned in your library. Can you find other scientifically important discoveries he made? What else did he do?

This story centers around the nature of electricity. What is electricity? Where does it come from? Is natural electricity different from that created in a power plant? Use **electricity**, **lightning**, and **static electricity** as key words to aid your library search for additional information. Can you guess who named the electric charges "positive" and "negative"?

This story also describes **Leyden jars**. See if your library has descriptions and pictures of different Leyden jar designs. Who was Leyden, and what else did he do besides invent the jars that bear his name?

Finally, the story mentions an electrical device called a **capacitor**. What is a capacitor? Are there capacitors in your radio, your stereo, your microwave? How big are commercial capacitors? What do they look like? How do they differ from other common electrical components such as resisters, diodes, or amplifiers?

References for Further Reading

The following references deal with the major characters, concepts, and processes in this chapter.

Alder, David. *Benjamin Franklin: Printer, Inventor, and Statesman.* New York: Holiday House, 1992.

Aliki. *The Many Lives of Benjamin Franklin.* New York: Simon & Schuster Books for Young Readers, 1985.

Asimov, Isaac. *The Kite That Won the Revolution.* New York: Houghton Mifflin, 1973.

———. *How Did We Find Out About Electricity?* New York: Walker & Company, 1973.

Clark, Ronald. *Benjamin Franklin: A Bibliography.* New York: Random House, 1983.

Daugherty, Charles. *Benjamin Franklin: Scientist & Diplomat.* New York: Macmillan, 1965.

Daugherty, James. *Poor Richard.* New York: Viking Press, 1961.

Davidson, Margaret. *The Story of Benjamin Franklin: Amazing American.* New York: Dell, 1988.

Draper, John. *The Life of Franklin.* Washington, DC: Library of Congress, 1977.

Fleming, Thomas. *The Man Who Dared the Lightning.* New York: William Morrow, 1971.

Franklin, Benjamin. *The Autobiography of Benjamin Franklin.* New York: Harper, 1964.

Meltzer, Milton. *Benjamin Franklin: The New American.* New York: Franklin Watts, 1988.

Osborne, Mary. *The Many Lives of Benjamin Franklin.* New York: Dial Books for Young Readers, 1990.

Potter, Robert. *Benjamin Franklin.* Englewood Cliffs, NJ: Silver, Burdett, 1991.

Randall, Willard. *A Little Revenge: Benjamin Franklin and His Son.* Boston: Little, Brown, 1984.

Sandak, Cass. *Benjamin Franklin.* New York: Franklin Watts, 1986.

Stein, R. *Benjamin Franklin: Inventor, Statesman, and Patriot.* New York: Rand McNally, 1972.

Stewart, Gail. *Benjamin Franklin.* San Diego, CA: Lucent Books, 1992.

Stone, A. *Turned On: A Look at Electricity.* New York: Prentice Hall Press, 1970.

Tamarin, Alfred. *Benjamin Franklin: An Autobiographical Portrait.* New York: Macmillan, 1969.

Tanford, Charles. *Benjamin Franklin Stilled the Waves.* Durham, NC: Duke University Press, 1989.

Tourtellot, Arthur. *Benjamin Franklin: The Shaping of Genius.* New York: Chelsea House, 1990.

Whyman, Kathryn. *Sparks to Power Stations.* Boston: Gloucester Press, 1989.

Wilson, M. *American Science and Invention.* New York: Bonanza, 1960.

Wright, Esmond. *Franklin of Philadelphia.* Cambridge, MA: Belknap Press, 1986.

Consult your librarian for additional titles.

From *Great Moments in Science: Experiments and Readers Theatre.* © 1996. Teacher Ideas Press. (800) 237-6124.

Friction in the Factory

Scientific Background

What is heat? You can't see it, touch it, taste it, or smell it. Where does it come from? Is heat created, or is it a physical part of a piece of wood like water content and cellulose fiber? You can feel hot. You can feel warmth. You can feel heat radiating from a fire. You can even feel the absence of heat (cold). But what is heat?

For centuries science struggled to understand the nature of heat. By the Middle Ages, alchemists had concluded that heat was a "thing." It existed as a physical part of any object that released heat, such as a piece of wood or skin that's warm to the touch. Different materials contained different amounts of heat, which they called "caloric."

Fire released caloric. The sun was on fire and so released caloric into the air, which traveled to the earth to warm us. Burning a log caused that log to release its caloric. When the log was completely burned and all its caloric had been released, it would no longer feel warm because it was no longer releasing heat. Caloric always flowed from greater caloric pools (heat) to smaller ones (cold).

This was the commonly accepted view of heat all through the seventeenth and eighteenth centuries. It seemed to explain what people could observe. No one questioned this view until Count Rumford (neither a count, nor really named "Rumford") visited the Bavarian cannon factory for which he was responsible. What he found there didn't match what scientists believed. He hastily conducted an experiment to find out where heat comes from and what heat really is.

What he uncovered was "friction." What he gave to science was a better understanding of how the natural world works.

Readers Theatre

Characters

Narrator

Nobleman and Hoser. A single reader can play the parts of a court nobleman, who represents all of Bavaria's nobility, and a second factory worker, who runs the cooling hoses.

Count Rumford. Thirty-eight-year-old self-proclaimed count. Arrogant, self-assured, condescending.

Frederick Weiss. The cannon factory foreman. He's 46 and shows great deference to the count, but is deathly afraid of the wrath of the king of Bavaria. Tries to keep the peace, please everyone, and produce the needed cannons.

Driller. An older factory worker who runs the boring drill and doesn't care about politics or science, only about doing his job and not getting fired.

Staging

Figure 6.1. Suggested placement of readers for *Friction in the Factory*.

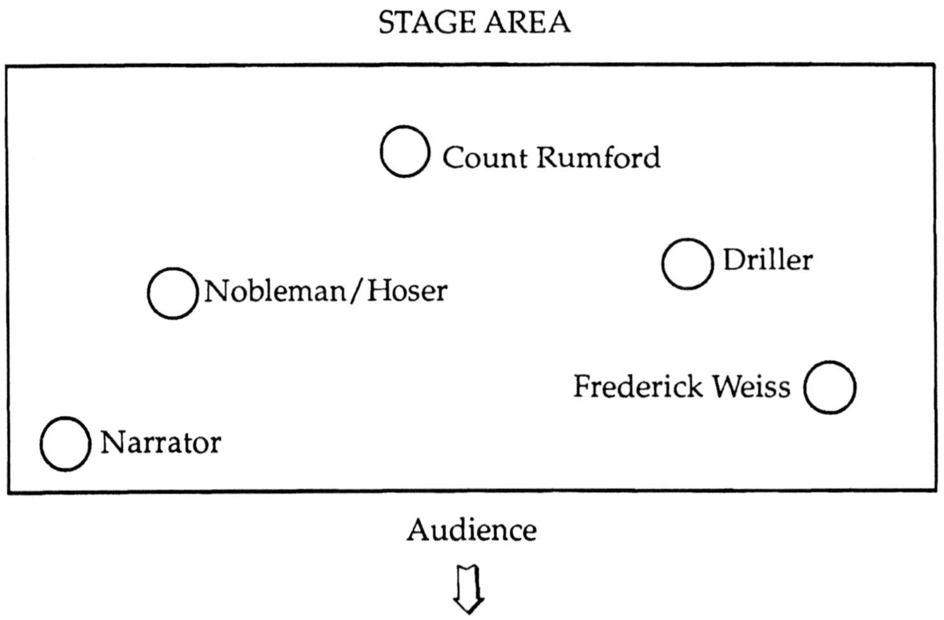

STAGE AREA

Audience

From *Great Moments in Science: Experiments and Readers Theatre*. © 1996. Teacher Ideas Press. (800) 237-6124.

Friction in the Factory

NOBLEMAN:
More cannons!

NARRATOR:
The king of Bavaria needed more cannons, and he needed them *now*.

NOBLEMAN:
More cannons, NOW!

NARRATOR:
The cry arose from ministers, dukes, earls, generals, and heralds.

ALL:
More cannons!

NARRATOR:
They were yelling at Count Rumford, the king's director of cannon manufacturing.

RUMFORD: (*Irritated*)
Cannon this. Cannon that. What a boring ruckus they raise.

NARRATOR:
Dashing Count Rumford had floated through the king's court for almost a year with a charming smile and a grand bow, and had won the favor of the king of Bavaria. Actually, the count was not really a count at all. He gave himself that title when he moved to Bavaria. But, then, Rumford wasn't his real name either.

The count had been born Benjamin Thompson in Massachusetts. During the Revolutionary War, he had been a well-paid spy for the British. As the colonists marched toward victory, Thompson fled to England. There he got an even better paying job spying on the British for the Prussians. By 1790 Thompson had to hotfoot it to Bavaria. There, he changed his name to Count Rumford, and he planned to settle down quite comfortably with his large stash of spy money and an easy job being in charge of the king's cannon factory.

ALL:
More cannons!

NARRATOR:
Then war broke out. The king wanted 1,000 new cannons on the front line.

RUMFORD: (*Disgusted*)
Bother! I suppose now I'll have to actually visit that smelly cannon factory.

From *Great Moments in Science: Experiments and Readers Theatre.* © 1996. Teacher Ideas Press. (800) 237-6124.

NARRATOR:
Despite his title, Count Rumford had never actually seen the cannon factory.

RUMFORD: (*Chuckling*)
I'll yell at the plant manager, twice as hard as everyone at court has yelled at me. That will fulfill my duties and be quite satisfying.

NARRATOR:
The factory was a huge, deafeningly noisy warehouse. On one side, next to a long row of eight billowing open hearths, metal wheel rims and mounting brackets were hammered into shape around wooden wheels and cannon carriages. Hammer blows on red hot metal strips echoed like high-pitched thunder across the plant. Steam rose from hissing vats as glowing metal plates were cooled in slimy water, only to be reheated in the shimmering hearths.

On the other side of the warehouse, great cannons, themselves, were forged. Molten metal, spewing like lava, was poured into huge molds. From these emerged solid cylinders for cannon barrels. Many were 14 feet long and more than 4 feet across. The inside of the cannon barrel was hollowed out by a rapidly turning boring drill, which scraped and gouged its way down the interior.

WEISS: (*Nervously*)
Count Rumford, so good of you to honor us with a visit.

RUMFORD: (*Shouting*)
What? I can't hear a word over this awful din.

WEISS:
I am the factory manager, Frederick Weiss. Welcome to the king's cannon factory.

NARRATOR:
Of course, the boring drills grew dangerously hot. Streams of water had to be constantly sprayed to keep them from melting. Hissing steam rolled out of each cannon barrel and billowed up to the ceiling, where it slowly condensed and dripped down onto the workers below.

The pounding noise of that factory was incredible.

RUMFORD: (*Sarcastic*)
What a fascinating place this is, Wright.

WEISS:
Weiss. Frederick *Weiss*, sir. Would you prefer to start with a tour of the factory or a review of our production books?

RUMFORD:
What? Speak up, Rice.

WEISS:

Weiss, sir! Do you want to see our books?

RUMFORD: (*Arrogantly*)

Books? Why on earth would I come to a factory to read books? You run along. I'm going to watch the drilling.

WEISS:

Ah, the boring out of each cannon barrel is a critical process. Our drillers are experts, the best in the world.

RUMFORD:

Why ever would I care about your workers? It is the heat that fascinates me.

WEISS:

The heat, sir?

RUMFORD:

Use your eyes, man. Do you not see great quantities of heat flowing into the air and water from those cannon barrels?

NARRATOR:

The subject of heat had interested the count for many years. As Benjamin Thompson, he and several scientist friends had studied heat in England in the mid-1780s. At that time all scientists believed that heat was an invisible, weightless liquid called "caloric." They believed that, as a substance grew hotter, its caloric overflowed and spilled out in all directions to heat whatever it touched.

RUMFORD:

How could so much caloric pour out of the metal of one cannon barrel? That is the question. (*Louder, to one of the workers*) You, there, driller, have you measured the amount of caloric flowing from each cannon barrel?

DRILLER:

Pardon, sir? Measured, sir? I just drill the barrels straight and true.

RUMFORD: (*Irritated*)

Yes, yes, I'm sure. But have you conducted this important heat experiment?!

DRILLER:

Experiment, sir? I just drill.

RUMFORD: (*Fuming*)

Weill, what do you have to say about this man?

From *Great Moments in Science: Experiments and Readers Theatre.* © 1996. Teacher Ideas Press. (800) 237-6124.

WEISS: (*Nervous and apologetic*)
Factory Manager Frederick *Weiss*, sir.

RUMFORD:
So, Mr. West, how do you account for the fact that your factory has ignored every opportunity to conduct this essential science experiment?

WEISS:
Science experiment, sir? We're a factory, sir. We make cannons. We don't do science, sir. . . . And it's *Weiss*, sir. Weiss!

RUMFORD:
In the king's cannon factory, we do what I say we will do. (*To Driller*) My good man, I know factory manager East has failed in his duty to conduct essential science. But surely you have at least closely watched the flow of heat from the metal barrels as you bore them out.

DRILLER:
Watched the *heat* sir?

WEISS:
Weiss, sir. *Weiss*! And I was never informed we were to conduct experiments. And I do not think I have failed.

DRILLER:
I watch the metal to make sure I'm drilling correctly. I didn't know I could watch heat. . . .

RUMFORD:
Look at the heat flowing so freely all around you: heat waves shimmer through the air, billowing steam obscures your view, hot water covers the floor. Have you never asked yourself how much heat can be in one of these barrels to begin with?

DRILLER:
No one told me to watch the heat. They just said to watch the drill.

WEISS:
I must insist, Count Rumford, that our job is only to produce quality cannons, and has nothing to do with science or heat.

RUMFORD:
Nonsense. I say our job is science.

WEISS: (*Distraught*)
But the king needs cannons, not science.

From *Great Moments in Science: Experiments and Readers Theatre.* © 1996. Teacher Ideas Press. (800) 237-6124.

RUMFORD:

Again, nonsense. If the king had a brain in his head, he would know he needs science most of all.

NARRATOR:

Count Rumford paced along the fiery line of cannon drillers. Factory Manager Weiss nervously trotted just behind.

RUMFORD:

Don't you see the opportunity we have here, man? The secrets of heat are locked in those cannon barrels. How much caloric does each one hold? How and where is it stored within the metal fabric? What releases it to flow out into water and air? By Jove! What knowledge we shall find here!

WEISS:

As long, of course, as it doesn't slow our production of cannons.

NARRATOR:

The count seemed to arrive at a decision. He cried in a loud voice . . .

RUMFORD:

All drillers cease work! This side of the factory is being diverted to conduct an experiment.

WEISS:

Oh, no! This will never do! The king will be furious!

RUMFORD:

All of you will work solely on the devices I need to accurately measure heat.

WEISS: (*Hopefully*)

Perhaps *several* of the drillers could be spared to produce cannons for the king . . . . We *do* have a production schedule to meet . . .

RUMFORD: (*Ignoring Weiss*)

You there, on the hoses, fetch three large and accurate thermometers.

HOSER:

Thermometers, sir?

RUMFORD:

Next, I need a cement wall and trough built around this cannon barrel. The wall will capture all water poured onto it during drilling. The trough will channel this flow of heated water so I can measure it.

From *Great Moments in Science: Experiments and Readers Theatre.* © 1996. Teacher Ideas Press. (800) 237-6124.

WEISS: (*Terrified*)

Oh, dear. But . . . but sir . . . What of cannon production?

RUMFORD:

Don't you see the brilliance of my plan, Whittle?

WEISS:

Weiss, sir.

RUMFORD:

By estimating water flow volume and by measuring its temperature change, I will calculate exactly how much caloric flows from this cannon barrel. Feel the barrel, man.

WEISS:

Yes, sir.

NARRATOR:

Plant Manager Weiss slid one hand behind Rumford's along the smooth, gray metal that would become a cannon barrel.

RUMFORD: (*Chuckling*)

It starts so cool. You'd think it couldn't hold very much caloric. Soon, we shall see. (*Louder*) Bring extra hoses.

HOSER:

Yes, sir. More hoses.

RUMFORD:

Begin the drilling!

DRILLER:

Drilling, sir.

NARRATOR:

With a deafening screech, the powerful bits of the boring drill ground their way into the metal cylinder. Hoses sprayed water from all sides.

RUMFORD:

Excellent! See my thermometers climb? 20 degrees, 30 degrees! (*To Weiss*) Whitt, how big would you say is this river of water flowing down my trough?

WEISS:

Weiss, sir! And I would say $\frac{1}{8}$ meter deep by $\frac{1}{2}$ meter wide.

From *Great Moments in Science: Experiments and Readers Theatre.* © 1996. Teacher Ideas Press. (800) 237-6124.

RUMFORD:

I agree. And see? Enough caloric flowed into each ounce of it to raise the water's temperature 30 degrees!

NARRATOR:

The drill bits ground deeper into the barrel. The metal glowed dull red.

RUMFORD:

More water!

HOSER:

The hoses are open full, sir.

RUMFORD:

Then more hoses! We cannot allow any heat to escape as steam and go uncounted through my trough!

DRILLER:

More hoses!

NARRATOR:

Eight thick hoses now flooded the barrel with cold water. Still the drill bit and cannon barrel glowed and hissed.

DRILLER:

I should change drill bits, sir. This one is dulling.

RUMFORD:

Continue to drill. My experiment is not yet complete.

WEISS:

But, sir, dull bits drill more slowly and put us farther behind the production schedule.

RUMFORD: (*Sourly*)

Driller, how long have you been working on this cannon?

DRILLER:

Half an hour, sir.

RUMFORD:

Cease work!

WEISS: (*Hopefully*)

And now we can go back to producing cannons?

From *Great Moments in Science: Experiments and Readers Theatre.* © 1996. Teacher Ideas Press. (800) 237-6124.

RUMFORD: (*Ignoring Weiss*)

Something is wrong, very wrong. I must think.

WEISS:

Perhaps you could think about the fact that the king demands more cannons!

RUMFORD: (*To himself*)

How can this much caloric flow from one gun barrel? When will all caloric flow out and leave only cold metal behind?

NARRATOR:

Then Rumford's face brightened. He pointed at a very dull, used drill bit against the plant wall.

RUMFORD:

Use *that* drill bit!

DRILLER:

But it's already dull, sir.

WEISS:

Very dull, sir.

RUMFORD:

Exactly!

DRILLER:

But, sir, it will take us forever to bore out a cannon barrel with that bit.

RUMFORD:

Now we'll see when this barrel runs out of heat, even if it *does* take us forever!

WEISS:

Forever? The king will have my head!

NARRATOR:

Again the grinding started. The scraping screech rattled walls across the factory. Both cannon barrel and dulled bit glowed and hissed like a fiery volcano. Water streamed into the barrel from nine hoses.

RUMFORD:

Look! Even more heat flows from the cannon! The water has been heated 50 degrees! Amazing!

From *Great Moments in Science: Experiments and Readers Theatre.* © 1996. Teacher Ideas Press. (800) 237-6124.

NARRATOR:
The dull drill bit inched its way deeper into the cannon barrel with agonizing slowness. The balding plant manager wrung his hands and quietly sobbed in fright.

RUMFORD:
So much heat! More than I ever dreamed could be held in the metal!

NARRATOR:
Again Rumford's face clouded.

RUMFORD:
Cease work!

DRILLER:
Another duller drill bit, sir?

RUMFORD:
Something is very wrong. . . . More than 8,000 liters of water have flowed down my trough. My thermometers say all of it has been heated by over 30 degrees. That's enough total heat to turn a cannon barrel into a bubbling pool of liquid metal many hundreds of degrees hot. Yet when I initially touched the barrel, it felt cool.

NARRATOR:
The workers stood like statues while Count Rumford paced, deep in thought.

RUMFORD:
No metal can hold more heat than is needed to melt it and still feel cool. Something is very wrong.

DRILLER:
May we go back to the good drill bit now?

WEISS:
May we go back to producing cannons for the king, sir?

RUMFORD: (*Indifferently*)
Do whatever you like. My experiment is finished. Now I must decide what it means.

NARRATOR:
Count Rumford sat in a corner of the warehouse and watched the driller resume work on his cannon barrel.

RUMFORD:
Still heat flows out!

From *Great Moments in Science: Experiments and Readers Theatre.* © 1996. Teacher Ideas Press. (800) 237-6124.

NARRATOR:

Watching steam and molten metal spray from the cannon barrel, a great discovery began to take shape in the count's mind.

RUMFORD:

Heat cannot be a liquid that is stored in matter. My experiment shows me that cannot be the case. So, if heat is not already stored in the metal fabric, it must be created right in front of my eyes! . . . But how, and by what?

NARRATOR:

He saw only the metal barrel, the metal drill bit, and the scraping motion of the second across the first.

RUMFORD: (*Excited*)

Motion! If heat is not a thing stored in every substance, perhaps it is created by motion—in this case the scraping motion of metal over metal. . . . But how?

NARRATOR:

Rumford raced across the factory to study the motion of the boring drill.

DRILLER:

I'd stand back, sir. Molten metal's hot enough to burn right through to the bone.

RUMFORD:

Cease work on this barrel and start a new one. I must be able to closely watch the motion of the drill.

WEISS:

Couldn't we finish this cannon first? It would be so nice to produce *one* for the king today. . . .

RUMFORD: (*Irritated*)

Certainly not. Important science must be completed!

NARRATOR:

Count Rumford peered closely at the drill bits as they chiseled into the tip of the new cannon barrel.

DRILLER: (*Aside*)

Standing that close his whole face will get fried to a crisp!

NARRATOR:

Still Rumford watched, fascinated.

From *Great Moments in Science: Experiments and Readers Theatre.* © 1996. Teacher Ideas Press. (800) 237-6124.

RUMFORD:

Movement is being converted into *heat*! The drill's overall motion must be converted into quick, tiny movements by the tiniest, individual particles making up the two metals. It is that movement, that ripping apart, by these tiniest of particles, and their crashing into each other, that creates heat.

NARRATOR:

Of course, no one believed Count Rumford's new theory on where heat came from for over 50 years. "What particles?" they demanded. "I see no tiny particles!" But as atoms and molecules were discovered, Rumford's theory suddenly made perfect sense, and became the foundation for our understanding of heat created by friction, or the rubbing of two substances against each other.

Of course, how the king of Bavaria fared in the war is another story.

From *Great Moments in Science: Experiments and Readers Theatre*. © 1996. Teacher Ideas Press. (800) 237-6124.

Related Experiments

Here is a series of simple experiments you can use to recreate the steps that led Count Rumford to his discoveries. These experiments will help you understand both the work of Count Rumford and the scientific concepts involved.

Necessary Equipment

- A double sink with hot and cold running water and an extra dishpan-sized bucket (or a single sink and two buckets).

- One sturdy, wide-mouthed bottle (like the old-style milk bottles).

- Enough marbles (or similarly sized smooth stones) to fill this bottle more than half full.

- A good water thermometer.

- A series of gradually rougher solid surfaces. Good examples include a steel tabletop, linoleum, polished wood, smooth plywood, plastic, fine and coarse sandpaper, nylon mesh (stockings), various fabrics, and bricks or unfinished wood.

- A bottle of vegetable oil.

➤ *The Hot and Cold of Heat Flow*

What You'll Investigate: In Count Rumford's day, scientists believed heat was a physical substance called "caloric" that flowed to a colder substance when released from a warmer one. Certainly heat is a hard concept to grasp because it is created in a variety of ways and does exhibit some of the properties of a physical substance, including always flowing from hot to cold (just as water always runs downhill). In this first experiment, you will look at the flow of heat and see how that flow can confuse its definition.

The Setup: Fill one pan or side of a double sink with water as hot as a human hand can stand. Fill the other side with cold water. Add ice to the cold side if you have some. Fill a third pan with warm water (around 80°F to 85°F). This pan should be the largest of the three.

What to Do: A student tester will be blindfolded and place one hand in the hot water and one in the cold. Just for the record the tester will declare the heat of the water (hot, warm, or cold) for each hand.

The tester leaves his or her hands in the water baths for 60 seconds. A second student lifts the hot water hand and places it in the warm water tub, without telling the blindfolded tester whether the hand is going to the cold or the warm tub. Have the tester declare the temperature of the water his or her hand is now in. Now lift the cold water hand and place it in the same warm water bath, making sure it doesn't touch the other hand. Again, have the tester declare the temperature of the water that the cold water hand has been shifted to.

What to Observe: The warm water bath will not feel warm to either hand. It will feel cold to the hand that was heated in hot water and is now sensing the flow of heat from the hand into the water. The warm water, however, will feel hot to the other hand because that hand was chilled in a cold water bath, which pulled heat from the hand. That hand now senses the flow of heat from the water into the hand and decides the water is hot.

The point is that we sense heat *flow* and describe things as cold, warm, or hot according to the direction and rate of this perceived heat flow. We don't sense heat itself, only its flow. This makes our understanding of heat more complicated as our direct experience of heat is relative, depending on heat flow, or the movement of heat, and not on heat itself.

Questions to Ask Yourself: What is the difference between the flow of heat and heat itself? How does the dictionary define heat? Where does heat come from? Can heat be created? How? Is there more than one way to create heat?

➤ *The Rub of Friction*

What You'll Investigate: We all have an intuitive sense of what friction is. It is the resistance to movement when two surfaces slide against each other. Count Rumford studied the friction of metal grinding against metal under high pressure. Heat is a chief by-product of this resistance to movement.

But do some surfaces produce more friction that others? How can you increase or decrease the friction between any two surfaces that move in contact with each other? These are the questions you will address in this experiment.

The Setup: Assemble the various surfaces you have collected in a random order on a long countertop or table. Number each surface to be tested. Identify three groups, each containing three friction testers and one recorder to compile their results.

What to Do:

1. Each tester in each group will rub his or her hand back and forth across each surface 10 times. At the end of this rubbing each tester will rank the amount of heat generated from a low score of 1 ("I don't really feel anything") to a high score of 10 ("My hand is burning up and I can hardly stand it"). If a student's hand begins to hurt during the rubbing, he or she should immediately stop. The recorder should then note how many rubs were completed, as well as the tester's evaluation of the heat generated.

   Begin the experiment with the first group of three testers. They should each maintain *medium* pressure with each surface as they rub their hand back and forth. The first tester in this group rubs his or her hand slowly across each surface 10 times. The second rubs at a medium speed. The third rubs fast.

   Immediately upon completing their rubs on each surface, each tester ranks that surface from 1 to 10 according to their sense of how much heat was generated during the rubbing. The recorder must record these rankings on a grid sheet with a separate column for each surface and a separate line for each tester.

From *Great Moments in Science: Experiments and Readers Theatre.* © 1996. Teacher Ideas Press. (800) 237-6124.

2. The second group of testers will now repeat the experiment, except they will each maintain *hard* pressure with each surface during their rubbing. Again, the first tester rubs slowly, the second at a medium speed, and the third rubs fast.

3. The third set of testers will also apply *hard* pressure during their rubbing. However, this group will pour a thick coat of vegetable oil onto their rubbing hand before they test each surface. As before, the first tester rubs slowly, the second medium, and the third rubs fast.

What's Going On?—Sources of Error: This is a qualitative (as opposed to quantitative) experiment. Error can be introduced into the experiment through each tester's differing interpretation of such qualitative words as "hard" versus "medium," or "slow" versus "fast." Still, you should be able to see consistent trends and patterns emerge.

A second type of error can creep into this experiment. Besides creating heat, friction also breaks down the two surfaces being rubbed against each other, which is why in the story the drill wore holes into the cannon metal. A soft or rough surface will wear down more quickly than a hard or smooth surface. For example, most of us have gotten rugburns from sliding across carpets or scraped skin from sliding across polished gym floor; our skin in these cases is softer than the rug or the gym floor. Some of a tester's perception of heat or discomfort could be due to the wearing down of the hand's skin by a rough surface such as sandpaper.

What to Observe: What creates frictional heat? Is it a function only of the surfaces involved? Does speed affect it? Does pressure? From the results of your class, can you tell if speed has a bigger effect on the rate of heat generation than pressure does, or if it is the other way around?

What effect did oil have on the rate of heat generation? Do you think that is why all moving parts in cars, motors, and gears are lubricated with oil or grease?

Questions to Ask Yourself: What controls how much heat is created when two surfaces rub against each other? Is enough heat created by friction to be a problem? Based on your results in this experiment, how would you design moving parts to minimize frictional wear and heat creation? Is there friction when you move your hand through air? Is frictional heat created? Why does the space shuttle or a meteorite grow so hot streaking back into the earth's atmosphere?

➤ *All Shook Up*

What You'll Investigate: The last experiment was purely qualitative. That is, you rubbed your hand across a series of surfaces and, by the relative feel of your hand, ranked each surface for how much frictional heat it produced. But how much heat did this friction really produce? How much heat does it take to heat up the palm of your hand?

When we think of heat, we first think of temperature and the Fahrenheit or Celsius scales. But heat is really a form of energy. Heat itself is not measured in temperature degrees, but in units that describe how much heat energy is being produced or consumed. Heat is measured in calories and in British Thermal Units (BTUs).

From *Great Moments in Science: Experiments and Readers Theatre*. © 1996. Teacher Ideas Press. (800) 237-6124.

A calorie is defined as the amount of heat required to raise the temperature of 1 gram of water 1 degree Centigrade. Thus, the more common measure, temperature, is an indicator of the amount of heat that has been added or removed from the substance being measured.

In this final experiment, you will measure how much heat friction can produce.

The Setup: Fill a widemouthed bottle ½ to ⅔ full with marbles and completely fill it with room temperature water. The class should stand in a circle.

What to Do: First measure the temperature of the water and record it. Seal the bottle so no water can escape and pass the bottle to the first student. Each student shakes the bottle hard 10 times and passes it to the next student.

After each student has had a turn, unseal the bottle and again measure the water temperature.

What to Observe: Shaking the bottle smashes the marbles back and forth so that they rub against each other and against the side of the jar. The heat created by this friction is trapped in the water, where you can measure it by noting the temperature rise of the water.

Can you calculate the amount of heat created by the marble's friction? Remember, 1 calorie is the amount of heat required to raise the temperature of 1 gram of water 1 degree Centigrade. Pour the water from your bottle into a large measuring cup. Multiply its volume (number of cubic centimeters, or centiliters) times its temperature rise to see how much heat you created.

The temperature rise of your water was probably small. But remember water acts as a lubricant, and you have already seen how a lubricant greatly reduces friction. Further, marbles are light, smooth, and round. Thus, there is very little surface contact between individual marbles, and they are not pressed together very hard, meaning there was relatively little pressure. In the previous experiment, these were all conditions which you found produced the least amount of frictional heat.

Questions to Ask Yourself: Does friction produce very much heat? How could you either increase or decrease the amount of frictional heat created when two surfaces rub against each other? Is there a limit to the amount of frictional heat a surface can create?

Friction is a mechanical source of heat. What else creates heat? Can you name chemical processes that create heat? Nuclear processes? Are there other kinds of heat-creating processes?

From *Great Moments in Science: Experiments and Readers Theatre.* © 1996. Teacher Ideas Press. (800) 237-6124.

Bridges to Books

This story deals with one aspect of our understanding of the physical world around us. You can learn much more about these concepts in your library. The following list gives you key words, concepts, and questions to begin your exploration in a school or public library.

Count Rumford is a colorful character in the history of science. See what other information you can find on him in your library. Did you find that he was born in Massachusetts, and that his real profession was being a spy? Did you find his real name? On what other scientific projects did he work? Is he credited with any other scientific breakthroughs?

This story deals with **heat** and more specifically with **friction**. Use those key words to assist in your search for further information in the library. Friction is one way to create heat. But how is that heat really created? Are there other ways to create heat? How many can you find?

References for Further Reading

The following references deal with the major characters, concepts, and processes in this chapter.

Adler, Irving. *Hot and Cold.* New York: Day, 1975.

Ardley, Neil. *Hot and Cold.* New York: Franklin Watts, 1983.

———. *Heat.* New York: New Discovery Books, 1991.

Asimov, Isaac. *Great Ideas of Science.* Boston: Houghton Mifflin, 1969.

Bowden, Frank. *Friction.* New York: Doubleday, 1975.

Brown, Sanborne. *Count Rumford: Physicist Extraordinaire.* New York: Anchor Books, 1972.

Darling, David. *Between Fire and Ice.* New York: Dillon Press, 1992.

Jennings, Terry. *Heat.* Chicago: Childrens Press, 1988.

Mellett, Peter. *Hot and Cold.* New York: Franklin Watts, 1992.

Pine, Tillie. *Friction All Around.* New York: Whittlesey House, 1970.

Orton, Vrest. *Observations on the Forgotten Art of Building a Good Fireplace.* New York: Sincere Press, 1969.

Santrey, Lawrence. *Heat.* Mahwah, NJ: Troll Associates, 1985.

Tattner, Ernest. *Architects of Ideas: The Story of the Great Theories of Mankind.* New York: Carrich and Evans, 1958.

Thompson, James. *Count Rumford of Massachusetts.* New York: Farrar & Rinehard, 1955.

TV Ontario. *Take a Look #2: Friction.* Chapel Hill, NC: TV Ontario, 1990. Videocassette.

Victor, Edward. *Friction.* New York: Follett, 1977.

Consult your librarian for additional titles.

A Gold Medal
Speck of Light

Maria Mitchell's discovery of a comet in 1847

Scientific Background

Stars were the first scientific love of humans. People have always studied the heavens—partly as practical aids to navigation, and partly to understand the stars themselves. Our desire to understand space has always been greater than the precision of available technology. Until the seventeenth century, humans had nothing more powerful than their own eyes with which to watch the heavens. Even then they learned much about the motion and nature of the planets and stars, but not nearly enough to answer all their questions about how and why heavenly bodies moved across the sky as they did.

Telescopes greatly enhanced astronomers' ability to learn from the stars. But for every question telescopes answered, two new ones seemed to be created. Even today, with high-powered radio telescopes and satellite-mounted telescopes, scientists still puzzle at the many mysteries they uncover and dream of the day yet another improved piece of equipment will give them the answers they seek.

In the world of astronomy, the greatest prize of all is the discovery of a new body in the heavens—star, planet, comet, or even an entire galaxy. With so many astronomers and so many powerful telescopes searching the skies for new discoveries, it is surprising how many discoveries have been made by amateurs working with unsophisticated equipment. Pluto, for example, was discovered by an American amateur astronomer working in his backyard.

More than high-powered equipment, what's needed to discover something new in heavens is steadfast watching and an intimate familiarity with the night skies so an observer will recognize that something is new, and lots of time spent staring through a telescope. One discovery, also made by an American amateur astronomer, was heard round the world, because in 1846 the king of Denmark offered a gold medal for the discovery of a new comet. This story is about how that medal was won.

Readers Theatre

Characters

Narrator

John Mitchell, Sr. A 54-year-old seaman who lives by the stars. Maria's father, he repairs ships' chronometers for a living.

King of Denmark. Now in his sixties, he is an avid amateur astronomer.

John Mitchell, Jr. Maria's 27-year-old brother. He is a fisherman on local fishing boats, not sea going whalers.

Maria Mitchell. A 29-year-old librarian and amateur astronomer. She's orderly, systematic, conscientious, and thorough but also somewhat quiet, plain, and unimaginative.

Susan Peale. Maria's 26-year-old library co-worker. She's a good friend but not an astronomer.

Staging

Figure 7.1. Suggested placement of readers for _A Gold Medal Speck of Light_.

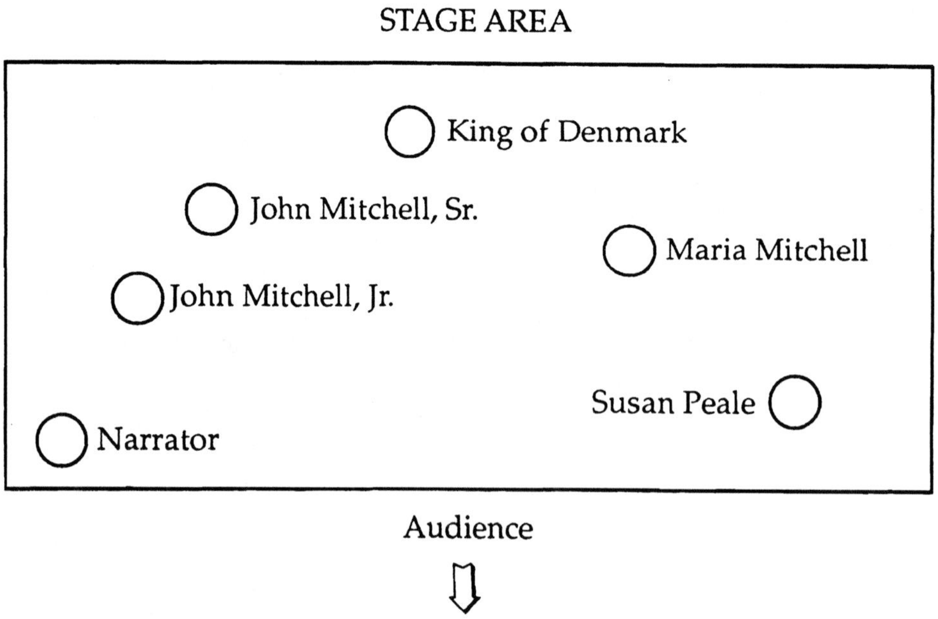

STAGE AREA

◯ King of Denmark

◯ John Mitchell, Sr.

◯ John Mitchell, Jr.   ◯ Maria Mitchell

Susan Peale ◯

◯ Narrator

Audience

⇩

A Gold Medal Speck of Light

JOHN, SR.:

From what I have seen, Your Majesty, your Denmark looks a lot like my Nantucket Island—flat and surrounded by the sea. Only Nantucket is much smaller.

NARRATOR:

John Mitchell, Sr.; his son, John, Jr.; his daughter, Maria Mitchell; and a friend of hers, Susan Peale, all stood at court before the king of Denmark in the spring of 1849. A sizable crowd had gathered to watch the king present a gold medal to amateur astronomer Maria Mitchell.

KING:

Everywhere in Denmark you can hear and smell the ocean.

JOHN, JR.: (*Eagerly and agreeing*)

That's just like home, your kingship . . .

JOHN, SR.: (*Whispered*)

Your *Majesty*, John!

JOHN, JR.: (*Embarrassed*)

Your Majesty, I mean. There's no place in Nantucket where you can't hear the creak of wooden decks, the clanging of channel buoys, the smell of salt air, and the screeching of gulls.

JOHN, SR.:

Flat, marshy ground stretches away from town on three sides. On the fourth, the harbor leads out to an endless, flat sea. The masts of whaling and cargo ships are the tallest points for miles in any direction.

NARRATOR:

Nantucket Island sat off the southern shore of Massachusetts. The island's one town, Nantucket, was a bustling ocean port. With most of the men at sea, Nantucket always looked like a town of women, children, and dogs.

KING:

Enough geography. We are here because of a comet. Miss Mitchell, do you also work by the sea?

MARIA:

I'm a librarian, Your Majesty.

KING:

How did a librarian come to discover a new comet in the heavens instead of in a book?

MARIA:

The library is my *job*. But my heart has always been an astronomer.

KING:

Ahh. Astronomy, rather than seawater, runs in your veins, eh?

MARIA:

I love to watch the stars, to map them, to mark their progress across the sky, to know that, although they are countless miles away, the light of each star travels faithfully straight to me on isolated Nantucket Island. The stars have always been my passion, Your Majesty.

KING:

Always?

MARIA:

Always, Your Majesty. Every person in Nantucket first learns to tell time by the stars. I have studied the stars since I was five. My father's job was to check, or calibrate, the chronometers for whaling ships before they put out to sea. To do that he made a series of precisely known observations over the course of an evening while his assistant—me—recorded and checked the chronometer's time for each event. I got my first telescope when I was eight. I could use a sextant when I was six.

KING: (*Impressed*)

Use a sextant at six?

MARIA:

Every Nantucket house has a sextant.

NARRATOR:

A sextant is a device used by ships at sea to measure position by the stars.

JOHN, SR.:

The lifeblood of our whole town beats with the ebb and flow of the tides.

SUSAN:

But there *are* some things in Nantucket that run according to the clock. The public library is one. Maria opens the wide front door precisely at noon each day, and closes exactly at 5:00. Except for Saturday when the library stays open until 8:00, and for Sunday when it's closed all day.

KING:

And you are?

SUSAN:

Susan Peale, Your Majesty.

From *Great Moments in Science: Experiments and Readers Theatre.* © 1996. Teacher Ideas Press. (800) 237-6124.

KING:

Ahh. Also a librarian?

SUSAN:

Yes, Your Majesty. I am Maria's assistant.

KING: (*To Maria*)

If you've been raised by the ebb and flow of the stars and sea, why are you a librarian?

MARIA:

I suppose there are three reasons. First, I love books and have read every book in the library. Second, I think reading is important, and I want to influence what the children of Nantucket read. Finally, my library job lets me stay up most nights, studying the stars, and sleep late each morning.

NARRATOR:

Maria was 29. She still lived at home with her father and three brothers. She still worked each day at the library. She still studied the stars each evening—if it was clear and if the moon wasn't out to obscure faint stars with its great wash of reflected sunlight.

KING: (*Enthusiastically*)

And now to the discovery. I had three full-time astronomers searching to discover a new comet. How did you find our comet before they did?

MARIA:

It was October 1st, 1847, Your Majesty. I remember because of what was happening at the library.

SUSAN:

Oh, yes. The inventory.

KING:

Inventory?

MARIA:

The annual inventory of books by the library trustees would begin the next day.

SUSAN:

We had to check and reshelve each book and straighten all the shelves.

MARIA:

And I had to sneak my stash of secret "lost" books back into the children's area.

KING:

Lost books?

MARIA:

Anytime I saw the children of Nantucket going after a book I deemed inappropriate for their reading, I would conveniently "lose" the book. All those "lost" books had to reappear on the shelves before the trustees' examination.

KING:

I see . . .

JOHN, JR.:

You're the one who always did that?

MARIA:

When I closed and locked the library doors at 5:15, I was dead tired. As I trudged home toward the setting sun, with the first hints of coming winter chill in the air, I realized it would be a crystal-clear night. The quarter moon would set before midnight. From midnight on, the sky would be perfect for stargazing!

I ate dinner with my father and brothers and lay down for a short nap, setting an alarm for 11:45.

SUSAN:

Late that night, I came over to sit with Maria while she stargazed. Partly to reminisce about the library struggles of the day, partly out of curiosity.

KING:

Curiosity?

SUSAN:

I wanted to see why she found white dots in the sky more fascinating than sleep.

MARIA:

The sky was crisp, clear, and pitch black. The stars seemed to leap out of the heavens at us.

JOHN, SR.:

Aye. I remember, the stars looked so close I felt I could touch them. I was tempted to sit up with Maria myself that night.

KING:

Are you also an astronomer?

JOHN, SR.:

Me, Your Majesty? No. The stars have always just been part of work and night to me—a way to calibrate my chronometers.

From *Great Moments in Science: Experiments and Readers Theatre*. © 1996. Teacher Ideas Press. (800) 237-6124.

MARIA:

I began my usual slow sweep across the constellations, noting and recording the position and reflectivity of each major star.

SUSAN:

I entered these values in Maria's notebook.

KING:

Ahh, yes. Accurate record keeping is the most important part of any astronomer's life.

MARIA:

Mars and Jupiter were both plainly visible. I could clearly see the famed canals on Mars and could even make out some detail on Jupiter's distant surface.

SUSAN:

Maria let me see both planets. I think planets are much more interesting than stars.

KING:

And planets move in much more interesting patterns across the sky. A pity there are so few to watch.

MARIA:

My favorite formations have always been nebulae . . . Your Majesty.

SUSAN:

She had me record their spectrum and light values.

MARIA:

The truth is, I just love to watch, to glory, and to wonder at these phenomenal formations.

KING:

But the comet discovery. When did that happen?

MARIA:

I finished my normal sweep of constellations, nebulae, and major stars about 1:00 A.M. and began to wonder what I would study in greater depth this sparkling evening.

SUSAN:

I asked Maria to show me Cassiopeia. I've read about it often and wanted to see what it looked like.

From *Great Moments in Science: Experiments and Readers Theatre.* © 1996. Teacher Ideas Press. (800) 237-6124.

MARIA:

I scanned toward Cassiopeia, and . . . and something caught my eye. I almost missed it because it wasn't supposed to be there: a faint white speck where there was supposed to be only black, empty space.

KING: (*Eagerly*)

Near Cassiopeia, you say?

SUSAN:

I remember she cried, "Oh, my!" And her hands began to tremble.

MARIA:

Had I not scanned that sector so often, I wouldn't have known the sky there should be black, and probably wouldn't have noticed such a faint speck at all. But because I could see that part of the sky so clearly in my mind, the new speck caught my eye.

SUSAN: (*Laughing*)

"Caught your eye?" Your Majesty, she actually gasped. I asked, "What's wrong? Can't you find Cassiopeia?" Maria didn't answer. Her eye was pressed against her telescope. Her hands shook as she adjusted the focus.

MARIA:

I remember my heart pounded.

SUSAN:

She began to pant.

MARIA:

Of course, I didn't know what it was yet. But it still thrilled me to see something I hadn't seen before.

KING:

And? Was it the comet?

MARIA:

As I stared at that tiny dot of light, I could tell it was something new. It hadn't been there two nights before when I scanned that same quadrant of the sky. What was it?

KING:

By thunder, what was it?!

MARIA:

I couldn't be sure with *my* telescope. It isn't powerful enough. I dashed inside for father's. It's more powerful than mine—not as good for general sweeps of the sky, but better for detailed study.

From *Great Moments in Science: Experiments and Readers Theatre.* © 1996. Teacher Ideas Press. (800) 237-6124.

SUSAN:

I had never seen her so excited. And still she hadn't said a word to me. "Maria!" I demanded. "What's going on?" She just mumbled over and over, "I have to hurry! I have to hurry!" But the faster she tried to adjust her father's telescope, the more her hands shook and fumbled.

MARIA: (*Laughing*)

My trembling hands made the telescope wiggle slightly and blurred my vision. It seemed an eternity before I correctly aimed and focused father's powerful telescope.

JOHN, SR.:

By this time, Maria's commotion woke me up. I stumbled outside. Maria was frantically bent over my telescope. Susan kept shouting, "What's the matter? What's going on?"

SUSAN:

I remember saying to Mr. Mitchell, "Something's happened. But Maria won't tell me what. Find out what it is."

JOHN, SR.:

And then Maria spoke.

MARIA:

I did? I guess I was too excited to remember that part.

JOHN, SR.:

You only said, "Be quiet!" But it was the power in your voice. It was a command a king would have obeyed—beggin' your pardon, Your Majesty.

MARIA:

I just remember staring into the eyepiece and thinking, "There it is. There it is . . ." I was looking at a heavenly body I had never seen before. I could make out a faint dust or ice trail stretched out behind. It had already moved relative to the stars near it. It could only be a comet!

KING:

The comet! And what time was this?

MARIA:

By now it must have been past 1:30.

SUSAN:

It was 1:40 A.M., Your Majesty. I checked.

MARIA:

I began to shout, "A new comet! A new comet!"

From *Great Moments in Science: Experiments and Readers Theatre.* © 1996. Teacher Ideas Press. (800) 237-6124.

SUSAN:

I said, "A comet? Let me see, Maria."

JOHN, SR.: (*Chuckling*)

I bellowed it. "A new comet! Let *me* see! Let *me* see!"

JOHN, JR.:

That's what woke me up. I rushed outside. There's Maria, eye glued to father's telescope, repeating, "It's a new comet! It's a new comet!" Everyone else is screaming, "Let me see! Let me see!"

KING:

What a thrilling moment! I would have given almost anything to have been there myself!

JOHN, SR.:

Maria wouldn't have let even you see, Your Majesty. We couldn't pry her away!

SUSAN:

And then Maria dashed inside without a word.

MARIA:

I had to see if there was a listing, a record for this comet on any of the charts, and I just hadn't noticed it before. I searched every book and table. No listing. I had read the papers that day at the library. There was no mention of a new comet sighting. (*Chuckling*) I remember fearing my new comet might be some conveniently "lost" star the heavens snuck back into place before a celestial inspection. It must have been 3:00 A.M. when I stepped back outside. The others were still clustered around father's telescope, repeating, "It's a comet. It's a comet."

JOHN, SR.:

I asked, "Maria, did you look it up? Which comet is it?"

MARIA:

I remember saying, "There is no listing for it." And my knees began to tremble.

SUSAN:

Her voice was a shrill whisper.

MARIA:

It suddenly hit me that I might be the first human to gaze at this chunk of rock as it hurtled through space. Now my heart truly pounded. Was it possible that a simple librarian in Nantucket, Massachusetts, with barely a high school education could discover a new comet?

From *Great Moments in Science: Experiments and Readers Theatre.* © 1996. Teacher Ideas Press. (800) 237-6124.

JOHN, JR.:

Every astronomer in the world knew the King of Denmark was offering a gold medal to the first person to discover a new comet. We began to wonder, "Could this be Maria's gold medal comet?"

SUSAN:

Three A.M. became 5:30 while we traced Maria's new comet across the sky. When the new day's light hid the stars, Maria rushed inside. . . .

MARIA:

I was far too excited to sleep.

SUSAN:

She started writing letters about her find.

MARIA:

My first two letters were to William Bond at the Harvard Observatory and to Joseph Henry, director of the Smithsonian Institution in Washington. Then I wrote to Your Majesty.

KING:

Then why didn't I get your letter or hear of your discovery sooner?

JOHN, SR.:

Nantucket mail has to wait for the twice-weekly mail boat to leave the island. Maria's letter did not leave Nantucket until October 4th.

KING:

So when an Englishman and Italian both claimed to have discovered the new comet on October 3rd, that's why their notice to me ran one day ahead of yours.

JOHN, SR.:

Exactly, Your Majesty.

NARRATOR:

A flurry of letters, claims, and charges sped back and forth for over a year before the Danish gold medal was officially awarded to Maria in early 1849. But as grand as the trip to Denmark and her shiny medal were, neither could compare with the thrill of that crystal-clear night of October 1, 1847, when Maria Mitchell realized the secret dream of almost every amateur astronomer. With the medal came fame and important offers to pursue her astronomy while teaching at a university. But that is another story.

From *Great Moments in Science: Experiments and Readers Theatre.* © 1996. Teacher Ideas Press. (800) 237-6124.

Related Experiments

Here is a series of simple experiments you can use to recreate the steps that led Maria Mitchell to her discoveries. These experiments will help you understand both the work of Mitchell and the scientific concepts involved.

Necessary Equipment

To build a sextant:

- One large (at least 6-inch) plastic compass—the semicircular 180-degree style.

- One plastic or wooden 12-inch ruler.

- One small weight (at least 4 ounces). Metal washers, a heavy eraser, or even a large bolt will do.

- Several feet of string, yarn, or thick, white thread.

- A magnetic compass.

- One wooden stake and two 6-foot lengths of thick string or light rope.

To track the stars:

- One homemade sextant per student.

- Notebook paper, polar coordinate graph paper, and a clear view of the night skies.

➤ *Your Own Sextant to the Stars*

What You'll Investigate: We now can use computers, telescopes, and satellites to locate our position relative to the stars and to track the movement of the stars. However, for centuries before, people used sextants, and before that quadrants, to chart the position of the stars. **Stars are located by their elevation angle and azimuth (direction).** Even a simple, homemade sextant is a powerful tool for charting the flow and cycles of the skies above. As the first part of this astronomy experiment you will build your own sextant and compare your results with those of your classmates.

The Setup: Gather ruler, compass, magnetic compass, string, weight, and tape.

What to Do:

Figure 7.2. A simple homemade sextant.

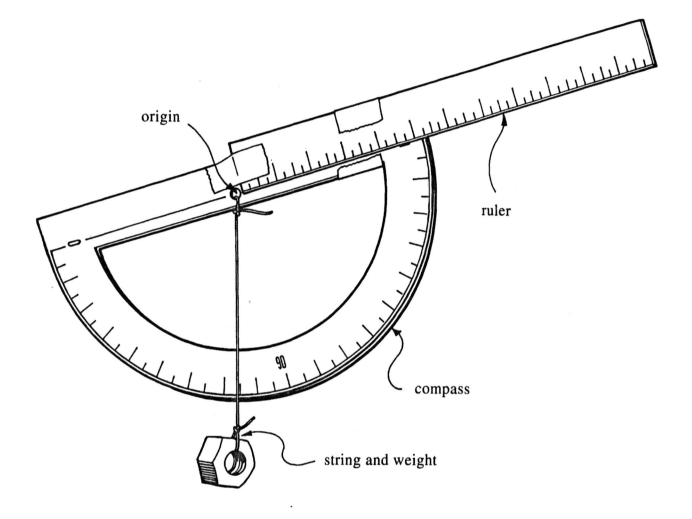

1. Tape your ruler onto the compass so that the ruled edge runs from the compass's origin point (center) through one zero degree mark and beyond. If placed correctly, you can now sight along the ruler and also be sighting along a zero degree line from the origin of the compass.

2. Next thread your string through the compass's origin hole and knot its upper end. Tape or tie the string's lower end to your weight. This line will fall as a plumb line straight toward the earth.

From *Great Moments in Science: Experiments and Readers Theatre.* © 1996. Teacher Ideas Press. (800) 237-6124.

3. Holding the compass with curved edge down, you have a simple, homemade sextant. To find the elevation angle of a star, sight along the ruler's edge at a distant star. Have someone else read the angle (in degrees) at the curved bottom of the compass where your string plumb line crosses the plastic arc of your compass. This angle, however, is not the elevation angle to your star, because you are holding the compass upside down. You must subtract this angle from 90 degrees to get the elevation angle to the star you measured.

Elevation angle is one of the two measures you need to locate a star. It tells how high the star is in the sky. The other measure is the direction, or azimuth, to the star. Azimuth is measured clockwise in a circle of 360°, with north at 0°, east at 90°, south at 180°, and west at 270°. There are two simple ways of measuring azimuth. You will try both and see which gives you better results. The first way is to use a magnetic compass. It is easy, but as you will see, a little awkward.

a. Align the magnetic compass so that the compass's floating arrow points north. Now hold your sextant over the compass and sight along the ruler to your chosen star. As you fix your eye on the distant star, have a helper watch the compass and sextant to ensure that the compass stays lined up with north and that you hold your sextant directly over the middle of the compass.

When the magnetic compass and sextant are correctly aimed and aligned, glance down and read the degree (angle) over which your sextant is resting. This is the azimuth to your star.

Your readings should be in the following form: azimuth—223 degrees, elevation—41 degrees. These readings would define a point about halfway up in the southwestern sky.

b. The second way to measure azimuth requires one stake, two 6-foot segments of thick, white string, and two rocks.

Pound the stake partway into the ground at the spot where you plan to stand for your measurements. Stand with both heels touching the stake and sight toward the North Star. Have a helper stretch the first of your strings along this line from your stake toward the North Star. This string points due north. Place a heavy rock on the end of this string to hold it in place.

Now sight from your stake toward a star. Have your helper stretch out the second string from the stake in line with your sighting toward this new star. Have your helper secure this line with a second rock.

Use your semicircular compass to measure the angle between these two strings. Is this angle the azimuth toward your chosen star? Maybe.

Remember, azimuth is measured in a clockwise circle of 360 degrees from north (0°), through east (90°), south (180°), and west (270°) before returning to north (360° or 0°). Your compass can measure only 180°. If you measured your string angle clockwise from north, the angle you measured is the azimuth to this star. If, however, you measured *counter*clockwise from north to the string pointing at your star, you must subtract the angle you measure from 360° to find the correct azimuth.

As a check on everyone's homemade sextants, all students should measure the elevation and azimuth to the same star at the same time on the same evening. Use both methods described above to calculate the azimuth. Compare readings during class the next day. Did everyone measure approximately the same elevation and azimuth?

From *Great Moments in Science: Experiments and Readers Theatre.* © 1996. Teacher Ideas Press. (800) 237-6124.

What's Going On?—Sources of Error: Errors of only a degree or two are probably a function of the sextants you are using. Yours are, after all, homemade and simple.

But readings that differ by more than 3 or 4 degrees indicate that an error was made somewhere. How many possible ways to create such an error can you think of? Did you include possible errors in the construction of your sextant as well as errors in using the sextant to measure a star's position?

Did both methods for measuring azimuth produce the same answers? Did everyone's string and magnetic compass measurements differ in the same way? Why do you think that might happen? The magnetic north pole of the earth is not in the same spot as the geographic north pole. Measuring to the North Star uses geographic, or "true," north. A magnetic compass measures to the magnetic north pole. Depending on where you are on the earth, these two readings could be as much as 5 or 6 degrees apart.

What to Observe: How do we mark the location of a star? What two measures do we need to use? Notice the degree of care necessary to take an accurate reading of a star. Any slip in aligning your equipment, even a slight wiggle of your hand, can result in a error of a degree or two. Simply not standing straight over your marking stake can create an error of several degrees.

All too easily these individual errors add up to an error of 5 to 10 degrees, resulting in a measurement that is next to worthless. Try to find ways to eliminate these errors from your readings. See if you can find how modern astronomers correct for errors as they mark the location of stars and distant galaxies.

Questions to Ask Yourself: Do you understand what two measurements are critical to fixing the position of a star in the sky and how those measurements are made? Does your simple homemade sextant give you a feeling for how ships at sea are able to calculate their position by measuring the angle from their ship to known stars? Can you see the advantage of knowing the stars and their positions if you were lost?

What are the drawbacks and limitations of your sextant? How would you make it better? What do you wish it could do? And what would it have to look like for it to work the way you'd like? Compare your dream version with real sextants in a museum or with pictures in your local library.

➤ *Tracking the Stars*

What You'll Investigate: Astronomy is the systematic study of objects we can see in the sky above us, of their motion, and of their composition. The first step in that study is to become familiar with the patterns of movement with which the various stars, planets, and galaxies cross the sky.

The Setup: You should choose five heavenly objects to study. At least one should be a planet (Mars and Venus are usually visible either in early morning or in the evening). Ease of identification should be an important selection criterion. You must be sure you are measuring the same stars even though they may move great distances between measurements. Another important criterion is to pick objects high enough in the sky so that they will be visible throughout the night without interference from trees, buildings, or mountains.

You'll want to begin this experiment around the time of a waning quarter moon. This way you'll have several weeks of a relatively moonless night sky to observe.

From *Great Moments in Science: Experiments and Readers Theatre.* © 1996. Teacher Ideas Press. (800) 237-6124.

Create a log book for your star readings. It should have separate pages for each object being studied. Each page should have columns for date, time, azimuth, and elevation angle.

Finally, find a good open spot from which to make your measurements. Remember, you will be working at night, so don't pick a spot very far from your home. But pick a spot that gives you the clearest view of the sky.

What to Do: You should select four times during the night to make measurements. These times should be at least one hour apart, all must be well after dark, and at least one should be in the early morning. This exercise is easier to do in the winter when there are more hours of darkness to choose from without interfering with sleep.

1. At each of your four designated times, use your homemade sextant to measure the azimuth and elevation angle to each of your chosen objects. Be as careful and precise as you can during these measurements. Repeat all five measurements to be sure you haven't made an error in your readings.

2. Repeat this process every other night for three weeks. If clouds prevent you from making your readings one night, add an extra night at the end of your study so that you will record the objects on at least 12 nights.

3. Now plot the movement of your chosen stars and planet on polar graph paper (graph paper that is organized around polar compass grid lines). Use a separate sheet for each heavenly object you are following.

   For the first object, place a dot on the graph to mark its location at each of your four first-night readings. Next, connect these dots for the first object with a smooth, curved line and label it "Day 1."

   Repeat this whole process for each of your other four objects, using a separate piece of graph paper for each. Did all five of your chosen objects move and shift their movement in the same way?

   On the graph for each object, mark the readings from each subsequent day so that each graph has 12 lines, one labeled for each day's readings. Now look for how the movement of this object (your lines) shifted east, west, north, or south over the three- to four-week span of your study.

What's Going On?—Sources of Error: There are only two possible sources of error that could make your plots jump all around the sky instead of following smooth, regular patterns. First, you are using a simple, homemade sextant. Real sextants are highly precise tools. It is understandable that your readings may drift randomly several degrees because of your equipment.

Any error greater than a few degrees, however, must be attributed to "operator error." That is, to *you*. You made a mistake. You rushed your readings. You misread your sextant. You took a reading at the wrong time, or you slipped and measured the wrong star.

If you take an occasional reading that doesn't make any sense, that doesn't fit with the pattern for that star, try to repeat the measurement. If it's too late to retake the readings, at least be very suspicious of these single abnormal readings.

From *Great Moments in Science: Experiments and Readers Theatre*. © 1996. Teacher Ideas Press. (800) 237-6124.

What to Observe: As you watch the stars and galaxies roll across the sky above you, first be aware that the stars seem to be in constant motion. Really, of course, it is the earth that is in constant motion, making the distant stars appear to move. The earth rotates on its axis once a day and revolves around the sun once a year. The sun is moving through space, dragging us with it, as it spirals around the center of the Milky Way galaxy. Finally, our whole galaxy is roaring through space at a speed of hundreds of miles per second. It is really this motion we see when we gaze at the stars.

Were you able to see how the stars seem to spin across the sky? Try to get a feel for how the whole heavens rotate above you from hour to hour during the night. Were you able to detect shifts in the position of your stars from night to night? Did they shift a little north or south? Did they cross the sky a little earlier or later? These are the markings of seasonal shifts in the night sky.

Did all five of your objects shift the same way over the span of your observations? Did the planet you studied move the same way as the stars? Can you think of any reason why a planet in our own solar system might appear to move differently from distant stars?

Questions to Ask Yourself: Do the stars above actually move? Do planets really move? Do they both move in the same way? What creates their apparent motion across the sky? Are there any stars that do not race across the sky during the night? Which one(s) and why?

Having watched the night skies for almost a month, do you have a feeling for the movement of the stars? Can you imagine how their pattern will shift in three months, or six months? Six months from now will you be able to see stars you cannot see now? Will some familiar stars during this season have disappeared from the night sky?

From *Great Moments in Science: Experiments and Readers Theatre.* © 1996. Teacher Ideas Press. (800) 237-6124.

Bridges to Books

This story deals with one aspect of our understanding of the physical world around us. You can learn much more about these concepts in your library. The following list gives you key words, concepts, and questions to begin your exploration in a school or public library.

Maria Mitchell is one of America's best known amateur astronomers. See if your library has information describing what happened to Maria after she received the king of Denmark's gold medal. Did she remain active in astronomy?

Maria Mitchell was a dedicated **amateur astronomer**. What other discoveries have been made by amateur American astronomers?

Astronomy is the oldest of all the sciences. See how far back you can trace the study of the stars. How have our beliefs about the stars and planets changed over the centuries? How have astronomer's tools and methods changed?

Maria Mitchell discovered a **comet**. Others have discovered planets, stars, galaxies, nebulae, white dwarfs, red giants, and black holes. Does your library have information describing these heavenly bodies and how many different types of astronomical phenomena exist? What are the differences between them?

This story talks about using **sextants** to chart the stars. What is a sextant? What's the difference between a sextant and a **quadrant**? Does your library have pictures of both?

References for Further Reading

The following references deal with the major characters, concepts, and processes in this chapter.

Asimov, Isaac. *Asimov on Astronomy.* Garden City, NY: Doubleday, 1975.

Baker, Rachel. *America's First Woman Astronomer: Maria Mitchell.* New York: J. Messner, 1980.

Berry, Erich. *Stars in My Pocket.* New York: Day Publishers, 1980.

Degani, Meir. *Astronomy Made Simple.* New York: Doubleday, 1976.

Ferris, Jeri. *What Are You Figuring Now?* Minneapolis, MN: Carolrhoda Books, 1988.

Fichter, George. *Comets and Meteors.* New York: Franklin Watts, 1982.

Fisher, David. *The Origin and Evolution of Our Particular Universe.* New York: Atheneum, 1988.

Fradin, Dennis. *Comets, Asteroids, and Meteors.* Chicago: Childrens Press, 1984.

Harwit, Martin. *Cosmic Discovery.* Cambridge, MA: MIT Press, 1984.

Hoyle, Fred. *Highlights in Astronomy.* New York: W. Freeman, 1975.

McPherson, Stephanie. *Rooftop Astronomer.* Minneapolis, MN: Carolrhoda Books, 1990.

Melen, Grace. *Maria Mitchell.* New York: Bobbs-Merrill, 1974.

Milton, Jacqueline. *Astronomy: An Introduction for the Amateur Astronomer.* Boston: Charles Scribner's Sons, 1978.

Moore, Patrick. *Comets.* Boston: Charles Scribner's Sons, 1986.

———. *The Amateur Astronomer.* New York: W. W. Norton, 1990.

Oles, Carole. *Night Watches: Inventions on the Life of Maria Mitchell.* Cambridge, MA: Alice James Books, 1985.

Overbye, Dennis. *Lonely Hearts of the Cosmos.* New York: HarperCollins, 1991.

Ridpath, Ian. *The Young Astronomer's Handbook.* New York: Arco, 1984.

Ronan, Colin. *Man Probes the Universe.* New York: Natural History Project, 1974.

———. *The Natural History of the Universe.* New York: Macmillan, 1991.

Serafini, Anthony. *Legends in Their Own Time.* New York: Plenum Press, 1993.

Wayne, Bennett. *Women Who Dared to Be Different.* Champaign, IL: Garrard, 1973.

Wilkie, Katherine. *Maria Mitchell, Star Gazer.* New York: Garrard, 1976.

Consult your librarian for additional titles.

Spontaneous War

Louis Pasteur's discovery of microorganisms in 1858

Scientific Background

Louis Pasteur is best known as the creator of the sterilization method for liquids that bears his name, pasteurization. He is also known for his development of vaccines for anthrax, cholera, and rabies, and for saving the French beer and wine industries with his work on fermentation.

Even more significant for our modern world, he opened the door to a whole new field of study: microbiology. He accomplished this partly through his work on fermentation, and partly through a scientific war he was dragged into by the strong forces touting the theory of spontaneous generation theory.

From earliest history, humans believed that certain organisms sprang into existence all by themselves from nonliving matter when conditions were suitable. They needed no parents. They simply materialized. Rats and mice, it was believed, spontaneously materialized from old rags and cheese, eels materialized from mud, and worms from rotting meat. The theory was called "spontaneous generation." By the mid-nineteenth century it was known that mice, worms, and eels couldn't spontaneously generate themselves. But it was still widely believed that microscopic organisms such as molds and bacteria could and did spontaneously generate. Pasteur didn't believe this, and so was forced to defend his beliefs, a war from which sprang the field of microbiology, or the scientific study of microscopic life.

Readers Theatre

Characters

Narrator

Louis Pasteur. A 38-year-old biologist and researcher. He's well known in his field and is determined, exacting, and calculating.

Juliet Villot. Pasteur's 25-year-old lab assistant. She's smart, inquisitive, a hard worker, but not well educated because women were not allowed to attend college at that time, so she's very grateful for the opportunity Pasteur has given her to study in his lab.

President Miranou. The president of the famed Ecole Normale University in Paris. He's 62 years old, heavy-set, tough, and a no-nonsense administrator.

Felix Pouchet. Outspoken biological researcher. He's 28, flamboyant, and cocky.

Staging

Figure 8.1. Suggested placement of readers for *Spontaneous War*.

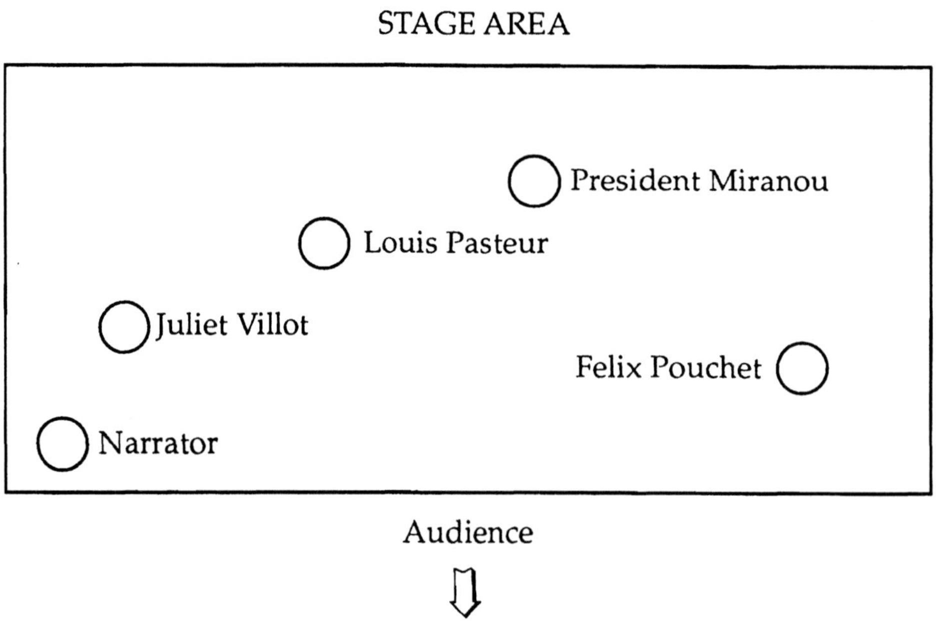

STAGE AREA

Audience

From *Great Moments in Science: Experiments and Readers Theatre.* © 1996. Teacher Ideas Press. (800) 237-6124.

Spontaneous War

PASTEUR: (*Angrily*)
I can't believe even *he* would write this!

VILLOT:
Who? Write what?

PASTEUR: (*Growing angrier*)
This is terrible! Pouchet hasn't supported any of these wild ideas!

VILLOT:
What ideas?

NARRATOR:
On a cold, gray, Paris day in early December, 1858, Louis Pasteur shifted in his chair near the one small corner window in his tiny attic lab. With first a snort, and finally a low growl, Pasteur furiously underlined Felix Pouchet's report, scribbling fierce exclamation and question marks in the margins. His assistant, Juliet Villot, was cleaning up the lab after a demonstration for some advanced students.

PASTEUR: (*Shaking the paper*)
I can feel a great battle brewing with this paper, Juliet, a very great battle.

VILLOT:
In two years of working here, I've never seen you like this. What could Felix Pouchet have written to upset you so?

PASTEUR:
It's nothing less than a call to war!

VILLOT:
War or no, just remember University President Miranou expects you to have the department budgets ready this morning—by *10:00.*

PASTEUR: (*Shocked*)
I forgot all about them.

VILLOT:
You *always* forget your administrative duties.

PASTEUR:
What time is it?

From *Great Moments in Science: Experiments and Readers Theatre.* © 1996. Teacher Ideas Press. (800) 237-6124.

VILLOT:

Almost 11:00.

PASTEUR:

Oh, dear.

NARRATOR:

Pasteur was Director of Scientific Affairs at the famed Ecole Normale University. It was an honored administrative position. He was supposed to be down in his second-floor office preparing university budgets and program plans. But Pasteur's heart was pure research chemist. He found an abandoned nook in the attic and commandeered it for his laboratory. To the university's dismay, he spent more time in that cramped attic lab than in his spacious director's office.

MIRANOU:

Pasteur! Louis Pasteur! Are you in that lab again?

PASTEUR: (*Resigned*)

President Miranou. Do come in. Sorry the room is so cramped.

MIRANOU:

Your second-floor office can seat 30! Why not spend some time down there where you belong?

PASTEUR:

I belong in my lab.

MIRANOU:

You're not hired to run a lab. You should be doing your administrative work instead of experiments!

VILLOT:

He was just finishing this year's budget, sir. Weren't you, Dr. Pasteur?

PASTEUR:

Actually, I was reading this outrageous report by Felix Pouchet.

MIRANOU: (*Trying to remember*)

Pouchet . . . I've heard of him. Isn't he one of the "Spontaneous Generation" crowd?

VILLOT:

What's spontaneous generation?

From *Great Moments in Science: Experiments and Readers Theatre*. © 1996. Teacher Ideas Press. (800) 237-6124.

PASTEUR:

A belief that microscopic organisms—bacteria—can spontaneously pop into being, all by themselves, with no parent or outside source of life. And it's rubbish! But Felix Pouchet claims to have proved it in this paper!

VILLOT:

So, *that's* what got you so upset.

MIRANOU:

Has he proved it?

PASTEUR:

Of course he hasn't! He's proved no such thing! The point is, this paper is the first broadside in a war.

VILLOT:

The first salvo?

MIRANOU:

A war?

PASTEUR:

The entire world of science will now be watching to see if I either surrender or fire back.

MIRANOU: (*Skeptical*)
They will?

PASTEUR:

Whether or not I want it, whether or not I feel it's good for science, Felix Pouchet has challenged me to a war. My reputation, the reputation of this university, the truth, itself, are all at stake!

MIRANOU: (*Growing more skeptical*)
He has? They are?

PASTEUR:

The point is, *this* is more important right now than administrative duties.

MIRANOU: (*Angrily*)
It is? . . .

PASTEUR: (*Interrupting*)
Let me read you Pouchet's conclusion. Where is it? . . . Ahh, yes. Here. Listen to this.

From *Great Moments in Science: Experiments and Readers Theatre.* © 1996. Teacher Ideas Press. (800) 237-6124.

POUCHET:

The microscopic organisms that appear during fermentation and putrefaction are produced by spontaneous generation. They have no parents. My research shows there were no organisms present in the meat at the beginning of the putrefaction process. Organisms formed spontaneously from the decaying material itself.

PASTEUR:

Rubbish! The experiments he describes don't support that conclusion at all. I can't let this report stand unchallenged.

MIRANOU:

You can't?

PASTEUR:

President Miranou, you will have to cover my administrative duties for a few days while this pack of lies is answered.

MIRANOU:

A few days? You're sure it will only take a few days?

PASTEUR:

I'll give you a full report by week's end. Good-day, Mister President.

VILLOT:

Is that all true, Louis?

PASTEUR:

Absolutely. Spontaneous generation is an unfounded, illogical theory that I plan to disapprove once and for all.

VILLOT:

All by week's end?

PASTEUR: (*Grinning*)

Perhaps it will take a *bit* longer. . . .

NARRATOR:

For thousands of years scientists had believed that some organisms spontaneously materialize from nonliving matter without any parents. Mice had been thought to spontaneously materialize from old rags and cheese, eels materialized from mud, and worms from rotting meat.

VILLOT:

We know now that those old beliefs aren't true. But how do you know microscopic organisms—bacteria, yeasts, and molds—don't spontaneously materialize? No one has found original parent spores in test meat or bread samples. They *seem* to just appear.

From *Great Moments in Science: Experiments and Readers Theatre.* © 1996. Teacher Ideas Press. (800) 237-6124.

PASTEUR:

What "seems to be," and what's *proven* to be are two very different things.

VILLOT:

But even some of your own early work seems to support spontaneous generation.

PASTEUR:

It may *seem* that way. But it's not true. Not at all.

NARRATOR:

Pasteur discovered that microscopic live organisms, such as bacteria called yeast, were always present during, and seemed to cause, the fermentation of beer and wine. However, many scientists still believed that these fermentation microorganisms spontaneously generated from the decaying molecules of organic matter. When something began to rot, yeast bacteria just appeared. Felix Pouchet had become the leading spokesman for this group of scientists.

VILLOT:

If yeast, molds, and bacteria don't spontaneously generate, where do they come from?

PASTEUR:

I don't know yet. But I *do* know Pouchet hasn't proved his case as he claims.

VILLOT:

What are you going to do?

PASTEUR:

Stop asking idle questions and start some careful, exacting science. It's time to go to work in this lab!

VILLOT:

Great! But what?

PASTEUR:

Some preliminary experiments have led me to a general theory: Bacteria float in the air and simply fall by chance onto food and all living matter. They rapidly multiply when they find a suitable decaying substance to use as nutrient for their growth.

VILLOT:

So it's settled then. Write this braggart, Pouchet, and tell him you've already proved him wrong.

PASTEUR:

I have no conclusive proof yet. This is still a general theory. But I think you're right. I will write a paper and let Felix Pouchet know the war is on!

From *Great Moments in Science: Experiments and Readers Theatre.* © 1996. Teacher Ideas Press. (800) 237-6124.

NARRATOR:

Within a day of first reading Pasteur's paper, Felix Pouchet fired back a scathing response.

POUCHET:

Your theory, sir, is ridiculous. You propose that microscopic organisms float freely through the air and settle on us like a thickening dust. If such an outlandish thing were true, by now these organisms would blanket every living thing and would have grown to form a mist as dense as iron across the whole of the world.

VILLOT:

That's as harsh a response as ever I've seen. Are you going to fire back?

PASTEUR:

Not yet. Rather than return this hostile fire, I'll quietly prove my theory in the lab.

VILLOT:

How?

PASTEUR:

Two questions are at the center of this fight. First, do living microbes float freely in the air as I propose?

VILLOT:

Do you really think they float free in *all* the air? All the time? Even the air I breathe? Even in the air right here in my hands?

PASTEUR:

Yes, microscopic bacteria must exist floating everywhere. First I must prove that. The second question is whether it is really impossible for microbes to grow spontaneously.

VILLOT:

But how can you prove *that*? Once you prove microbes are everywhere, how will you decide if a microbe spontaneously generated or just happened to be floating there to begin with?

PASTEUR:

Ahh, good question, Juliet. Shows you're thinking. I'll have to create a sterile environment in some closed container—a space where there are no microbes.

VILLOT: (*Becoming excited*)

I think I see. Then if any microbes appear, they must have spontaneously generated, because there were none there when the experiment began!

PASTEUR:

Exactly. Those are the two questions. If both answers go our way, I win. If both answers go against us, Pouchet wins.

VILLOT:

What if one answer goes your way and one goes his?

PASTEUR:

Then the war drags on. But now to work! Bring me a glass tube and some guncotton.

VILLOT:

Guncotton?

PASTEUR:

That dense cotton wadding in the corner cabinet. Bottom shelf as I recall.

VILLOT:

Yes. I see it.

PASTEUR:

I've got the Bunsen burner. If you could fetch a small square of old bread with a few drops of sugar water on it.

VILLOT:

You're hungry for soggy sugar bread?

PASTEUR:

Not me. Bacteria. It will be a good medium for some fast-growing mold.

NARRATOR:

Pasteur plugged the open end of the glass tube with a thick wad of guncotton and heated the tube to sterilize both it and the air inside.

VILLOT:

Why not use a glass stopper instead of cotton?

PASTEUR:

We must allow outside air to leak in as the air inside the tube cools and condenses.

VILLOT: (*After a moment's thought*)

But won't microbes drift in with that outside air and ruin the experiment?

PASTEUR:

The dense cotton wadding should filter out any microbes and keep them outside the tube.

From *Great Moments in Science: Experiments and Readers Theatre.* © 1996. Teacher Ideas Press. (800) 237-6124.

VILLOT: (*After another moment's thought*)
But what about the microbes already in the tube and on the bread? Why won't they multiply and ruin the experiment?

PASTEUR: (*Smiling*)
You're determined to catch me today, aren't you? Good! A good scientist always is. But remember, I heated the tube, the bread, and the guncotton. And I made sure they got hot enough to kill all bacteria. Most microbes are very sensitive to temperature, you know. The tube is now sterile and free of microscopic organisms.

VILLOT:
Now what?

PASTEUR:
We wait.

VILLOT:
And what do we watch for?

PASTEUR:
Mold growth on the outside of the guncotton shows microbes were floating freely in the air. Mold growth inside the tube proves they generated spontaneously.

VILLOT:
What should we do while we wait?

PASTEUR: (*With a long sigh*)
There are those budgets I'm supposed to prepare.

NARRATOR:
Ten o'clock the next morning, Pasteur and his assistant returned to the attic lab.

PASTEUR:
Look! Good news!

VILLOT:
The outside of the guncotton has turned dingy gray.

PASTEUR:
Mold growth from free-floating microbes has concentrated on the guncotton as air filtered down into the tube.

VILLOT: (*Amazed*)
But the inside of the tube is crystal clear.

From *Great Moments in Science: Experiments and Readers Theatre.* © 1996. Teacher Ideas Press. (800) 237-6124.

PASTEUR: (*Smugly*)

No spontaneous generation.

VILLOT:

You proved it! You won!

PASTEUR:

Not so fast. You never prove anything by doing an experiment once. It must be repeatable. We'll do the experiment at least a dozen times, varying the filter material and growth medium, so no one can claim these results were a fluke.

VILLOT: (*Alarmed*)

A dozen times? But that will take . . . weeks.

NARRATOR:

Each time the experiment worked exactly as Pasteur had predicted it would.

PASTEUR:

Question number 1 is answered! . . .

MIRANOU: (*Interrupting*)

The question I want answered is why aren't you down in your office doing the work you are paid to do?

PASTEUR:

Ahh, President Miranou. You're just in time to help celebrate. I've shown that microbes *do* float free in the air and do not exist in a sterile environment. I'm halfway to proving Pouchet completely wrong.

MIRANOU:

Only *half* way? You said this whole thing would only take a few days!

PASTEUR:

And we've just about got him! Only one more experiment to go.

MIRANOU:

You're sure only one more?

PASTEUR:

One short, easy experiment.

MIRANOU:

And then you get down to your office where you belong!

From *Great Moments in Science: Experiments and Readers Theatre.* © 1996. Teacher Ideas Press. (800) 237-6124.

PASTEUR:

Now for question number 2.

VILLOT:

Isn't this question going to be harder? It seems impossible to prove something *doesn't* happen.

PASTEUR: (*Thoughtfully*)

In a way you're right. We have to set up a sterile ideal growing environment, a place where microbes would surely spontaneously generate if ever they were going to.

VILLOT:

Then when nothing grows you'll have proved they can't spontaneously generate at all.

PASTEUR:

That's our plan.

VILLOT:

But that sounds just like the first experiment.

PASTEUR:

Close. But this time we have to create the best possible temperature and growth medium, and give it more time.

NARRATOR:

Pasteur mixed a nutrient-rich bouillon, which is a favorite food of bacteria, in a large beaker with a long, curving glass neck. Then he furiously boiled the bouillon until the glass glowed. This step killed any bacteria already in the bouillon or in the air inside the beaker.

VILLOT:

Now we wait again?

PASTEUR:

Not yet. Room temperature is too cool for ideal growing conditions. We'll use the incubator.

VILLOT:

What incubator?

PASTEUR:

The warming oven.

From *Great Moments in Science: Experiments and Readers Theatre.* © 1996. Teacher Ideas Press. (800) 237-6124.

VILLOT:

Right.

NARRATOR:

Because of a slanted attic roof and limited lab space, Pasteur had to jam this oven far back under the sloping eaves. He had to crawl on hands and knees to reach the oven door. Almost lying on his stomach, he slid the beaker into his incubation oven and noted the time and day in a log book, 9:00 A.M., Tuesday.

At 9:00 A.M. Wednesday, Pasteur crawled back to his oven and checked the beaker.

VILLOT:

Nothing. The bouillon is still crystal clear. You've won!

PASTEUR:

Not yet. We'll give it more time.

NARRATOR:

He checked again on Thursday and on Friday. He carefully checked every day for eight weeks. Nothing grew at all in the beaker.

PASTEUR:

Bacteria do not spontaneously generate.

VILLOT: (*Suddenly worried*)

But what if you ruined the bouillon when you boiled it, and nothing would grow in it whether spontaneously generated or not?

PASTEUR: (*Impressed*)

Very good, Juliet! You'll make a first-rate scientist yet. Break open the neck of the beaker and let in some microbes from the room air. We'll see if they multiply on our bouillon.

NARRATOR:

By 10:00 A.M. the next morning, the surface of the bouillon was covered with the thick tufts of fuzzy mold.

VILLOT:

So the bouillon was good. Now you've won! . . . Haven't you?

PASTEUR: (*Triumphant*)

Yes. Now we've proved it. I have won the war! Without original airborne microbes floating into contact with a nutrient, there can be no bacterial growth. Now to publish our results.

From *Great Moments in Science: Experiments and Readers Theatre.* © 1996. Teacher Ideas Press. (800) 237-6124.

NARRATOR:

Within a week the white flag of surrender fluttered from Pouchet's camp.

POUCHET:

Upon careful review and repetition of the described experiments, it does seem probable that microbes cannot spontaneously generate but need free-floating parents to start a colony in a suitable growth environment.

NARRATOR:

The war was over. Pasteur had won. More importantly, microbiology, the study of all those microscopic organisms floating all around us, became a brand new field of study. But how the process of removing those microscopic organisms from milk came to be called "pasteurization" is another story.

From *Great Moments in Science: Experiments and Readers Theatre.* © 1996. Teacher Ideas Press. (800) 237-6124.

Related Experiments

Here is a series of simple experiments you can use to recreate the steps that led Louis Pasteur to his discoveries. These experiments will help you understand both the work of Pasteur and the scientific concepts involved.

Necessary Equipment

- Thirty-three sealable sandwich bags

- A fresh loaf of commercial white bread, three oranges, and three fresh lettuce leaves

- Three small strips of cardboard

- A thin strip of a soft wood, split into three sections each 3 or 4 inches long

- A small bottle of vinegar

- Water in a spray bottle

- Masking tape and marker pens

- A toaster

➤ *Making Happy Mold*

What You'll Investigate: Pasteur studied the growth of common bread molds to discover that molds do not spontaneously generate from decaying organic material. To learn if molds would spontaneously grow under sterile but otherwise ideal growth conditions, he had to know what those ideal growth conditions were.

That is, he had to already know what conditions encourage or discourage the growth of common molds. This experiment will demonstrate the conditions that foster or inhibit mold growth.

The Setup: Assemble all equipment on a convenient work surface.

What to Do: All molds take a day or two to grow into colonies large enough to be clearly visible to a human eye. You will assemble 33 separate growth chambers and watch their relative growth rates to assess which variety of factors might influence mold growth rates. If the class is divided into groups, each group should prepare, store, and monitor all 33 samples. Then groups may compare results to see if they all detected the same growth patterns.

The four factors you will investigate are moisture level, temperature, acidity, and salinity (saltiness). Each of the growth chambers (sealed bags) will be prepared, sealed, and stored for your regular observation.

From *Great Moments in Science: Experiments and Readers Theatre.* © 1996. Teacher Ideas Press. (800) 237-6124.

Listed below are 11 sets of contents for your bags. You will prepare three identical bags for each listed content and store one bag of each content in a refrigerator (cold), one at room temperature, and one warmer than room temperature (in an incubator, on top of a water heater, by a radiator, or next to a heat duct in winter). You will not need to test extreme heat as Pasteur proved that high heat kills molds, which led to the process known as pasteurization.

Prepare three bags each of the following foods:

1. White bread moistened with water (use spray bottle).
2. White bread soaked and soggy with water.
3. White bread moistened with vinegar.
4. White bread that has been dried for a day.
5. White bread sprinkled on both sides with salt.
6. White bread moistened with water and sprinkled on both sides with salt.
7. White bread toasted fairly dark and allowed to cool for one minute.
8. A whole, fresh orange.
9. A leaf of fresh lettuce.
10. A piece of moistened cardboard.
11. A piece of moistened soft wood.

Remember to prepare three bags of each set of contents. Seal the bags and place a long strip of masking tape across the top. Label each bag on the masking tape by its contents, by the temperature at which it will be kept, and finally, by the time and date you sealed it.

Place all 33 bags in their appropriate storage sites.

Set up log sheets for each bag to note the date and time of every inspection you make, and the size, color, and condition of any mold growth you detect. Do not open the bags during these inspections. Leave them sealed throughout the experiment. Inspect each bag at least three times a day for seven days and record your observations. What do your results teach you? What conditions increase mold growth? Which decrease mold growth?

What's Going On?—Sources of Error: Did your group obtain the same results as other groups? If not, can you think why not? Were your contents the same as the other groups? Were they all correctly labeled?

If one group observed more mold growth on their orange than other groups, does this indicate an error? Why might one orange or one piece of bread exhibit mold growth before another?

Do you think everyone used the same amount of water when creating a "moistened" piece of bread? Would that affect the final results? How could you be sure?

What to Observe: Is mold growth increased by cold or by warmth? Does mold grow better in moist, very wet, or dry conditions? Does it grow well in salty or acid (vinegar) surroundings? All the materials you tested were organic. On which did you note the best (largest) mold growth?

Does mold grow as quickly on cardboard as on bread? What about on wood? Why do you think this is?

If you wanted to grow a colony of mold as quickly as possible, what conditions would you set up? What conditions would you avoid?

One factor you didn't test is light sensitivity. Light, especially direct sunlight, causes greater evaporation and dryer conditions. However, some molds are also photophobic. That is, light itself inhibits their growth. How would you test to see if the kinds of molds you grew were photophobic?

Questions to Ask Yourself: Do you have a feeling for what conditions encourage and discourage mold growth? Instead of measuring the amount of growth, your evaluation was qualitative. That is, you decided if there was "a lot of growth" or "a little growth." Could you actually measure the amount of mold growth? How? Could you find *ideal* growing conditions for your mold?

Where did the molds you grew come from? What started their growth? Preservatives have been mixed into most commercial breads. How do preservatives protect bread? What do they preserve it from? If your bread had preservatives in it, were your results affected? Would you expect more or less mold growth on bread with no preservatives?

From *Great Moments in Science: Experiments and Readers Theatre.* © 1996. Teacher Ideas Press. (800) 237-6124.

Bridges to Books

This story deals with one aspect of our understanding of the physical world around us. You can learn much more about these concepts in your library. The following list gives you key words, concepts, and questions to begin your exploration in a school or public library.

Louis Pasteur is one of the giants of biological and medical sciences. He discovered many important scientific and medical concepts, including **vaccines.** How many vaccines did he invent? How many other important concepts did he uncover? Can you find stories about lives he saved? See what your library has on this important person from our past.

This story was about the study of microscopic organisms (**microorganisms**). These are organisms too small to see without using a microscope. This field of study is called **microbiology.** An important subfield is **bacteriology,** the study of bacteria. Use these three key words to assist your study in the library of Pasteur's work.

Pasteur's first great discovery came during his study of the process called **fermentation.** What is fermentation? What products use fermentation? Pasteur's most famous development was a sterilization system for liquids called **pasteurization.** What can you find in the library on these two key concepts?

References for Further Reading

The following references deal with the major characters, concepts, and processes in this chapter.

Bains, Rae. *Louis Pasteur.* Mahwah, NJ: Troll Associates, 1985.

Birch, Beverly. *Louis Pasteur.* Milwaukee, WI: G. Stevens, 1989.

Brock, Thomas. *Biology of Micro-organisms.* Englewood Cliffs, NJ: Prentice-Hall, 1991.

Burton, Mary June. *Louis Pasteur: Founder of Microbiology.* New York: Franklin Watts, 1973.

Dubos, Rene. *Louis Pasteur: Free Lance of Science.* Boston: Charles Scribner's Sons, 1976.

———. *Pasteur and Modern Science.* Madison, WI: Science Tech Publishers, 1988.

Duclaux, Emile. *Pasteur, the History of a Mind.* Metuchen, NJ: Scarecrow Reprint, 1983.

Green, Carol. *Louis Pasteur: Enemy of Disease.* Chicago: Childrens Press, 1990.

Johnson, Spencer. *The Value of Belief in Yourself: The Story of Louis Pasteur.* New York: Value Communications, 1976.

Latour, Bruno. *The Pasteurization of France.* Cambridge, MA: Harvard University Press, 1988.

Lovett, Sarah. *Micro-Monsters*. Santa Fe, NM: John Muir, 1993.

Morgan, Nina. *Louis Pasteur*. New York: Bookwright Press, 1992.

Nardo, Don. *Germs: Mysterious Organisms*. San Diego, CA: Lucent Books, 1991.

Newfield, Marcia. *The Life of Louis Pasteur*. Frederick, MD: Twenty-First Century Books, 1992.

Paget, Stephen. *Pasteur and After Pasteur*. London: A & C Black, 1974.

Reynolds, Moira. *How Pasteur Changed History*. Bradenton, FL: McGuinn and McGuire, 1994.

Sabin, Franceen. *Microbes and Bacteria*. Mahwah, NJ: Troll Associates, 1985.

Tames, Richard. *Louis Pasteur*. New York: Franklin Watts, 1990.

Winner, Harold. *Louis Pasteur and Microbiology*. London: Priory Press, 1974.

Wood, Laura. *Louis Pasteur*. New York: Julian Messner, 1968.

Consult your librarian for additional titles.

From *Great Moments in Science: Experiments and Readers Theatre*. © 1996. Teacher Ideas Press. (800) 237-6124.

Green Pea, Yellow Pea

Gregor Mendel's formulation of the theory of heredity in 1865

Scientific Background

What color eyes do you have? Are they the same color as one or both of your parents? Do your brothers and sisters have the same color eyes as you? Are your parents' eyes the same color as their parents' eyes? If the answer to any of these questions is "no," why not?

Why don't you look exactly like your parents? Why isn't your hair the same, your nose the same, your height the same, your build the same? Why do some characteristics seem to show up every generation in a family and some pop up only every now and then? Why don't all the members of a family in the same generation all have the same characteristics?

Charles Darwin first opened the door to our modern study of heredity in the eighteenth century by discovering that species evolve over time. That is, new characteristics can be introduced into one or two members of a species and slowly spread out from generation to generation to appear in the entire population. Other characteristics are introduced and never appear again. Darwin's work launched a great study of how characteristics are passed on from generation to generation. The first researcher to gain any real understanding of this complex process was an Austrian monk named Gregor Mendel.

Mendel didn't study people because people are far too complicated and because it isn't possible to experiment on people and crossbreed people for the sake of an experiment. He chose to study pea plants. In many ways this was a very lucky choice of study subjects. Mendel didn't initially understand the process he was trying to study. No one did. But as he slowly came to understand, he realized that peas were one of the best choices he could have made. Their simple genetic structure allowed him to isolate individual characteristics and watch how they were passed from generation to generation. From his small plot of peas grew our basic understanding of heredity and of dominant and recessive genes.

149

Readers Theatre

Characters

Narrator

Abbot Barthol. Head abbot of the monastery. In his late sixties, he's meek and has an administrator's mind.

Brother Michael and **Head of the Bruun Society for Natural Studies.** A single reader can play these two supporting roles.

The Bishop of Prague. Pompous, sarcastic bishop in his early sixties.

Gregor Mendel. Plump, inquisitive Austrian monk in his early forties. A thoughtful and thorough investigator. Intolerant of those who neither understand nor appreciate good science.

Staging

Figure 9.1. Suggested placement of readers for *Green Pea, Yellow Pea*.

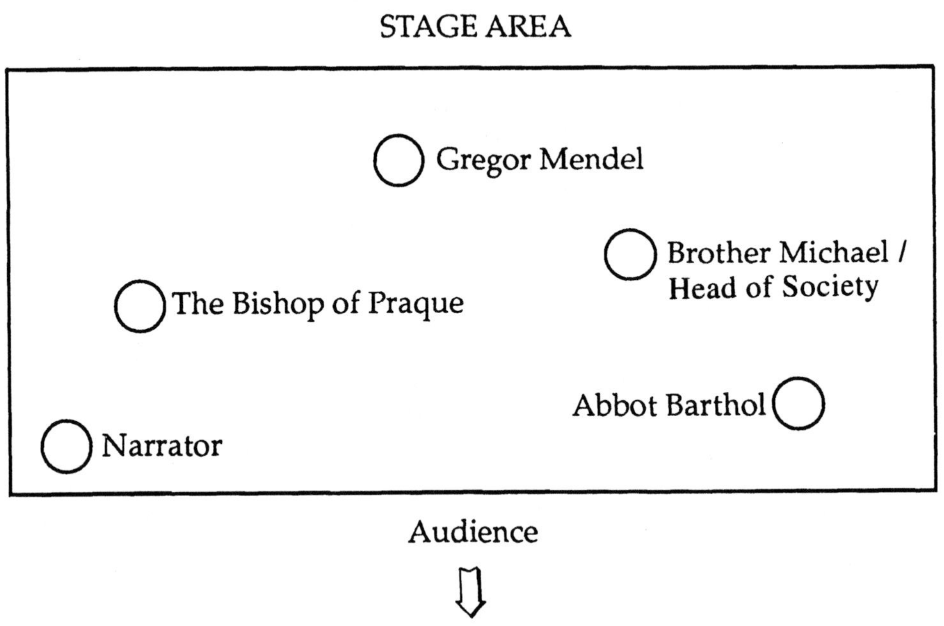

STAGE AREA

◯ Gregor Mendel

◯ Brother Michael / Head of Society

◯ The Bishop of Praque

Abbot Barthol ◯

◯ Narrator

Audience

⇩

From *Great Moments in Science: Experiments and Readers Theatre.* © 1996. Teacher Ideas Press. (800) 237-6124.

Green Pea, Yellow Pea

ABBOT:

Quickly, everyone, line up. I see his carriage coming!

MICHAEL: (*Muttered*)

What a waste of a lovely spring day—standing out here in the dust so the bishop can gawk at us.

ABBOT:

Quiet please! Now everyone look your best. This is important for our monastery.

NARRATOR:

On a bright spring morning in early May of 1865, the Bishop of Prague's open-topped carriage pulled leisurely along the gently sloping dirt road, up to the main gate to the Austrian Monastery of Bruun. The Abbot assembled his monks to meet this high dignitary. It was a rare opportunity for the monastery to show its efforts and to promote its programs to the church hierarchy for more support and funding.

ABBOT:

Your Grace, welcome to the Monastery of Bruun. It is such a pleasure to have you grace our humble monastery.

BISHOP: (*Droll, bored, and grumpy*)

Yes, I'm sure. Pity the place is so . . . dusty.

ABBOT: (*Apologetically*)

Well, it is a dirt road you're standing on, Your Grace.

BISHOP:

As I said, "dusty."

ABBOT: (*Nervous and embarrassed*)

Of course, Your Grace. We will gladly sweep it immediately. (*Louder*) Brother Michael! Sweep the entry road.

MICHAEL:

Sweep? Sweep a dirt road?

ABBOT:

Quickly and graciously, Brother Michael.

MICHAEL: (*Mumbled*)

What a waste of a spring day.

From *Great Moments in Science: Experiments and Readers Theatre.* © 1996. Teacher Ideas Press. (800) 237-6124.

NARRATOR:

By mid-afternoon the bishop's tour of the monastery led him to the gardens and fields.

BISHOP:

The sun here is so . . . so hot.

ABBOT: (*Worried*)

But, Your Grace, I'm afraid I can't do anything about the sun. . . .

BISHOP:

And why should you? It feels wonderful. Prague has been so damp and dreary.

ABBOT: (*Relieved*)

We are forever pleased that the sun here pleases you, Your Grace.

NARRATOR:

They passed a small 120-foot by 20-foot plot used by one of the monks, Father Gregor Mendel, for his experiments on heredity; that is, on how individual traits are blended from an individual through successive generations into a population.

BISHOP:

Ahh, peas for dinner, I see.

MENDEL:

Oh, no, Your Grace!

BISHOP:

"No?" What was that? "No?"

ABBOT: (*Nervous*)

Of course, he doesn't mean to refuse Your Grace. . . .

NARRATOR:

The plump monk working in his thick rows of peas, Gregor Mendel, wiped his small round glasses.

MENDEL:

My peas are not for eating, Your Grace. They're my experiment in heredity.

BISHOP:

Heredity, you say? That would be "science," wouldn't it?

MENDEL:

Yes, Your Grace.

From *Great Moments in Science: Experiments and Readers Theatre.* © 1996. Teacher Ideas Press. (800) 237-6124.

BISHOP:

Pity. "Peas" sound so much more useful than "science."

NARRATOR:

The bishop rocked back and forth, hands clasped behind his back, his face upturned to better soak in the warm spring sunshine.

BISHOP:

I thought that English fellow, Darwin, settled all the hubbub about heredity.

MENDEL: (*Patiently*)

Darwin's work did, indeed, explain much of evolution. But it never successfully addressed *how* characteristics are passed down through each generation.

BISHOP:

And why do we care how characteristics are passed as long as the peas taste good?

ABBOT:

I promise Your Grace that we will serve an abundance of tasty peas this evening for dinner.

MENDEL:

Some traits dominate in every generation, some randomly pop up only every now and then. Why and how does this happen? That's what I am studying.

BISHOP: (*Bored*)

And you expect to learn this by growing peas?

MENDEL:

Yes, Your Grace. Peas are an excellent subject for study.

BISHOP:

Yes, of course. . . . And how does it happen?

ABBOT:

How does *what* happen, Your Grace?

BISHOP: (*Irritated*)

The traits, man. How are they inherited from generation to generation?

NARRATOR:

Mendel shrugged his shoulders and turned his eyes to the rows of pea plants just beginning to stretch their vine-like arms up and around the supporting trellises.

From *Great Moments in Science: Experiments and Readers Theatre.* © 1996. Teacher Ideas Press. (800) 237-6124.

MENDEL:

The answer, Your Grace, is somewhere in my new crop of peas.

NARRATOR:

Continuing on his official tour, the bishop grunted over his shoulder.

BISHOP:

Who cares what a pea inherits besides flavor? Peas . . . such an odd place to look for heredity. He should study people. We care about what people inherit. (*Laughing*) Especially if it's money!

NARRATOR:

On a hazy, muggy August day that same year, church business brought the bishop back to Bruun.

ABBOT:

Ahh, Your Grace! We are blessed as always by your presence.

BISHOP:

Yes. I'm sure.

NARRATOR:

Near the end of his stay at the monastery, he found Gregor Mendel diligently weeding his garden plot.

BISHOP:

Ahh, Father Mendel. Have your peas whispered any secrets to you this summer?

MENDEL: (*Irritated*)

They have, Your Grace. I crossed a strain of tall pea plants from the far row with one of short pea plants from this row. What do you think I got?

BISHOP:

Medium-sized peas, I suppose.

MENDEL:

Wrong!

ABBOT:

He, of course, doesn't mean to say that Your Grace could be . . . "wrong." He means that . . .

MENDEL:

Cross short plants with tall plants and you get a second generation of all tall plants.

From *Great Moments in Science: Experiments and Readers Theatre.* © 1996. Teacher Ideas Press. (800) 237-6124.

BISHOP:

Really? Why not medium-sized . . .

MENDEL: (*Interrupting*)

All tall. And when I planted the seeds of those tall plants what do you think I got for the third generation?

BISHOP: (*Now irritated himself*)

More tall plants, I suppose. (*Now more blasé and bored*) This really isn't very interesting work, Father Mendel.

MENDEL: (*Emphatically*)

Wrong again!

ABBOT: (*Wringing his hands*)

I'm sure he didn't mean to say *you* could be wrong, Your Grace. It's probably his fault.

MENDEL:

The next generation was *mostly* tall plants with a few short plants. The short trait returned in the third generation.

BISHOP: (*Now fascinated*)

Really? How many short ones did you get?

NARRATOR:

But Mendel was already pointing at the next row and the next demonstration.

MENDEL:

And now guess what happened when I crossbred yellow peas with green peas?

BISHOP:

Yellow-green peas?

MENDEL:

Wrong!

ABBOT:

Father Mendel, I think you've used that word quite enough with His Grace.

MENDEL:

The second generation was *all* yellow peas. But in the third generation, I got *mostly* yellow with a few green peas. But never a yellow-green. The traits don't mix.

BISHOP:

Really? Never? And how many green peas did you get?

From *Great Moments in Science: Experiments and Readers Theatre.* © 1996. Teacher Ideas Press. (800) 237-6124.

MENDEL: (*Surprised*)

How many, Your Grace? Well, let me see.

NARRATOR:

Mendel adjusted his glasses and flipped through the pages and careful notes of his ledger.

MENDEL:

Why, it's exactly three yellow peas to one green.

BISHOP:

Ahh. And which tastes better: green or yellow? That is the point, I assume: to produce a tastier pea?

ABBOT: (*After a pause*)

Father Mendel! The Bishop has asked you a question.

NARRATOR:

But Gregor Mendel was lost in other pages of his ledger.

MENDEL:

Yes! In the third generation, there were also three tall plants to every short one. Three to one again . . .

BISHOP:

Really? Both the same? Exactly 3 to 1?

ABBOT: (*Worried*)

Does this result displease Your Grace?

BISHOP:

On the contrary. This would seem to be even more important than my dinner. (*To Mendel*) This neat and constant 3-to-1 ratio in your results would seem to defy the very laws of nature.

MENDEL:

More probably, Your Grace, it is those same laws of nature that create this result. We just do not yet understand the ways of nature. (*Turning back to his notebook*) Yes, here again. Three smooth-skinned peas to one wrinkled-skin pea in the third generation . . . always 3 to 1. . . . But why? Why always that ratio?

NARRATOR:

The mathematician's wheels spun wildly inside Gregor's head as he paced his small room that night.

From *Great Moments in Science: Experiments and Readers Theatre.* © 1996. Teacher Ideas Press. (800) 237-6124.

MENDEL:
Why 3 to 1? Why always 3 to 1?

NARRATOR:
A knock interrupted his thoughts.

MICHAEL:
Are you busy, Father Gregor?

MENDEL:
Ahh, Brother Michael, come in. Come in.

MICHAEL:
I enjoyed watching you humble the mighty bishop a peg or two today. But even more, I was fascinated by your conversation. Have you discovered why the ratio of traits is always 3 to 1 in the third-generation plants?

MENDEL:
Not yet, I'm afraid. But do join me. We'll pace together. (*After a long pause*) Maybe the answer isn't in my garden.

MICHAEL:
Where else could it be?

MENDEL:
In the numbers. Three to one is a simple mathematical ratio. Maybe the answer is in mathematics.

NARRATOR:
Mendel froze mid-stride, overwhelmed by the glorious blaze of sudden insight and understanding.

MENDEL:
Mathematics! It's a simple math ratio. It's suddenly so obvious! How could I have missed it all this time? (*Chuckling*) How odd. It took six years of careful digging and planting to uncover the obvious. 3 to 1. It doesn't *defy* nature. It *defines* nature's way.

MICHAEL:
What defines nature's way? *What's* obvious?

MENDEL: (*Still excited*)
It's easy to follow, Brother Michael. For each characteristic, a plant inherits one trait, or gene, each from father and mother plants. But what if one of those traits is always stronger, or dominant, and one weaker, or recessive? Then, when the traits mixed, second-generation plants would always show the dominant characteristic, such as all yellow or all tall, because they would all have one gene with that trait.

From *Great Moments in Science: Experiments and Readers Theatre.* © 1996. Teacher Ideas Press. (800) 237-6124.

MICHAEL:

So if every second-generation pea plant got one tall gene and one short gene, and if the tall gene is dominant, then every second-generation plant will be a tall plant. I see!

MENDEL:

But 3 to 1 . . . That happens in the *third* generation. In that generation there can be four possibilities.

MICHAEL:

Four?

MENDEL:

Yes, four. In the second generation there is only one possibility. *Every* second-generation plant gets a dominant gene from one parent and a recessive gene from the other. They all have one of each kind of gene. When I crossbreed to create the third generation, each second-generation plant will give one gene to its offspring. Now which gene will each second-generation plant give?

MICHAEL:

I don't know. I suppose it could be either.

MENDEL:

Exactly! Either father or mother can give either dominant or recessive gene. There are four possibilities: either the dominant or recessive gene from either the father or the mother. Now think, Brother Michael. In how many of those four possible combinations will at least one of the dominant genes be present?

NARRATOR:

Brother Michael began to pace as he thought, fingers tapping out possibilities in the air.

MICHAEL: (*Unsure*)

I think a dominant trait will be present in three of the four possible combinations.

MENDEL: (*Excited*)

Exactly! 3 to 1. The third-generation plants will always show the dominant trait except in that one-in-four chance that both parents give it the recessive gene. 3 to 1.

MICHAEL:

And that's exactly what happened in your pea plants!

NARRATOR:

Peas, mathematics, and a seventh year of testing in the garden confirmed Gregor Mendel's answer.

From *Great Moments in Science: Experiments and Readers Theatre.* © 1996. Teacher Ideas Press. (800) 237-6124.

MENDEL:

Traits do not mix. They are inherited from generation to generation and appear only when they are dominant in an individual plant.

MICHAEL:

Then traits from countless ancestors flow into each of us, in separate packages, called "genes," unblended for us to pass on even if the traits doesn't "show" in our generation.

NARRATOR:

In the fall of 1866 Gregor Mendel presented his findings to the Bruun Society for Natural Studies.

MENDEL:

Inherited traits follow simple mathematical laws, either dominating or recessing in any given generation according to simple mathematical probabilities.

NARRATOR:

He expected either the light of understanding to fire in their eyes, or the anger of disagreement to echo through the hall.

He got only blank stares. The Head of the Society said only . . .

HEAD OF SOCIETY:

Father Mendel. Mathematics and botany have absolutely nothing to do with each other. What, in heaven's name, are you talking about?

MENDEL: (*Frustrated*)

Mathematics describes nature. The generations of my pea plants follow a simple mathematical progression.

HEAD OF SOCIETY:

Nature is not constrained, Father Mendel, not by mathematics, not by you. You aren't making any sense.

NARRATOR:

No amount of explaining and lecturing made Mendel's generation understand. It was not until 34 years later, in 1900, that the Dutch scientist Hugo deVries realized Mendel's great gift to the world with his insights on heredity. But that is another story.

From *Great Moments in Science: Experiments and Readers Theatre.* © 1996. Teacher Ideas Press. (800) 237-6124.

Related Experiments

Here is a series of simple experiments you can use to recreate the steps that led Gregor Mendel to his discoveries. These experiments will help you understand both the work of Mendel and the scientific concepts involved.

Necessary Equipment

- Twenty-two small paper bags (the "lunch bag" size works best).

- Thirty-two white and 32 black marbles, all the same size.

► A Look at Your Past

What You'll Investigate: Gregor Mendel identified a universal process through which each generation passes traits and characteristics to the next generation. Mendel worked with a genetically simple species. In his peas, each trait was distinct and obvious. Peas were either green or yellow; they were either tall or short. Humans, however, are much more difficult to study. Their genetic structure is immensely complex. Traits can lie dormant for generations before surfacing, seemingly at random. Still, see if you can detect the principles of this process at work in your own family.

The Setup: Create a family tree listing you, your brothers and sisters, your parents and their brothers and sisters, your grandparents, and your great-grandparents. Optionally, include your cousins on this family tree.

What to Do:

1. Select five physical characteristics you want to track. Each trait should be physically apparent and easy to describe. A good example set would include hair color, hair texture, eye color, height, and nose shape or style.

2. Identify each selected trait for every person on your family tree. Use pictures and the memory of other family members to help you describe family members you are not able to see directly.

3. Search for the flow of traits through your family tree. Identify dominant traits that show up over and over again. Often your family will already know these, calling them "family traits." Note recessive traits that have surfaced more than once. Can you track them through the different generations as recessive genes? Can you predict any traits that the next generation of your family will probably exhibit?

From *Great Moments in Science: Experiments and Readers Theatre.* © 1996. Teacher Ideas Press. (800) 237-6124.

What's Going On?—Sources of Error: Was it difficult to identify family characteristics, or certain dominant traits that seem to show up over and over again? If so, it may be that each generation's dominant traits enter from outside the family through spouses.

It could also be that, with the many generations that have contributed to your heritage, a complex web of traits is surfacing in a pattern that doesn't become apparent without analyzing many more generations. Can you think of other reasons new traits could be introduced into your family to complicate the pattern of dominant and recessive traits?

What to Observe: This is an exercise in pattern identification. You are trying to track the flow of traits through your family. Did you find any traits so dominant that they almost always show up? Are there others that show up in only one person in your whole family?

Questions to Ask Yourself: What are your family's dominant traits? Where do the random traits that show up only once or twice come from? How do traits spread out across a whole population? Moving beyond the five traits you tracked in this experiment, can you find traits that are dominant across whole segments of our population? Can you find any universal human traits?

➤ *The Dominant Probability*

What You'll Investigate: Gregor Mendel found that biology and mathematics meshed in the process of passing traits from one generation to the next. He discovered that one trait for each plant characteristic was given to a new plant by each parent. If those two traits differed, one tended to be dominant (direct the development of that new plant), and one recessive (not appear, or be actively present in the new plant, but still be carried by that plant).

With that information, his mathematics predicted, and his pea plants confirmed, that if he started with two first-generation plants showing different traits, second-generation plants would all show the dominant trait, as would three out of four of the third-generation plants. The remaining quarter of the third-generation plants would show the recessive trait even though it hadn't shown up at all in the second generation. This experiment will show you how this mathematical process works.

The Setup: Label one paper bag "First-Generation Father" and another "First-Generation Mother." Place eight white marbles in the Father bag and eight black marbles in the Mother bag. Each marble represents a possible trait for the plant's color characteristic. For this experiment, assume that the black marble trait is dominant and the white marble trait is recessive. That is, if any plant possesses any of the black marble trait, it will be a black plant. Plants will be white only if they possess no black marble trait.

Finally, label four bags "Second-Generation Plants" and number them 1, 2, 3, and 4.

What to Do:

1. Assess the first-generation plants. The Mother plant (bag) has black marble trait and so is a black plant. The Father plant (bag) contains nothing but white marble trait and so is a white plant.

2. Cross-pollinate the Father and Mother plants to create the second-generation plants. One student closes his or her eyes, reaches into the First-Generation Mother bag and draws out a marble (trait), and drops it into the first of the Second-Generation Plant bags. Repeat this for the other three Second-Generation bags.

   Another student does the same thing for the traits each second-generation plant receives from the Father bag.

3. Assess the second-generation plants. What traits did each second-generation plant receive? One black and one white, right? Therefore, all four second-generation plants will be black plants. This is what Mendel predicted.

4. Prepare the third generation. Label 16 bags as "Third-Generation Plant" and number them 1–16. Remember, each second-generation plant has an equal number of white and black traits, and each will pass on only one trait to each of their third-generation offspring. So each has an equal chance of passing on either a white or black trait to any of the third-generation plants.

   Load eight white and eight black marbles into each second-generation bag as an initial stock of traits, or genes, to pass on. This is enough marbles to ensure that each time a marble is drawn from a second-generation bag, it will have approximately the same chance of being either white or black.

5. Crosspollinate the third generation. You must figure out how to pollinate the third generation following these three rules: First, each third-generation plant (bag) must receive one trait (marble) from each of two different second-generation plants. Second, you also must make sure each second-generation plant pollinates the same number of third-generation plants. Third, you want to ensure that each possible combination of second-generation parents is used—as closely as possible—the same number of times. Note that more than one third-generation plant will have the same two parents.

   Write the numbers of the two second-generation parents on each third-generation bag. An example of a numbering scheme that works (the first digit represents the number of the mother bag, the second digit represents the number of the father bag) is: 12, 13, 14, 12, 21, 23, 24, 23, 31, 32, 34, 34, 41, 42, 43, 41.

   Now with your eyes closed, pick marbles (traits) one at a time from each second-generation parent and drop them into the appropriate third-generation bags.

   One student should act as "Mother Nature" to oversee this process and ensure that one marble from each of the correct second-generation bags is deposited in each of the correct third-generation bags.

6. Assess the third generation. Each third-generation bag should have two marbles (traits), one from each of two different second-generation parents. Take the two marbles from each third-generation bag and decide if that plant will be a white or black plant. Write the color of each plant on its bag. How many third-generation plants of each color did you have? Gregor Mendel and probability mathematics say you should have 12 black and 4 white plants.

From *Great Moments in Science: Experiments and Readers Theatre.* © 1996. Teacher Ideas Press. (800) 237-6124.

Turn all the bags around to the clean side, start over with the First Generation, and repeat the whole experiment, but use more marbles (the same number of each color) when seeding the second-generation bags in step 4. Did you get the same results? If not, why could the same process produce different outcomes?

What's Going On?—Sources of Error: If your Third Generation differed from Mendel's 3-to-1 ratio, there are two possible explanations. First, maybe your "Mother Nature" wasn't careful enough and allowed some incorrect pollinating.

Second, and more likely, the process you have used and probability theory do not *guarantee* that each specific group of plants will come out a certain way. They say that *on average* they will. The larger the number of plants, the greater the probability that your plants will follow the general average.

Sixteen is a very small number of plants, and the probability that your specific results for such a small sample will differ from average is substantial. It would not be at all surprising if at least one of your experiments turned up 11 black and five white, or 13 black and only three white plants.

What to Observe: Watch for the mathematical patterns to emerge in your bags as they did for Mendel in his rows of pea plants. Those same patterns, ratios, and probabilities operate to direct human heredity, which is the passing on of traits through human families. Those patterns are very difficult to detect in humans, however, because there is such a complex variety of possible traits that could be carried by, and passed on by, either parent, grandparent, or great-grandparent.

Questions to Ask Yourself: You have now tracked the occurrence of one dominant and one recessive trait through three generations of a plant. If the dominant trait appeared in three of every four plants in the third generation, can you predict what would happen in the fourth generation? In the fifth?

Can you find examples in your own family, or in the flowers and plants around you, of dominant traits that show up in plant after plant and family member after family member? Can you find recessive traits that have appeared in one person or plant that didn't appear in either parent?

Bridges to Books

This story deals with one aspect of our understanding of the physical world around us. You can learn much more about these concepts in your library. The following list gives you key words, concepts, and questions to begin your exploration in a school or public library.

Gregor Mendel was a brilliant and thoughtful researcher. See if you can find more about his life and work. What other plants did he study? What other discoveries did he make?

Gregor Mendel's work dealt with what we call **heredity** or **genetics**. He tracked the passage of **traits**, or **genes**, from generation to generation in his pea plants. Use these four key words to find what information your library has on these general topics.

Mendel's great contribution to our knowledge lay in the discovery of **dominant** and **recessive** traits. He was the first to unravel the mystery of how traits could lie dormant for generations and then seemingly spring out of nowhere in some future member or members of a population. Can you find references to dominant and recessive traits or characteristics in your library?

References for Further Reading

The following references deal with the major characters, concepts, and processes in this chapter.

Asimov, Isaac. *How Did We Find Out About Genes?* New York: Walker, 1978.

Bendick, Jeanne. *How Heredity Works.* New York: Parents Magazine, 1975.

Bornstein, Sandy. *What Makes You What You Are.* Englewood Cliffs, NJ: Julian Messner, 1989.

Byczynski, Lynn. *Genetics, Nature's Blueprints.* San Diego, CA: Lucent Books, 1991.

Dawkins, Richard. *The Selfish Gene.* New York: Oxford University Press, 1989.

Edelson, Edward. *Genetics and Heredity.* New York: Chelsea House, 1990.

Edlin, Gordon. *Genetic Principles.* Boston: Jones and Bartlette, 1984.

Fradin, Dennis. *Heredity.* Chicago: Childrens Press, 1987.

Gardner, Eldon. *Principles of Genetics.* New York: John Wiley, 1984.

George, Wilma. *Gregor Mendel and Heredity.* Howe, England: Wayland, 1975.

Morrison, Velma. *There's Only One You.* New York: Julian Messner, 1978.

Olby, Robert. *Origins of Mendelism.* New York: Schochen Books, 1966.

Oleksy, Walter. *Miracle of Genetics.* Chicago: Childrens Press, 1986.

Patent, Dorothy. *Grandfather's Nose: Why We Look Alike or Different.* New York: Franklin Watts, 1989.

Pomerantz, Charlotte. *Why You Look Like You, Whereas I Tend to Look Like Me.* New York: W. R. Scott, 1969.

Sootin, Harry. *Gregor Mendel: Father of the Science of Genetics.* New York: Vanguard Press, 1959.

Webb, Robert. *Gregor Mendel and Heredity.* New York: Franklin Watts, 1973.

Webster, Gary. *The Man Who Found Out Why.* New York: Hawthorne Press, 1963.

Consult your librarian for additional titles.

From *Great Moments in Science: Experiments and Readers Theatre.* © 1996. Teacher Ideas Press. (800) 237-6124.

Launching a Scientist

Robert Goddard's attempts to develop a rocket in 1888

Scientific Background

Fireworks were first launched into the sky more than a thousand years ago by the Chinese. The Chinese also fired artillery shells as rockets during battle as early as the thirteenth century. Roger Bacon discovered gunpowder for the European scientific community in the mid-thirteenth century. European artillery shells and early rockets gained rapid popularity as military weapons, although they were notoriously inaccurate. They created great battlefield noise and smoke and tore gaping holes in walls and fortifications; however, they rarely did much damage to opposing troops.

In the early nineteenth century the English inventor, Roger Congreve, developed the first metal casings for launched projectiles, a spin stabilization system for rockets, and the first launch pad. By the end of that same century, rockets were employed for nonmilitary as well as battlefield use. Their first commercial assignment was to carry a lifeline to a floundering cargo ship near shore.

All these shells, rockets, and fireworks have one characteristic in common: They all used solid fuel. They are launched by the explosion of a solid propellant like gunpowder. The problems with such fuels are that they are heavy (especially for the amount of propellant force they produce) and they explode all at once, rather than burn evenly over an extended flight.

American scientist Robert Goddard changed how the world viewed rockets by inventing liquid-propelled rockets. This advance allowed the world to enter an age of rockets that traveled thousands of feet into the air, rather than hundreds, and many miles downrange, rather than fractions of a mile. It also allowed humans to escape the earth's gravity and enter space. But Robert Goddard's path to the successful launch of a liquid-fueled rocket did not begin in an engineering class or in a rocket and testing design program. It began in his front yard.

Readers Theatre

Characters

Narrator

Percy Long. Six-year-old best friend of Bobby and already a confirmed skeptic.

Bobby Goddard. At six years old, Robert Goddard is a confident, if somewhat overly enthusiastic, young scientist.

Mother. Bobby's mother, Fannie Goddard, is a concerned, suburban mother. Not very impressed by Bobby's science efforts, she sees danger and mischief.

Father. Bobby's father, George Goddard, is a little aloof from the day-to-day running of the family, but he's a true scientist at heart, and a great source of support and encouragement for Bobby's scientific efforts.

Staging

Figure 10.1. Suggested placement of readers for *Launching a Scientist*.

STAGE AREA

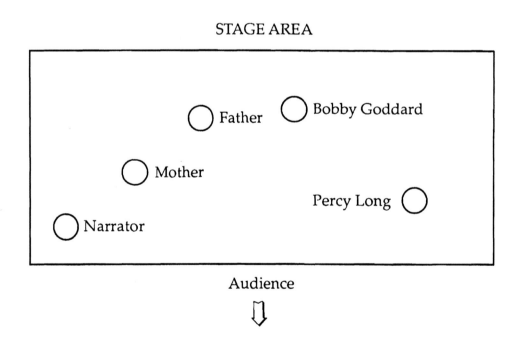

Audience

From *Great Moments in Science: Experiments and Readers Theatre*. © 1996. Teacher Ideas Press. (800) 237-6124.

Launching a Scientist

NARRATOR:

On a brisk Saturday afternoon in Boston in September 1887, with the leaves just beginning to turn, two six-year-old boys played in front of a modest two-story house. One lounged in the front yard, laughing through a face full of freckles and past bushy red hair.

PERCY: (*Laughing and confident*)

I keep telling you, it won't work, Bobby.

NARRATOR:

The other boy planted his feet on the front porch like an immovable rock, determined and convinced of his experiment.

BOBBY:

It will too work, Percy!

PERCY: (*Becoming irritated*)

You can't fly, Bobby. Only birds fly.

NARRATOR:

But young Bobby Goddard was not going to back down. When it came to science, he never doubted one bit.

BOBBY:

With science I can do anything. And that includes flying. You just count once I take off from the front porch railing.

NARRATOR:

Bobby fished a 10-inch-long shiny zinc rod out of his pocket. It was as thick around as his wrist.

PERCY:

What's that thing?

BOBBY: (*Confident*)

It's what'll help me fly. Now you just remember to count. . . . Get ready!

NARRATOR:

Bobby slammed open the front door and dashed into the living room. There, he slid his shoes along the thick wool carpet, shuffling back and forth across the room.

PERCY:
Hurry up! I can't wait around all day.

BOBBY:
Just a second! I need more charge.

NARRATOR:
Bobby shuffled two more laps across the living room carpet.

BOBBY:
Here I come!

NARRATOR:
Bobby Goddard sprinted back out the open front door, bounded once on the low bench he had positioned next to the railing, once on the railing itself, and, with a mighty leap, launched himself into space. He thrust the zinc rod high over his head with both hands.

BOBBY: (*Shouting*)
Count!

PERCY:
One . . . two . . .

ALL:
THUD!

NARRATOR:
Bobby slammed into the soft dirt of his mother's flower bed, just below the railing.

PERCY: (*Laughing*)
Yup. You fly just like a bird—a *dead* bird.

NARRATOR:
Percy Long laughed so hard he almost fell over. Bobby had crumpled two flower bushes, flattened half a dozen blooming primroses, and left deep holes where his elbow and knees hit.

PERCY: (*Still laughing*)
I told you you couldn't fly.

NARRATOR:
Bobby sat up thoughtfully and rubbed his sore knee.

From *Great Moments in Science: Experiments and Readers Theatre.* © 1996. Teacher Ideas Press. (800) 237-6124.

BOBBY:
Maybe I didn't get enough electric charge.

NARRATOR:
Bobby climbed out of the crushed flowers and back onto the front porch.

PERCY:
You giving up?

BOBBY:
Course not. I'll keep trying 'till it works. This time I'll get a better static electricity charge. So you be ready to count!

NARRATOR:
Bobby stepped into the house and shuffled across the living room carpet. Back and forth, scraping his leather shoes across the carpet.

BOBBY:
Here I come again!

NARRATOR:
Being careful not to touch anything and lose his electrical charge in a harmless spark, Bobby raced back onto the front porch. One foot on the bench. One foot on the railing. And six-year-old Bobby Goddard launched into the clear blue sky again. Again he lifted the zinc rod high over head.

BOBBY:
Count!

PERCY:
One . . . two . . . three . . . four . . .

ALL:
SMASH!

NARRATOR:
Bobby wiped out two hydrangea bushes as he crashed down and rolled out onto the grass.

PERCY: (*Laughing*)
Give it up before you kill yourself.

NARRATOR:
But Bobby leapt triumphantly to his feet.

From *Great Moments in Science: Experiments and Readers Theatre.* © 1996. Teacher Ideas Press. (800) 237-6124.

BOBBY:

Don't laugh. I flew longer that time! It worked better.

NARRATOR:

Percy squeaked to a stop in the middle of his laugh. It was true. Bobby had stayed up almost twice as long that time.

MOTHER: (*Irritated*)

Bobby Goddard, I have told you a thousand times not to leave this door open!

NARRATOR:

Mrs. Goddard stormed out the front door after her son. She reached the porch railing, looked over, and gasped.

MOTHER:

Land sakes! What have you done to my flowers?

PERCY: (*Snickering*)

He was crashing, Mrs. Goddard.

BOBBY:

I was *flying*, Mom.

MOTHER:

Flying? Where on earth do you think you're going to fly to?

BOBBY: (*Pleading*)

Not on earth, mom. I'm going to fly to the moon.

MOTHER: (*Exasperated*)

So far it looks like you've only managed to get as far as my flower beds.

PERCY: (*Sarcastically*)

That's where he did his crashing, Mrs. Goddard.

MOTHER:

And right now, young man, you will fix the damage you've done.

BOBBY: (*Sadly*)

Yes, ma'am. Sorry, Mother.

FATHER:

What's all the commotion out here? It's so loud I can't read the paper.

From *Great Moments in Science: Experiments and Readers Theatre.* © 1996. Teacher Ideas Press. (800) 237-6124.

NARRATOR:

Bobby's father marched out onto the porch, still carrying the newspaper he had been reading.

MOTHER:

Bobby's been wrecking my flower beds. That's what!

BOBBY:

I was trying to fly, Dad.

PERCY:

Mostly, he was crashing, Mr. Goddard.

NARRATOR:

Mr. Goddard squatted down on the porch and smiled at his son standing before him.

FATHER:

How were you trying to fly, Bobby?

BOBBY: (*More excited now*)

Electricity, dad. If I could only get a big enough electric charge.

FATHER:

So that's what all that shuffling across the living room was about. You were building up a static electricity charge. And here I thought you were just wearing out the rug.

MOTHER:

He's wearing out my patience.

NARRATOR:

Mr. Goddard smiled at his son and thought for a moment.

FATHER:

Why did you think static electricity would help you fly? And that zinc rod—what was it supposed to do?

BOBBY: (*With a sigh and a shrug*)

You told me yesterday that when I shuffle my feet on a rug, electricity rises up from the carpet to my feet. I knew zinc was a good conductor, so I figured if I held a zinc rod up real high when I jumped, maybe the electricity would rise up through me to the zinc. And maybe it would carry me up with it as it went.

NARRATOR:

Mr. Goddard clamped both hands over his mouth to cover up the laugh that threatened to jump out of his throat. Bobby looked glum and dejected.

From *Great Moments in Science: Experiments and Readers Theatre.* © 1996. Teacher Ideas Press. (800) 237-6124.

BOBBY:

Well, it sort of worked. I flew longer the second time. (*Sigh*) Maybe I just jumped harder.

NARRATOR:

Mr. Goddard rose and turned to his wife.

FATHER: (*Proudly*)

Now what do you think of our boy, Fannie? I tell him one thing about electricity, and he puts it together with two or three other ideas and comes up with an experiment!

MOTHER:

What he came up with was the destruction of my flower bed!

PERCY:

What he came up with was mostly crashing.

FATHER: (*Kindly*)

So your experiment was a failure, eh, son?

BOBBY:

I guess so . . .

FATHER:

Good! That's what I want to see!

BOBBY:

What?

FATHER:

Failure is how a scientist learns, Bobby. You try something. It flops. That leads you to a better idea for the next try. The important thing is to never stop trying. Now before your next try, you might spend some time thinking about what kind of force is strong enough to overcome gravity and push something up into the air. I think it's time I told you about Sir Isaac Newton and his laws of motion.

PERCY: (*Softly to Bobby*)

Yuck! That sounds boring. (*Louder to all*) I, uh, think I have to go home now.

NARRATOR:

Mr. Goddard threw an arm around his son's shoulders and led him toward the house.

FATHER:

I think you are going to find Isaac Newton very exciting!

From *Great Moments in Science: Experiments and Readers Theatre.* © 1996. Teacher Ideas Press. (800) 237-6124.

MOTHER:

Oh, no, he won't! At least not until he's fixed my flower beds!

NARRATOR: (*After a brief pause*)

On a cloudy afternoon three days later, Mrs. Goddard climbed the basement stairs with a load of wash and glanced out the kitchen window.

MOTHER:

Land sakes! What on earth does he think he's doing now?

NARRATOR:

She dropped the laundry basket and dashed for the back door. Her son balanced on top of the high wooden backyard fence. In his hands, Bobby held two enormous balloons.

MOTHER:

He'll break his neck! He must be six feet off the ground.

NARRATOR:

Bounding onto the back porch, she screamed,

MOTHER:

Bobby Goddard, you get down from there this instant! . . . But be careful!

NARRATOR:

Percy Long had already started his countdown.

PERCY:

Three . . . Two . . . One . . . GO!

NARRATOR:

Mrs. Goddard's scream was heard as Bobby leapt from his precarious perch, high into the air.

BOBBY:

Count, Percy!

NARRATOR:

As he jumped, Bobby relaxed his tight grip on the necks of the two, bulging, 24-inch balloons. With a piercing, high-pitched screech, air rushed out the bottom of each balloon.

PERCY:

One . . . two . . . three . . . four . . . fi-

From *Great Moments in Science: Experiments and Readers Theatre.* © 1996. Teacher Ideas Press. (800) 237-6124.

ALL:

THUD!

NARRATOR:

Bobby crashed to the soft grass. The whine of his two balloons slowly died away to a faint hiss as the balloons deflated.

MOTHER: (*Angry but relieved*)

What on earth do you think you were doing?

NARRATOR:

Bobby sat up and shook his head to clear away the stars before his eyes.

BOBBY: (*Dazed*)

I was flying, Mom.

PERCY:

You mean you were crashing again.

NARRATOR:

At dinner that night, Mr. Goddard asked his glum and dejected son,

FATHER:

What's this I hear about your trying to fly again, Bobby?

MOTHER:

He just about broke his neck, is what he did.

PERCY:

He's getting real good at crashing, Mr. Goddard.

NARRATOR:

Percy had stayed for dinner, eager to see if Bobby would get yelled at.

BOBBY:

I was using balloons for thrust, Dad, like what you told me Mr. Newton said. When the air rushes out the bottom of the balloons, it pushes the balloons up. I figured they'd take me up with them.

FATHER: (*Proudly*)

Did you hear that, Fannie? What do you think of our boy now?

MOTHER:

I think he'll break his neck before he turns seven.

From *Great Moments in Science: Experiments and Readers Theatre.* © 1996. Teacher Ideas Press. (800) 237-6124.

PERCY:

I think he should enter the state fair for crashing.

BOBBY:

Is this another failure, Dad?

FATHER:

You just need more lift, son, more power. A lot more power. Oh, and maybe it's time to stop sending yourself up with your rockets. Safer for you to watch from the ground. Yup. A few more experiments and a little more power. I think you'll get it.

NARRATOR:

Forty years later, on March 16, 1926, Robert Goddard launched the world's first liquid-fueled rocket. It rose 50 feet from the ground. By 1937 one of his rockets thundered more than 9,000 feet into the air, and the space age was launched for mankind. In another 35 years, rockets regularly blasted free of earth's gravity to place satellites and manned capsules in orbit. But that is another story.

From *Great Moments in Science: Experiments and Readers Theatre.* © 1996. Teacher Ideas Press. (800) 237-6124.

Related Experiments

Here is a series of simple experiments you can use to recreate the steps that led Robert Goddard to his discoveries. These experiments will help you understand both the work of Robert Goddard and the scientific concepts involved.

Necessary Equipment

- Several softballs

- Tape measure

- A number of large balloons (14-inch or larger)

- One small tank of helium

- Thin galvanized wire (28 gauge is best)

- Aluminum foil

- Lengths of string

- Short candles

- A number of small, uniform weights. Smaller Lego® building blocks are about the right size and weight.

- One magic marker per group

- One balance scale for weighing small weights

- A hair dryer

➤ *Why Do You Need Lift?*

What You'll Investigate: What is *lift*? Lift is a force that overcomes gravity and makes something rise. How much lift do you need to raise an object one foot off the floor? Do you need more lift to make that same object rise a hundred feet? A thousand feet? What forces does lift have to overcome to make something continue to rise? These are the first questions you will investigate.

The Setup: This is an outdoor exercise. All you'll need is one softball per group. Start with each softball on the ground in front of the student doing the exercise.

What to Do:

1. Overcoming Gravity. First see if you can overcome the force of gravity that holds your softball to the earth. Reach down and lift the ball chest high. Have you just overpowered gravity? Yes. You applied a greater upward force than gravity exerts downward on the ball. Because the force you applied was greater, the ball rose. As you hold the ball steady at chest level, the upward force you apply exactly equals the downward force of gravity. They cancel each other out, and the ball sits motionless.

    What is another name we commonly use for the downward force of gravity? The answer is weight. The weight of an object is a measure of the force with which gravity holds that object to the earth.

2. Launching the Ball. Throw the ball as close to straight up as you can. First, it rises into the sky. Then it slows, stops, and finally falls again to earth. Why? Why didn't it continue to climb? What slowed and then stopped it?

    The answer is, of course, the force of gravity. While the ball remained in contact with your hand, you could push the ball faster and faster through the air. You pushed it upwards much harder than gravity pulled it down. As soon as you released the ball, though, there was no longer any force pushing it upwards. There was only the momentum the ball had already gained from your throw.

    However, two other forces continued to tug on the ball and slow its upward motion: gravity and air resistance, or drag. As long as the ball is within earth's gravitational field, gravity will continue to pull it down. You can easily overpower the force of gravity. However, the ball will only rise as long as you continue to push the ball upward or until the momentum you have given it finally runs out. The only reason you can't throw a ball into space is that humans can't impart enough momentum into a ball to overcome gravity and drag and continue to carry it upwards until it escapes the earth's clutches.

What's Going On?—Sources of Error: This is a qualitative experiment. Don't look for errors. Rather look for an understanding of the way gravity acts on an object and of how we routinely deal with gravity's effect.

What to Observe: The force of gravity is measured by the weight of an object. If you can lift that object, you can overpower the force of gravity. When you throw a ball skyward, the force of your throw imparts enough momentum to carry the ball into the air. But the force of gravity continually pulls down on the ball, slowing its speed, and finally drags it back to earth.

A more significant measure is "work." Work is the application of a force over a certain distance. For example, if you lift a 1-pound ball 2 feet into the air, you have performed 2 foot-pounds (ft.-lb.) of work. If you lift it 4 feet, you have performed 4 ft.-lbs. of work. To make an 8-ounce ($\frac{1}{2}$ lb.) softball escape earth's gravity, you would have to apply at least $\frac{1}{2}$ lb. of force continuously over a 40- or 50-mile journey from the earth's surface into open space, which is more than 105,000 ft.-lbs. of work ($\frac{1}{2}$ lb. x 40 miles x 5,280 ft./mile). That's a lot more energy than you can apply in one throw.

From *Great Moments in Science: Experiments and Readers Theatre.* © 1996. Teacher Ideas Press. (800) 237-6124.

Questions to Ask Yourself: What is lift? What is weight? How do work and force relate to each other? How does gravity pull downward on an object? How could you continue to apply upward force to a ball after you release it during a throw?

➤ *Giving Yourself a Lift*

What You'll Investigate: Can you lift yourself up with greater force than the gravity that holds you down? How high can you lift yourself? Do you always need the same amount of force to overcome gravity and lift yourself higher? How much force would it take to make you rise forever? These are the next questions to investigate.

The Setup: All students should line up the students at the bottom of a set of stairs.

What to Do:

1. Can you overpower gravity's force holding you to earth? Step up on the first step. Did you just overpower gravity? Yes. You pushed upward with your leg muscles harder than gravity pulled down. So your body rose.

2. Now climb to the top of the stairs. Did you accomplish work while climbing? Yes. You exerted a force over a distance. If the stairs were 15 feet high, and you weighed 80 pounds, you would have performed 15 ft. x 80 lbs., or 1,200 ft.-lbs. of work while climbing. No wonder your heart rate increases while you climb stairs.

    How much work would you have to perform to lift yourself into space? If you weigh 80 lbs. and if we say it is 40 miles to open space, then you would have to perform 80 lbs. x 40 miles x 5,280 ft./mile, or nearly 18,000,000 ft.-lbs. of work! If the stairway were long enough, you could lift yourself into space. Your legs would, however, grow pretty tired climbing 314,000 stairs!

3. Stand next to a wall on which marks 1 foot, $\frac{1}{2}$ foot, and $\frac{1}{4}$ foot high have been drawn from the floor. Jump as high as you can, keeping your legs straight while you are in the air. Have other students watch to see how high your feet rise above the floor. Make three jumps and average their heights.

    Now decide who in your class can perform the most work while overpowering gravity during a jump. Is it the person who jumped highest? No. Work is measured by raising a weight over a distance, which is your weight times the height you jumped. Measured in foot-pounds, see whose leg muscles were able to perform the most work during this jump.

What's Going On?—Sources of Error: Again, this experiment is primarily qualitative: Rather than measuring, you are primarily gaining a sense, a feel, for the force of gravity and of how you routinely work to overpower it.

The only place errors can enter is in measuring the height of each student's jump. These jumps happen quickly, and it's hard to tell exactly when someone reaches the top of their jump. They might have bent their legs as they reached the top and thus appeared to propel their body higher than they actually did. What can you do to minimize the possible error from this measurement?

From *Great Moments in Science: Experiments and Readers Theatre.* © 1996. Teacher Ideas Press. (800) 237-6124.

What to Observe: Can you overcome the gravitational force that holds you to the earth? If you can lift yourself up, the answer is "yes." Virtually every person has enough strength to exert a greater lifting force on his or her body than gravity exerts in an effort to hold it down.

How much extra force can you exert in lifting your own body? This can be measured by seeing how much momentum you can impart into your body to fly upward when you jump. The more force your leg muscles exert, the more momentum will be imparted, and the higher you will fly.

Questions to Ask Yourself: The force of gravity is proportional to the mass of two objects and to the distance between them. Would you weigh less 60 miles up than you do standing on the ground? Why do people weigh less on the moon than on earth? Would you weigh more or less on Jupiter?

One example earlier in this experiment showed that it would take 18,000,000 ft.-lbs. of work for an 80-pound person to climb into space. How much work is that? How many times would you have to lift a 10-pound weight 2 feet into the air to accomplish the same amount of work? The answer is 824 times a day every day for three years. Can you make that calculation?

➤ *Balloon Magic*

What You'll Investigate: Lift often comes from *thrust*. Thrust is a name given to an internally generated force that pushes, or propels, an object forward. Robert Goddard tried to use balloons as a source of thrust and lift. It's time to investigate how much thrust and lift you can create with a balloon.

The Setup: Each group should bend a length of wire into a loop about ½ inch in diameter and attach other wire pieces as supporting rods as shown in Figure 10.2. Place a piece of aluminum foil across the bottom of this support structure as a platform for weights and candles. This aluminum foil should be doubled to provide adequate firmness.

Each group should have a dozen large balloons. Fourteen-inch (or larger) balloons are readily available and large enough to provide good results. Also each group needs a small votive-style candle (regular votive candles are too heavy for one balloon to lift), a length of string, and a series of small, uniform weights (such as small Lego® building blocks).

Figure 10.2. Balloon support frame.

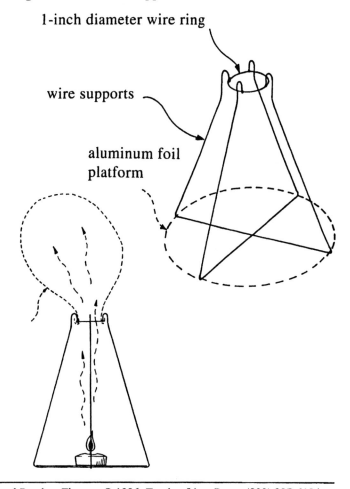

1-inch diameter wire ring

wire supports

aluminum foil platform

From Great Moments in Science: Experiments and Readers Theatre. © 1996. Teacher Ideas Press. (800) 237-6124.

What to Do, Part 1 (Thrust):

1. First blow up a balloon and tie its open end. Release it. Does it rise? Do you get any lift from this balloon? No? Why not?

2. Now blow up a second balloon and hold the end closed. Point it upwards and let it go. Does it fly? Does it propel itself through the air? Why? What creates the thrust to power this flight?

   Actually, the air rushing from an open balloon creates thrust in the same way a jet engine does. It's an example of Newton's second law of motion. The force of escaping air pushing in one direction creates an equal and opposite force pushing in the opposite direction. Jet engines create more force than your balloon by forcing much more hot gas through the engine's exhaust.

3. How much lift did your balloon create when you let it go? To find out, see how much weight it will carry. Blow up this same balloon again while holding the balloon high up on its neck. While you hold the balloon closed and point it upwards, have a second student measure how big the balloon is by looping a string around its fattest part and by marking the string at the point where it has completed one circumference around the balloon.

   A third student should attach the loop frame to your balloon and place several weights on the platform. Now release the balloon. Did it fall or rise? That is, was the force of the escaping air greater than the pull of gravity on the balloon, platform, and weights?

   Repeat this test and adjust the number of weights you place on the platform. Make sure you blow the balloon up to the same point each time by using the marked string as a guide. Your goal is to find the amount of weight needed to make the balloon hold still for a second or two when released, rather than rise or fall. Weigh the platform and those blocks. This weight equals the amount of upward thrust your balloon created.

What to Do, Part 2 (Lift):

Everyone has seen pictures of hot-air balloons drifting over the countryside. What makes a hot air balloon rise? In the previous experiment, your balloon moved because air rushing out of its open end created thrust. Hot air balloons rise because air expands when heated and so becomes lighter. It rises up, or floats up on top of the heavier, cooler air around it. Now see how much lift you get from heating the air that goes into your balloon.

1. Fit the end of a balloon over the nozzle of a warmed-up hair dryer. Turn the dryer to its hottest setting and inflate the balloon. Tie it off and let it go. Did it rise?

   Quickly tie your wire loop and platform onto this balloon with string. Does this hot-air balloon create enough lift to hold up the platform? Will it also lift any weights? Try to find out exactly how much weight your hot-air balloon will support. This is the amount of lift it creates.

From *Great Moments in Science: Experiments and Readers Theatre.* © 1996. Teacher Ideas Press. (800) 237-6124.

2. Now fill a balloon with helium. We all know that helium balloons rise because helium is lighter (less dense) than either oxygen or nitrogen, the two major components of air. But will helium create more lift than hot air?

   Tie your wire loop and platform onto this helium balloon and see if it will lift more weight than the hot air balloon from step 1. If the air in your hot-air balloon had been superheated to hundreds of degrees, would it have created more lift?

3. Here is one final question to answer in this experiment. Will putting more helium in your balloon create more or less lift? Fill a balloon about half full with helium. Use your string to measure its circumference. Make marks on the string 3, 6, and 9 inches beyond the length of this circumference.

   Now attach the loop and platform and record how much weight this half-filled balloon will support. Fill a second balloon so that its circumference is 3 inches larger than your half-filled balloon. Record how much weight this balloon holds.

   Repeat this process for two more balloons, one 6 inches larger, and one 9 inches larger than the first. Do you see a pattern? As the amount of helium increases, do you see a proportional increase in the amount of lift? Remember that the volume of helium inside your balloon is proportional to the cube of the circumference, so that relatively small increases in balloon circumference can represent a much greater increase in the volume of helium inside.

   Having measured the weight that one helium balloon can lift, figure out how many balloons it would take to lift you off the ground. Is this number larger than you thought it would be? One helium balloon doesn't create very much lift. Maybe that's why helium blimps, or dirigibles, have to be so large.

What's Going On?—Sources of Error: Did you have trouble measuring any lift from your balloons? Hand-held balloons provide very little lift. Sometimes it's hard to measure small quantities. Air currents swirling through the room might have a greater effect on the balloon's movement than lift from the gases inside.

When would you get more lift from a balloon—during the heat of summer or during a subfreezing spell in January? Which experiment would give you a more accurate measure of the lift potential of a balloon? Should you account for the room temperature and humidity if you wanted a very accurate measure of a balloon's lift?

What to Observe: Watch for what gives a balloon lift. Does a hot-air balloon or a similarly sized helium balloon create more lift? Why? The lift of a balloon is created by pressure differences between the gas inside the balloon and the air outside. During all of the experiments you have performed, this pressure difference was small, and so the resulting lift was also small.

Questions to Ask Yourself: Your muscles, hot air, and helium all create lift. What else creates lift? What gives an airplane enough lift to rise off the runway? Do its wings create lift? How? What creates lift for a Saturn rocket carrying a space shuttle into orbit? Is this lift closer to a helium balloon or to air escaping from the open end of a balloon? Can you find examples of other kinds of lift?

From *Great Moments in Science: Experiments and Readers Theatre.* © 1996. Teacher Ideas Press. (800) 237-6124.

Bridges to Books

This story deals with one aspect of our understanding of the physical world around us. You can learn much more about these concepts in your library. The following list gives you key words, concepts, and questions to begin your exploration in a school or public library.

Robert Goddard based most of his early research on the laws of motion developed by **Sir Isaac Newton**. Use these two names to begin your research. What can you find about their lives and work? Can you find other discoveries made by either man?

Rockets, planes, birds, and all things that fly require **lift** to overcome gravity. They also need **thrust** to propel them through the air. Finally, a flying object must be **stable**, so that its flight won't drift wildly and erratically. Use these terms as key words to research what makes flight possible and how flight works.

Goddard developed **liquid-fueled rockets**, a propulsion system still used on planes and rockets flown from the earth. But rockets have a long and fascinating history. See what information you can find in the library on the history, development, and growth of **rockets**.

References for Further Reading

The following references deal with the major characters, concepts, and processes in this chapter.

Asimov, Isaac. *Rockets, Probes, and Satellites*. Milwaukee, WI: G. Stevens, 1988.

Baird, Ann. *The U.S. Space Camp Book of Rockets*. New York: Morrow Junior Books, 1994.

Coil, Suzanne. *Robert H. Goddard*. New York: Facts on File, 1992.

Cox, Donald. *Rocketry Throughout the Ages*. New York: Winston, 1979.

Daughtery, Charles. *Robert Goddard: Trail Blazer to the Stars*. New York: Macmillan, 1964.

Dewey, Anne. *Robert Goddard, Space Pioneer*. Boston: Little, Brown, 1972.

Farley, Karin. *Robert H. Goddard*. Englewood Cliffs, NJ: Silver, Burdett Press, 1991.

Furniss, Tim. *Space Rockets*. Boston: Gloucester Press, 1988.

Hendrickson, Walter. *Who Really Invented the Rocket?* New York: Putnam, 1974.

Lampton, Christopher. *Rocketry: From Goddard to Space Travel*. New York: Franklin Watts, 1988.

Lehman, Milton. *This High Man: The Life of Robert Goddard*. New York: Farrar, Straus, 1973.

Lomask, Milton. *Robert H. Goddard.* New York: Garrard, 1972.

Maurer, Richard. *Rocket! How a Toy Launched the Space Age.* New York: Crown, 1995.

Quackenbush, Robert. *The Boy Who Dreamed of Rockets.* New York: Parents Magazine, 1978.

Richards, Norman. *Dreamers and Doers.* New York: Morrow Junior Books, 1984.

Verral, Charles. *Robert Goddard: Father of the Space Age.* Englewood Cliffs, NJ: Silver, Burdett Press, 1991.

Von Braun, Wernher. *The History of Rockets and Space Travel.* New York: Thomas Y. Crowell, 1966.

Consult your librarian for additional titles.

A Glowing Discovery

Marie Curie's discovery of radioactivity in 1897-1901

Scientific Background

What would you do if you stumbled onto something new, something the world had never seen? What if it were something the world hadn't even imagined could exist? Would you rush in to explore and study your find, or would you back away from the unknown, fearing that it might harm you? Marie Curie, probably the most famous of all female scientists, chose to rush in.

By 1895, 78 elements had been discovered. That same year Roentgen detected the first rays ever produced by, or radiating from, a metal. He named these invisible rays "X-rays." The world of science was astounded, both to find that some metals could produce radiance and to learn that these rays might be invisible. Invisible rays might be whizzing right past us all the time, and we'd never know it. Roentgen's discovery started a wild scramble to search for other naturally produced rays emitted by different metals. Only two types of natural radiation were found: fluorescence and phosphorescence.

Then an aging Parisian scientist accidentally stumbled onto a new kind of radiation flowing from a sample of uranium in his desk drawer. He shared this mysterious find with Marie Curie. After five years of hard work, she had discovered two new elements, discovered radioactivity, proved that an atom was not the smallest thing in the universe, and opened the door to the atomic age.

Readers Theatre

Characters

Narrator

Jeannette Reme. The 35-year-old wife of a biology professor, she is a good friend of Marie's and sometimes helps her sift and sort her samples.

Charles Reme. A 40-year-old biology professor. He's very droll, hard to excite, and skeptical, even a bit sarcastic.

Pierre Curie. Marie's 34-year-old husband. A college professor and dreamer.

Monsieur Becquerel. Older Parisian scientist, now in his sixties. Very excitable.

Marie Curie. A 29-year-old graduate student. She's practical, hardworking, and pragmatic.

Staging

Figure 11.1. Suggested placement of readers for *A Glowing Discovery*.

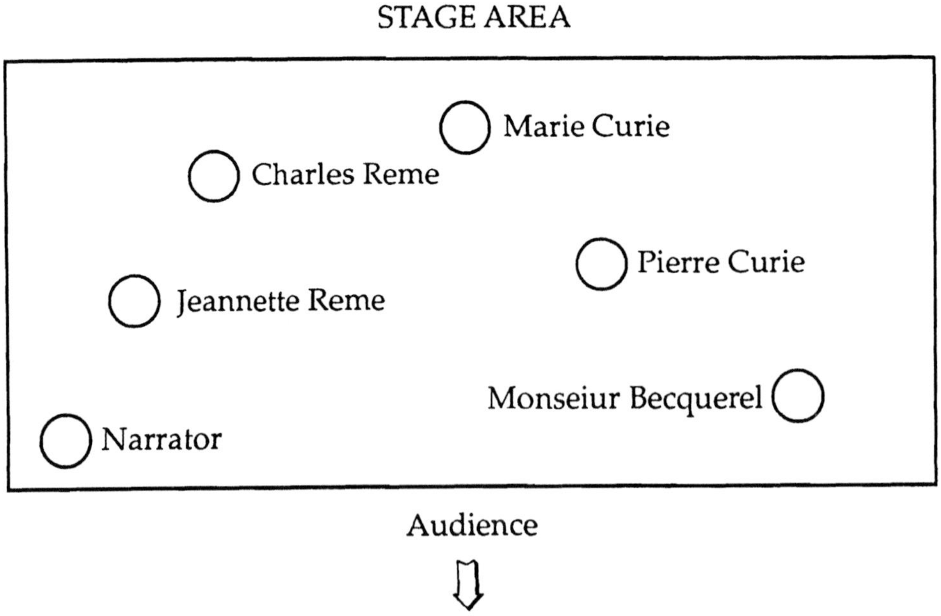

STAGE AREA

○ Marie Curie

○ Charles Reme

○ Pierre Curie

○ Jeannette Reme

Monseiur Becquerel ○

○ Narrator

Audience
⇩

From *Great Moments in Science: Experiments and Readers Theatre.* © 1996. Teacher Ideas Press. (800) 237-6124.

A Glowing Discovery

JEANNETTE:

Isn't it dark enough yet?

REME:

You know the Curies. They won't open the doors 'till we've all frozen to death.

JEANNETTE:

I'm cold *now*. Can't we start the tour?

NARRATOR:

A gray Paris afternoon had faded into a damp February 1901 twilight. Gas lamps glowed to life through countless city windows. A growing line of eager university professors and students again snaked across the frozen campus grass. At the head of this long, expectant line stood a dilapidated shack.

JEANNETTE:

Tell me again what makes the little vases glow.

REME:

They're "test tubes," not vases. And it's some chemical compounds of that new element, radium, that Marie discovered.

JEANNETTE:

But why do they glow?

REME: (*With a shrug*)

Don't ask me. I'm a biologist. I don't know chemistry. Marie calls it "radioactivity." Ask her.

JEANNETTE:

I did. But she went on and on about subatomic emissions, formulas, and chemical names. It might as well have been Greek.

REME:

That's physicists for you. All foreign-sounding mumbo jumbo. They're not practical like biologists.

From *Great Moments in Science: Experiments and Readers Theatre.* © 1996. Teacher Ideas Press. (800) 237-6124.

NARRATOR:

By now everyone at the university knew. Marie Curie had found some new metal buried in a ton of dirt borrowed from Czechoslovakia. And this new metal glowed! Not like a fluorescent glow. This new metal glowed all on its own, even at night, a soft, ethereal, fairy-like glow.

Twenty-nine-year-old Marie Curie and her 34-year-old professor husband, Pierre, had worked, strained, and struggled in this dilapidated shack for three years to isolate the new metal, radium.

PIERRE:

I still can't believe three years of our lives have been spent in this dump.

MARIE: (*Laughing*)

It *is* pretty dismal.

PIERRE:

Was dismal, until you created your radium-salt lights. (*After a slight pause*) Gad! They're magical, Marie—like fairy lights. No wonder everyone wants to see.

NARRATOR:

Marie hung test tubes of the wondrous substance she'd discovered from the ceiling of her shack to brighten it up. As darkness fell each evening, a procession of fascinated visitors marched through the shack, faces and hands bathed in warm pastel glows from the radium and polonium compounds. Yellow from one test tube, a faint pink from the next, luminescent green from a third. Gasps of wonder and delight rose from each person passing slowly through the shed in awe as Marie and Pierre stood proudly by the door.

JEANNETTE: (*Calling to her friend*)

Marie? Marie! The shack is beautiful tonight! It grows more enchanting every day.

REME:

First time I almost froze to death standing in line to see a light.

JEANNETTE:

Admit it, Charles. You're impressed by these lights too.

REME:

Oh, all right. The old shack does glow. But what can you *do* with this stuff?

NARRATOR:

Each night this once ugly shack was transformed into a radioactively glowing fairyland. In 1901 no one knew that radioactivity was deadly. They only knew it was new, it was exciting, and it was beautiful.

From *Great Moments in Science: Experiments and Readers Theatre.* © 1996. Teacher Ideas Press. (800) 237-6124.

JEANNETTE:
These . . . tubes . . . are like nothing the world has ever seen before . . . just incredible.

MARIE: (*Mostly to herself*)
"Incredible." . . . When did I first hear radioactivity described that way? Oh, yes. It was three years ago, and *I* was the one who said it.

NARRATOR:
It had been a warm summer afternoon three years before when the front door of Pierre and Marie Curie's Paris apartment burst open without so much as a knock.

BECQUEREL:
Marie! Pierre! Look at *this*!

MARIE:
Monsieur Becquerel. What is it?

PIERRE: (*Chuckling*)
I guess it is too late to say, "Come in."

NARRATOR:
Monsieur Becquerel, an elderly physicist and good friend of the Curies, stood in the midst of their tiny living room, out of breath and red-faced. As always when Monsieur Becquerel was excited, his little white beard quivered with emotion.

BECQUEREL:
Marie, Pierre. Look at this photograph!

PIERRE:
It looks like a fuzzy white blob in the middle of pure black.

MARIE:
That's a photograph? It's not very good. . . .

BECQUEREL:
What? It's incredible! That's why I'm here.

PIERRE:
Calm down before you burst something, Becquerel. Have a seat.

BECQUEREL: (*With a sigh*)
Thank you.

PIERRE:
Now, what's all this about a photograph?

From *Great Moments in Science: Experiments and Readers Theatre.* © 1996. Teacher Ideas Press. (800) 237-6124.

BECQUEREL:

As you know, I've been experimenting with natural phosphorescence and fluorescence.

NARRATOR:

After Roentgen discovered X-rays in 1895, many European scientists rushed to see if naturally created phosphorescent and fluorescent light rays were similar to Roentgen's electrically created ones.

BECQUEREL:

Anyway, I decided to test uranium ore. Well, no one else had, and so I thought to myself, "Well, why not?" I mean . . .

MARIE: (*Interrupting*)

So what happened?

BECQUEREL:

Ahh, well, that's why I'm here. My piece of uranium ore had been wrapped in thick black paper for several weeks. So there was no possibility of any fluorescent or phosphorescent activity. I was about to start my experiment when two cousins stopped by for a visit. Well, you know how it is. Relatives can talk and talk. . . .

MARIE:

So, what happened?!

BECQUEREL:

Ahh. Well, that's why I'm here. As I left the lab to visit, I placed the uranium—still wrapped—on top of a photographic plate in a drawer no light could have penetrated. Several days later I went back to the uranium. There sat the photographic plate. I really don't even know why I did it. I had no real reason to expect anything. . . .

MARIE:

So what happened?

BECQUEREL:

Ahh, yes. Well, that's why I'm here. I developed that photo plate . . . and here it is.

NARRATOR:

Again Monsieur Becquerel held out the photograph in his hands.

PIERRE:

Uranium did *that* all on its own? Some natural rays came out of your uranium and exposed the photograph? That's just like Roentgen's X-rays, only better.

From *Great Moments in Science: Experiments and Readers Theatre.* © 1996. Teacher Ideas Press. (800) 237-6124.

MARIE:

No. Not like X-rays at all. X-rays are created by a strong electrical current and stop as soon as the current is shut off. Phosphorescence and fluorescence are only created when light strikes a metal. This invisible radiance came from the uranium—all on it's own. How incredible! . . . How incredible . . .

PIERRE:

Marie. I know that look in your eye. You want to study this radioactivity, don't you?

MARIE:

I *have* to.

BECQUEREL:

But how, Marie? Absolutely nothing is known about radioactivity. It's never been studied.

MARIE:

That's the point. It's new. It's exciting. No one has ever studied natural radioactivity. But *I* will. As a start, I'll search for it in every known metal.

PIERRE:

I have a better question, Marie. How will you *pay* for this research? You'll need equipment, samples, and chemicals. We can barely afford to eat.

MARIE: (*Unsure of herself*)

I'll find a way . . . somehow. . . . But I *will* do this study!

NARRATOR:

Marie found a broken-down shed on campus she could use for free. The biology department had abandoned it because of its sagging roof, dirt floor, and leaky walls.

MARIE: (*Enthusiastically*)

Over here, Pierre. I found our new research center!

PIERRE:

This hovel? This dump is worse than my worst nightmares! Marie, how can we work here?

MARIE:

Cheaply.

NARRATOR:

The thrilling rush of a new idea quickly turned into the drudgery of long, hard work.

From *Great Moments in Science: Experiments and Readers Theatre.* © 1996. Teacher Ideas Press. (800) 237-6124.

JEANNETTE:

Marie! How is it going?

MARIE:

Slowly. It's taken us six months just to test all 78 known elements.

JEANNETTE:

Why did it take so long?

MARIE:

Look at where we have to work. I have to stop every time it rains because the walls leak like sieves. Besides, most of our time was spent searching for, and begging for, tiny samples of the many elements we couldn't afford to buy.

JEANNETTE:

And? . . . What have you found?

MARIE:

Only two are radioactive: Becquerel's uranium and thorium.

JEANNETTE:

Now what?

MARIE:

I'm not sure. I still have a dozen samples to test. Then we'll try to learn something about radioactivity from uranium. It's easier to get than thorium.

JEANNETTE:

But what's so interesting about invisible rays that pop out of a substance?

MARIE:

Two things, Jeannette. First, they radiate out all on their own. They're the first thing discovered in our natural world to do that. Second, they seem to come from *inside* the uranium atom itself!

JEANNETTE:

So?

MARIE:

So?! Jeannette, what is the smallest thing in the universe?

JEANNETTE:

Everyone knows that, Marie. It's the atom.

From *Great Moments in Science: Experiments and Readers Theatre.* © 1996. Teacher Ideas Press. (800) 237-6124.

MARIE:

But, if radioactive rays come from *inside* the uranium atom, then these rays, and maybe other particles inside an atom, have to be smaller!

JEANNETTE: (*Amazed*)

You mean you, a mere graduate student, might disprove all the greatest minds of science and show that the atom is not the smallest thing in the world?

MARIE:

Pretty exciting, huh?

JEANNETTE:

Wow! What's the next sample to test?

MARIE:

You saw that big dirt bin outside? It's a weak uranium ore from eastern Europe called pitchblende. That one's next.

JEANNETTE:

I'll stay and help.

NARRATOR:

With sieves, chemicals, washes, and a huge boiling cauldron, the two women steadily sifted out the nonmetal elements of their pitchblende sample. Using chemical tests, Marie determined that it contained no thorium and only trace amounts of uranium.

MARIE:

Now to measure its radioactivity.

JEANNETTE:

How?

MARIE:

With that electrometer on the counter.

NARRATOR:

After carefully measuring radioactivity from this sample, Marie frowned.

MARIE:

That can't be right.

JEANNETTE:

What's wrong?

From *Great Moments in Science: Experiments and Readers Theatre*. © 1996. Teacher Ideas Press. (800) 237-6124.

MARIE:
I must have made a mistake. This radioactivity reading is way too high for the amount of uranium I measured.

JEANNETTE:
So what do we do?

MARIE: (*After a long sigh*)
We start over and do it all again.

BECQUEREL:
Marie, I thought I'd find you here. Hello, Mrs. Reme. Why the long faces?

MARIE:
I've—we've—retested this pitchblende six times—six! Every time I get the same massive radioactivity reading. But it's many times too high for the trace of uranium I measure. A whole day—wasted.

BECQUEREL:
Very mysterious.

MARIE:
And I have no idea what I'm doing wrong.

BECQUEREL:
Perhaps Pierre will know when he comes to the shack after class.

PIERRE: (*After a pause*)
Why so glum, Marie?

MARIE:
I can't make this sample work. Massive radioactivity, but only a trace of uranium.

BECQUEREL:
Quite a mystery.

JEANNETTE:
It's really frustrating to waste so much time and effort.

PIERRE:
Perhaps, Marie, you didn't make a mistake.

MARIE: (*Angrily*)
Then how do you explain the radioactivity?

From *Great Moments in Science: Experiments and Readers Theatre.* © 1996. Teacher Ideas Press. (800) 237-6124.

PIERRE:

Something other than uranium.

MARIE:

But what? We tested all known elements and only uranium and thorium showed radioactivity.

PIERRE:

Exactly. "What" is the question.

NARRATOR:

Marie's mouth dropped open, and her face began to glow. She trembled with excitement.

JEANNETTE:

What is it, Marie?

MARIE:

Our tests weren't wrong, Jeannette. There has to be something *else* in this pitchblende.

JEANNETTE:

But what?

MARIE:

A new element. We've discovered a new, radioactive element!

NARRATOR:

Marie Curie had stumbled upon the greatest scientific prize of all: the discovery of a new chemical element in the makeup of the earth.

BECQUEREL:

To suspect the presence of a new element is one thing. To actually find that new element and prove it to be different from all others is quite another.

PIERRE:

Especially when all we have is a broken-down shed and one ton of donated pitchblende.

JEANNETTE:

What will you do?

MARIE:

Simple. We'll separate every known metal in our pitchblende. Whatever is left at the end and is radioactive should be our new mystery element.

BECQUEREL:

Humph. She calls that simple?

From *Great Moments in Science: Experiments and Readers Theatre.* © 1996. Teacher Ideas Press. (800) 237-6124.

NARRATOR:

They had no money for lab equipment and so used a large, borrowed iron cauldron to boil solutions of pitchblende. This they had to do outside; summer or winter; heat, rain, or snow, since they had no other way to vent the noxious fumes that rose up off the bubbling cauldron. Marie spent many days mixing that boiling mass with a long iron rod almost as tall as she was until her arms felt more leaden than the stir rod. Between aching groans she often giggled:

MARIE: *(Laughing)*

I must look just like a witch of old, hunched over a bubbling cauldron.

JEANNETTE:

Why's it taking so long, Marie?

MARIE:

There may only be a few specks of this new radioactive element in this whole ton of pitchblende, and those may be hidden, locked in some chemical compound.

JEANNETTE:

Still, you've been working two years now.

MARIE: *(With a sigh)*

It's this shed, Jeannette. Every test I've tried this week has been ruined by contamination from leaking rain water, or by leaves, dirt, and dust that swirled in through the cracks in the shed walls. Every time I have to throw the sample away and start over.

JEANNETTE:

Why don't you get a better lab?

MARIE:

We have no money for a better lab.

NARRATOR:

What should have taken weeks, dragged into long months because of their dismal working conditions. Finally, in her third year of work, Marie's ton of pitchblende gave up its secrets. Marie had found not one, but *two* new radioactive elements: polonium, named after Marie's native Poland, and radium, so named because it was by far the most radioactive element ever discovered.

REME:

And that's when she discovered that radium compounds glowed. As Marie isolated more and more of these beautiful, radioactive metals, she began to hang test tubes of radium salts around the shed to brighten the dumpy hovel. I, for one, was glad to see Marie do something practical with the stuff after all the work it took to find it.

From *Great Moments in Science: Experiments and Readers Theatre.* © 1996. Teacher Ideas Press. (800) 237-6124.

JEANNETTE:

Soon others noticed a bewitching glow spilling out of the Curies' shed, washing the drab winter snows in rich pastel sheens.

REME:

Friends began to gather, standing spellbound in the wondrous light. And then long evening lines started, and everyone wanted a peek into Marie and Pierre's enchanted castle.

NARRATOR:

For a time, Marie Curie's incredible discoveries were almost lost in the magical glow of her radioactive lanterns. Still, that one ton of pitchblende led Marie and Pierre Curie to two monumental discoveries. First, they found two, new, naturally radioactive elements.

Second, they shattered the belief that the atom was the smallest thing in the universe. If radioactive rays came from *within* an atom, there had to be something else inside the atom, something smaller. Marie's discovery cracked open the door to our whole atomic age of nuclear power, nuclear medicine, and nuclear weapons. But that, of course, is another story.

Related Experiments

Here is a series of simple experiments you can do that accomplish the same kind of chemical separation Marie Curie used during her discoveries. These experiments will help you understand both the work of the Curies and the scientific concepts involved.

Necessary Equipment

Each group of four to six students will need:

- One bucket

- A sifting screen (window screens are about the right mesh size)

- Fifteen coffee filters

- One large glass beaker with lid (a coffee pot with a lid or a large jar with a lid will do)

- A scale capable of measuring weights and weight changes of less than one ounce

- Half a dozen small glass bowls or dishes

- One microscope capable of detecting microscopic organisms

- One hair dryer and old newspaper for drying

- One hammer and large, heavy cloth for rock pulverization

- One turkey baster

- Safety goggles

- One butter knife to scrape samples into test dishes

- Dishwashing detergent

- Masking tape and a pen

- Vinegar (slightly diluted)

- One strong magnet

- One ultraviolet ("black") light

From *Great Moments in Science: Experiments and Readers Theatre.* © 1996. Teacher Ideas Press. (800) 237-6124.

➤ *Prospecting for Hidden Treasure*

What You'll Investigate: Marie Curie began her experiments with a one-ton pile of dirt and rock and asked the question, "What's in here? What is this dirt made of?" You'll do the same. Only you will use a modest shovelful of dirt, gravel, sand, and rock you scoop from near your school.

Marie used an intricate, complex, and often dangerous series of physical and chemical processes to separate out each individual chemical element in her pitchblende. On a more limited—and safer—scale, you will do the same. You will not be able to isolate each metal and chemical element. But you will be able to make some important discoveries about what either is, or is not, in your shovelful of dirt. More importantly, you will gain a feeling for the arduous process of chemical separation, and begin to see why it took Marie Curie several years to sift through her ton of borrowed dirt.

The Setup: Avoiding heavily vegetated areas, find an area to collect a shovelful of dirt. Seek out areas with a variety of rocks, shale, grit, shell, and sand as well as dirt, or soil.

Each group should pre-weigh their bucket and then collect one shovelful of dirt, including as rich a variety of inorganic material as they can find. Again weigh the bucket with the dirt sample to obtain the weight of the collected sample.

First you will sort your dirt sample to conduct a physical inventory. Then you'll dry it to remove water and conduct a much finer sifting by particle size and density before beginning chemical analysis.

What to Do, Part 1 (Physical Inventory):

1. Sort rocks and pebbles, dirt and sand, and organic material (roots, leaves, sticks, twigs, and living organisms) into separate piles. Sift your sample through a coarse screen (like a window screen) for this process. Weigh each pile and record this general makeup of your original dirt sample.

2. Use a microscope to examine half a dozen small samples from the dirt pile to search for microscopic organisms. In this experiment you will not be able to separate these organisms from inorganic dirt. Still, it is worth even qualitatively determining whether such organisms are present and in what quantity. Record your findings on the sheet where you are listing the composition of your dirt sample. See if your library has directions for a process to collect and separate these organic organisms from inorganic dirt.

3. Spread your dirt and organic piles on newspaper and carefully dry, using a hair dryer and then allowing the samples to dry out for several days. Now re-weigh each pile. Record this dry weight and calculate the weight of water that evaporated from your sample. Record this water content as one of the major components of your sample. You may now discard the organic matter. It contains carbon, oxygen, nitrogen, and other trace elements but nothing of great interest to this analysis.

4. Finally, you must crush, or pulverize, the rocks and pebbles in your sample so that elements and minerals locked inside the rock will respond to the tests you will conduct. To do this, wear safety goggles and place each rock under a large, heavy cloth before using a hammer to break the rock into a pile of fine-grained particles. The cloth prevents small chips and flecks from flying away, and will prevent both injury from flying particles and experimental inaccuracies. The one grain of your target element might be found in a single particle; none can be lost.

5. Your remaining sample now contains dried dirt, pulverized rock, sand, ground shell, grit, and other unknown materials. You must sort this sample by grain size before continuing.

   Thoroughly mix this sample to ensure that each component is evenly spread throughout. Place about one-quarter of your total sample in a large glass beaker or jar. Be sure this sample fills the beaker no more than one-quarter full.

6. Add water so that the beaker is about three-quarters full, and seal it. Thoroughly stir, shake, and agitate the beaker so that all the sample material is suspended in the water column.

7. Set the beaker down and let the suspended material slowly settle. Heavier, more dense grains will settle first. Lighter material will hold in suspension longer. In this way the sample will sort itself with heavier particles settling to the bottom, and progressively lighter material forming layers after layer on top. After 24 hours the water should be virtually clear, and all material should have settled to the bottom. There will be three exceptions:

   a. Some material might have gone into *solution*. That is, some elements might have chemically bonded with water molecules to form aqueous compounds. These will never settle to the bottom of the beaker. There are chemical tests you can perform to detect such compounds. See if you can find information on *"water soluble"* elements and how to detect their presence.

   b. Some material might float on the water's surface. Make sure this material isn't being held at the surface by adding a drop or two of dishwashing liquid to break surface tension. Any material remaining on the surface is lighter (less dense) than water. Search the library for information on common materials that are lighter than water and see if any are present in your sample.

   c. Some very light particles might still be in suspension, or physically held in the water column. A "cloudy" look to the water is a good sign that suspended material is still present.

Note the presence of still-suspended and floating material on the sheet listing your sample's composition. Now you're ready to conduct tests on the various layers of settled material at the bottom of this beaker.

From *Great Moments in Science: Experiments and Readers Theatre.* © 1996. Teacher Ideas Press. (800) 237-6124.

What to Do, Part 2 (Chemical Assessment):

1. Use a turkey baster to suck up small samples from the various layers in your beaker. While the number of layers in your specific sample may vary, a good general plan is to conduct each of the following three tests on the following five layers: floating material, suspended material, fine-grained material from the top layer of the beaker's sediment, medium-grained material from the middle of the sediment, and coarse material from the very bottom of the beaker.

    Surface floating material may be skimmed from the beaker. Each of the other layers must be carefully sucked up into a turkey baster. Expel most of the air from the baster and slowly work its tip into the layer you want to sample. Remember, any rapid movement will re-stir the top sediments and force you to delay until they resettle.

2. Once the baster's tip is in the layer you want to collect, carefully suck up a small amount of material and lift the baster out of the beaker. Expel this material into a coffee filter and let the water drip through into a sink. Remember, you need three samples from each layer (one for each of the following three chemical tests) so keep them as small as practical.

3. Once all free water has drained through the filter, use a butter knife to scrape the sample into a small glass dish. Write the layer and test on a strip of masking tape and stick it onto the side of this dish.

4. Your first assessment will be to detect the presence of calcium. This is an indicator that your sample contained chalk, or limestone. This test is conducted with a mild acid. You will use vinegar. Pour enough dilute vinegar over the sample in the glass dish to cover the sample particles.

5. Gently stir to expose the entire sample to this acid. Carefully observe the dish for the formation of bubbles. Bubbles indicate carbon dioxide gas freed when the acid broke down calcium carbonate into a calcium salt and CO_2 gas. Record whether or not you detected calcium in the sample from that particular layer.

6. Repeat this test with samples from each of the five layers from your beaker.

What to Do, Part 3 (Ultraviolet Assessment):

Most minerals become luminescent when struck by ultraviolet light. It is by far the easiest test for the presence of minerals in your crushed rock samples. Again you will test samples from each of the five layers in your beaker.

1. Carefully extract each sample, remove water with a coffee filter, and dry the sample with a hair dryer. Spread the sample into a thin layer and expose it to an ultraviolet light. Watch for any fluorescent glow from mineral flecks in your sample. It will help to darken the room and turn the light on and off several times to be able to detect a faint glow from

From *Great Moments in Science: Experiments and Readers Theatre.* © 1996. Teacher Ideas Press. (800) 237-6124.

minute mineral particles. Also search for any particles that continue to glow after the ultraviolet light has been turned off. This indicates the presence of phosphorous. (We have all seen stars and T-shirts that glow in the dark. Phosphorous is the element that emits this glow.)

2. Record your findings for the sample from each layer. That is, record whether or not you detected minerals and phosphorous.

What to Do, Part 4 (Magnetic Assessment):

Magnetic fields affect iron. This test will detect the presence of that metal in your sample.

1. Collect and dry a sample from each layer of your beaker as described above.

2. Spread each sample into a thin layer and slowly pass a strong magnet over the sample. Did any particle move? Such movement would indicate the presence of iron. The greater the movement, the greater the amount of iron present.

What's Going On?—Sources of Error: Did you detect *anything* in your dirt sample? If you did, wonderful! If not, does that mean you made an error? Repeat the tests with another quarter of your original sample. Would you expect to get the same results? Would you be surprised if your results were different? What would that mean? How many repeat samples would you need to test to be sure you had accurately analyzed your original sample?

Can you see where misassessment or misdiagnosis could enter this process? How might you prevent or minimize it?

What to Observe: You have analyzed water content and organic content of your original sample, have determined floating material and long-term suspended material, have weighed rock and dirt content, and have chemically searched for the presence of calcium, minerals, phosphorous, and iron. Which of these did you find?

Did you detect any stratification of these elements? Was all iron in the beaker's bottom layers? Was calcium found in higher (lighter) layers? Did you detect anything in the floating or long-term suspended material? How did rock and dirt settle out in the bottom of the beaker? How does that compare with the distribution of elements you detected?

What has this analysis shown you about the composition of your dirt sample?

Questions to Ask Yourself: You performed an initial coarse separation, did one check for the presence of minerals, and tested for calcium and iron. Can you imagine having to isolate and quantify every known element in your dirt sample? Can you envision how many separate samples you would have to use or the detailed record keeping you would have to employ? Does this give you a better appreciation for Marie Curie's painstaking work to isolate her two unknown elements? Do you see why it took her a long time?

See if you can find tests for other elements in the library. Which would be of greater interest—metals or nonmetals?

From *Great Moments in Science: Experiments and Readers Theatre.* © 1996. Teacher Ideas Press. (800) 237-6124.

Bridges to Books

This story deals with one aspect of our understanding of the physical world around us. You can learn much more about these concepts in your library. The following list gives you key words, concepts, and questions to begin your exploration in a school or public library.

> **Marie Curie** is often considered the greatest female scientist of all time. See what you can find in the library on this remarkable woman and her work. What did she do after she discovered radium? Also see if you can find any listings for her husband and fellow researcher, **Pierre Curie.**

> This story deals with **radioactive elements** and **radioactivity.** What is radioactivity? How many radioactive elements are there? Who first used the word "radioactivity"?

> Four radioactive elements are mentioned in this story: **uranium, radium, polonium,** and **thorium.** See what you can find on these four elements. Which is the most radioactive? Which do we use the most? What do we use it for?

> There are two kinds of nonradioactive natural emissions mentioned in this story: **fluorescence** and **phosphorescence.** What is the difference between these two? What are they? What elements and materials emit them?

References for Further Reading

The following references deal with the major characters, concepts, and processes in this chapter.

Birch, Beverly. *Marie Curie: The Polish Scientist Who Discovered Radium and Its Saving Properties.* Milwaukee, WI: G. Stevens, 1988.

Brandt, Keith. *Marie Curie, Brave Scientist.* Mahwah, NJ: Troll Associates, 1983.

Bryan, Jenny. *Health and Science.* New York: Hampsted Press, 1988.

Bull, Angela. *Marie Curie.* London: Hamilton, 1986.

Conner, Edwina. *Marie Curie.* New York: Bookwright Press, 1987.

Curie, Eve. *Madame Curie.* New York: Doubleday, 1937.

DeLeeuw, Adela. *Marie Curie, Woman of Genius.* New York: Garrard, 1970.

Dunn, Andrew. *Marie Curie.* New York: Bookwright Press, 1991.

Fisher, Leonard. *Marie Curie.* New York: Macmillan, 1994.

Fox, Ruth. *Milestones of Medicine.* New York: Random House, 1985.

Giround, Francoise. *Marie Curie, a Life.* New York: Holms and Meier, 1986.

Grady, Sean. *Marie Curie.* San Diego, CA: Lucent Books, 1992.

Green, Carol. *Marie Curie: Pioneer Physicist.* Chicago: Childrens Press, 1984.

Johnson, Ann. *The Value of Learning: The Story of Marie Curie.* New York: Value of Communications, 1978.

Keller, Mollie. *Marie Curie.* New York: Franklin Watts, 1982.

McGowen, Tom. *Radioactivity: From the Curies to the Atomic Age.* New York: Franklin Watts, 1986.

Montgomery, Mary Ann. *Marie Curie.* Englewood Cliffs, NJ: Silver, Burdette and Ginn, 1990.

Parker, Steve. *Marie Curie and Radioactivity.* New York: HarperCollins, 1992.

Pflaum, Rosalyn. *Grand Obsession: Marie Curie and Her World.* New York: Doubleday, 1989.

Poynter, Margaret. *Marie Curie: Discoverer of Radium.* Hillside, NJ: Enslow, 1994.

Quinn, Susan. *Marie Curie: A Life.* New York: Simon & Schuster, 1995.

Sabin, Louis. *Marie Curie.* Mahwah, NJ: Troll Associates, 1985.

Tames, Richard, *Marie Curie.* New York: Franklin Watts, 1989.

Wymer, Norman. *Inventors. Englewood Cliffs, NJ: Silver, Burdett, 1982.*

Consult your librarian for additional titles.

A Crystal-Clear
View of Science

Dorothy Hodgkin's discovery of the composition of penicillin in 1943

Scientific Background

Imagine the frustration of having a miracle cure in your hands but being unable to use it because it's too difficult and slow to grow or produce. This is exactly where the world found itself in the early 1940s with penicillin.

Alexander Fleming discovered the penicillin mold in 1923. Testing over the next decade confirmed its ability to destroy a wide variety of deadly germs and bacteria. By the mid-1930s, medical science thought it was poised to eliminate much of the world's suffering and disease with this wonder-weapon. But the near impossibility of mass producing the penicillin mold soured bright hopes into bitter disappointment. Only a tiny fraction of the total demand for penicillin could be met by naturally grown supplies. The mold couldn't be synthetically produced because the penicillin molecule proved far too complex for researchers to chemically unravel.

Then the world was plunged into World War II, and battlefield deaths from infection soon outnumbered deaths from enemy bullets. The world needed synthetic penicillin. But how to unlock the structure of the penicillin molecule?

Soon after X-rays were discovered in 1885, it was learned that their extremely small wavelengths could be used to "see" microscopic objects. Work by many researchers during the early twentieth century greatly improved science's ability to use X-rays to peer inside smaller and smaller objects—like molecules. One of these researchers was Dorothy Hodgkin, who specialized in studying the structure of crystals. The molecules in a crystal are lined up in a rigid, regularly repeating pattern. This repetition allowed her to successfully peer into increasingly complex molecules. Then in 1943 the British Army got the idea to see if her methods could unlock the hidden structure of a molecule as complex as penicillin. The world has ever after been a healthier place.

Readers Theatre

Characters

Narrator

Dr. Ernst Chain. Soft-spoken government researcher in his early fifties.

Colonel Jeffrey Stanton. Classic spit-and-polish British Army officer in his mid-thirties. Very proper and pompous.

Dr. Dorothy Hodgkin. Chemistry professor and researcher in her mid-forties. Independent, confident.

Barbara Lowe. Dorothy's 23-year-old research assistant. Serious and duty-oriented.

Staging

Figure 12.1. Suggested placement of readers for *A Crystal-Clear View of Science*.

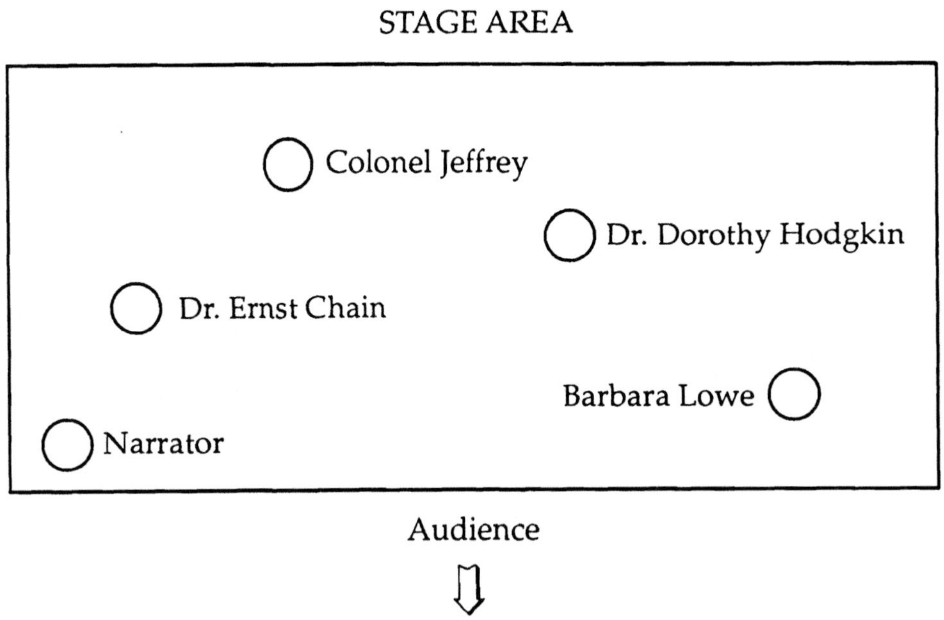

STAGE AREA

○ Colonel Jeffrey

○ Dr. Dorothy Hodgkin

○ Dr. Ernst Chain

Barbara Lowe ○

○ Narrator

Audience
⇩

A Crystal-Clear View of Science

CHAIN:

This way, Colonel Stanton.

STANTON:

What in the blazes? This is no top-notch research facility. This looks like a dusty museum. I said I want top-drawer, first-class.

CHAIN:

First, this *is* a museum. Second, Dr. Hodgkin is the best in the world.

NARRATOR:

A great booming echo reverberated off the cavernous museum walls as Dr. Ernst Chain and Colonel Jeffrey Stanton rushed in out of the cold English rain. The heels of Colonel Stanton's stiff military boots clicked like slow-motion machine-gun fire on the marble floor. Above their heads spectral skeletons of ancient whales and dinosaurs hung from the dimly lit Oxford University museum ceiling.

STANTON:

Well? I haven't got all day. Where is he?

CHAIN:

She.

STANTON:

She?

CHAIN:

Yes. Dr. Hodgkin isn't a "he." She's a "she."

STANTON:

You're asking me to entrust a national top-priority project to a *woman*?

NARRATOR:

Dr. Chain led the colonel to a small side door along one wall of the museum. Opening it, he nodded toward the narrow stairway and dim basement hall beyond.

CHAIN:

Dorothy Hodgkin's office is down here.

STANTON:

Down *here*?! Your "top-flight" researcher is hidden in a dungeon cubbyhole?

From Great Moments in Science: Experiments and Readers Theatre. © 1996. Teacher Ideas Press. (800) 237-6124.

HODGKIN:

Good afternoon, gentlemen. Come in Ernst, Colonel.

STANTON:

Come in *where*?

NARRATOR:

One of five rooms along this little-used basement corridor, Dr. Dorothy Hodgkin's office was a tiny, cramped alcove, hardly big enough for the three of them to sit without moving piles of books and reports and rearranging stacks of test equipment. Dorothy's large brown eyes sparkled with amusement, watching the colonel's face turn up in disgust as he surveyed her jumbled domain. Colonel Stanton stood stiffer than his starched uniform. His thick, red mustache quivered as he spoke in crisp, precise diction.

STANTON:

By gad, this is 1943, Dr. Hodgkin. The war lingers on. Good English lads—soldiers— are dying every day.

HODGKIN:

In battle?

STANTON:

Many, yes. But too many of them die from battlefield infections, rather than German bullets. We need a steady supply of those . . .

NARRATOR:

The colonel fumbled for the right word and then gestured imploringly to Dr. Chain.

CHAIN:

Antibiotics.

STANTON:

Precisely! Antibiotics. We need antibiotics to save our lads. And we need them now!

HODGKIN:

But why come to me? I'm a chemical researcher.

NARRATOR:

Dorothy Hodgkin was a tall, slender woman with short brown hair, and she looked like she sat at a desk two sizes too small for her lanky body.

STANTON:

Ah, precisely. It has everything to do with you and your . . . your X crystals . . . your radio . . . rays. Confound it!

From *Great Moments in Science: Experiments and Readers Theatre.* © 1996. Teacher Ideas Press. (800) 237-6124.

CHAIN:

X-ray diffraction crystallography.

STANTON:

Ah, precisely . . . but exactly what is that, Dr. Hodgkin?

HODGKIN:

We shoot X-rays at the molecules locked in a crystal structure and watch how the various atoms bend, or diffract the X-rays.

STANTON:

I see . . . and this bending does . . . what?

HODGKIN:

It gives us an insight into the structure of the molecule that diffracted the X-ray.

STANTON:

Ah, precisely! Well . . . I'll let Dr. Chain tell you precisely what we want.

CHAIN:

What we need is penicillin, the most powerful known antibiotic. Following Dr. Fleming's original work, I have tried to develop a way of growing penicillin as fast as it is needed. But it grows far too slowly. The problem is we can't synthetically create penicillin in a laboratory, because we don't know what's in it. We don't know the arrangement of atoms in a penicillin molecule, or even which atoms are in there to be arranged.

HODGKIN:

And you're hoping I can find out using X-ray diffraction on penicillin crystals.

STANTON:

Precisely! (*Now unsure*) What precisely is it you do with crystals? My wife collects them, you know.

HODGKIN: (*Laughing*)

Crystals are all around us, Colonel. Table salt is a crystal. So is sugar. So are snowflakes. Aspirin forms crystals. Copper can form some beautiful blue crystals. Some single crystals are as large as two thousand tons. Some are microscopic. If I could get my hands on a penicillin crystal, I believe I could tell you what's in it.

CHAIN:

Just what I hoped you'd say.

From *Great Moments in Science: Experiments and Readers Theatre.* © 1996. Teacher Ideas Press. (800) 237-6124.

NARRATOR:

Dr. Chain opened a briefcase chained to his wrist. He lifted out a small padded case, much like a jewelry box, and slowly opened the lid.

CHAIN: (*Proudly*)

Will these do?

HODGKIN:

Those look like crystals. (*Growing excited and amazed*) Penicillin?

NARRATOR:

Three tiny crystals sat on fluffy cotton wadding. Each shone with the pale milky translucence of pearls. Very carefully Ernst lifted one and set it in Dorothy's outstretched hand.

CHAIN:

The first penicillin crystals ever made. This stuff doesn't crystallize very easily. Took me two months to make a batch crystallize after I ground and boiled it.

NARRATOR:

Colonel Stanton leaned forward and grabbed Dorothy Hodgkin's wrist, his eyes filled with harsh urgency.

STANTON:

This is a national top priority, Dr. Hodgkin. We need the formula for penicillin. And we need it now!

NARRATOR:

Four days later Colonel Stanton's polished heels again clicked across the Oxford museum floor and down the narrow side stairway. As he marched into Dorothy's small office, he heard the whir of fan motors and the whine of test equipment from an even smaller lab beyond. His mustached face poked through the doorway just in time to see Barbara Lowe, Dorothy Hodgkin's somber research assistant, climb a ladder jammed against one wall.

LOWE:

What are the new settings, Dr. Hodgkin?

HODGKIN:

Uhh . . . rotate the crystal 15 degrees clockwise and 30 degrees down, please, Barbara.

STANTON:

Gadzooks. What a jumble! You couldn't cram any more equipment in here if you tried!

From *Great Moments in Science: Experiments and Readers Theatre.* © 1996. Teacher Ideas Press. (800) 237-6124.

NARRATOR:

Stacks of black-boxed test equipment were bolted to the walls and hung from the ceiling. Trays of pungent chemicals climbed up one wall, stacked atop each other. Cables and cords snaked across chairs and were tacked over the door. Two large adding machines perched on the one table, with long tails of used paper trailing out across the floor.

HODGKIN: (*Smiling*)

Come in, Colonel Stanton.

STANTON:

Any progress toward a penicillin formula for us yet?

HODGKIN:

You're just in time to watch us shoot some more film.

STANTON:

Ahh, good show, doctor. I'll catch the light.

LOWE:

Hey! Who turned out the lights?!

STANTON:

Dark and ready to shoot when you are.

LOWE:

Turn on the lights! I'm stuck on top of this ladder and I can't see what I'm doing!

HODGKIN: (*Laughing*)

Sorry, Barbara, I'll get the light.

X-ray film, Colonel, is not sensitive to visible light, only to high-frequency X-rays. We don't normally darken the room.

STANTON:

Ahh, precisely, yes . . . Wait. I don't see any crystals. My wife wanted me to note the size and kind you use so she could buy the same ones. She said that if they were good enough for national research, she wanted to hang some in her window.

HODGKIN: (*Laughing*)

The crystals your wife buys in small crystal shops are only one kind of crystal. A crystal is any solid whose molecules are locked into a regular, repeating pattern and shape. It is that repeating regularity that lets us look inside the crystal's molecules the way we do.

STANTON:

I see. And what, again, do X-rays have to do with it?

From *Great Moments in Science: Experiments and Readers Theatre.* © 1996. Teacher Ideas Press. (800) 237-6124.

LOWE:

The crystal is realigned. I'll reload the film.

HODGKIN:

Thank you, Barbara. (*To Colonel Stanton*) X-rays are smaller than visible light waves. They can see things our eyes and visible light can't see. X-rays can actually see atoms. They greatly extend what we can look at.

LOWE:

Film's loaded. Ready to shoot. I'm coming down.

NARRATOR:

Barbara Lowe fitted a 10-inch-high, 30-inch-long strip of X-ray film onto a semicircular wooden bracket. Dr. Hodgkin had cut a paper-thin sliver of penicillin crystal with surgical saws. It hung in a glass mount right in the center of that circle. The cone-shaped black nozzle of an X-ray gun stood several inches away, aimed at the crystal sliver.

NARRATOR:

Dorothy reached for a large red button mounted on the wall near her.

HODGKIN:

All clear?

LOWE:

Clear and ready!

STANTON: (*Worried*)

Should I duck?

HODGKIN: (*Chuckling*)

You're fine where you are, Colonel.

NARRATOR:

Dorothy hit the button. Motors whirred. There was a loud "Ka-lunk!" Barbara climbed the ladder to retrieve this new piece of exposed film.

STANTON:

That was it? I didn't see anything.

HODGKIN:

Sorry to disappoint you, Colonel. But X-rays are outside the visible spectrum.

LOWE:

I'll have this film developed in a couple of minutes.

From *Great Moments in Science: Experiments and Readers Theatre.* © 1996. Teacher Ideas Press. (800) 237-6124.

NARRATOR:
Barbara developed the film in the chemical trays stacked on one wall.

HODGKIN:
Bring the film straight over here, Barbara. I'll click on the light box.

NARRATOR:
Colonel Stanton peered over the two women's shoulders at the X-ray.

STANTON:
Ahh, pity. Bad shot. Nothing but a maze of fuzzy white splotches on a black background. No pictures of atoms or molecules there. You'll do better next time, I'm sure.

HODGKIN:
I'll measure this time, Barbara. You enter the numbers.

NARRATOR:
Dorothy busily measured the size of and distance between each white speck in this pattern of fuzzy white dots. As she called out each measurement, Barbara hurriedly punched it into the adding machines. Paper tape rolled out across the floor.

STANTON:
You're not going to tell me those blobs *mean* something? . . . What, precisely, can fuzzy blotches possibly tell you?

HODGKIN:
Imagine this, Colonel. Forty people stuffed into the middle of a room. One light somewhere along a wall shines onto those people, casting their shadow across to the far wall. Just looking at a picture of their collective shadow, could you correctly identify and place all 40 people in the room?

STANTON:
Certainly not.

HODGKIN: (*Smiling*)
Let's hope we can do better than you would then. Because that is exactly what we are doing. By rotating that penicillin crystal sliver to get different views of the shadow of its atoms, and by knowing what the X-ray shadow of different individual atoms looks like, we can slowly piece together a map of where the atoms must be in each regular, repeating penicillin molecule, and how they are connected—all just from looking at the repeating shadows of the atoms. I suppose it's like finding only a fingerprint on the wall, and trying to figure out the height, weight, and age of the person who made it.

From *Great Moments in Science: Experiments and Readers Theatre.* © 1996. Teacher Ideas Press. (800) 237-6124.

STANTON:

Egad! You can do that? I mean, you'll really unlock the structure and composition of penicillin from just these fuzzy shadows?

NARRATOR:

It took more than two years of constant work to identify and place the 30 atoms in a basic penicillin molecule and the almost 70 atoms in several of the salts of penicillin. However, that hard-won discovery has saved countless millions of lives and won the 1964 Nobel Prize for Dr. Dorothy Hodgkin. Her work led to a much better understanding of how crystals function and also to the invention of that now commonplace electronic crystal, the transistor. But that is another story.

From *Great Moments in Science: Experiments and Readers Theatre.* © 1996. Teacher Ideas Press. (800) 237-6124.

Related Experiments

Here is a simple experiment you can use to recreate the steps that led Dorothy Hodgkin to her discoveries. This experiment will help you understand both the work of Dr. Hodgkin and the scientific concepts involved.

Necessary Equipment

For each group:

- Three sheets of paper, two at least 18 inches high and 30 inches long and one at least 16 inches square.

For the whole class:

- About 12 three-dimensional objects from 2 to 6 inches high each. Use geometric shapes, balls, crumpled papers, cups, bowls, pitchers, rocks, boxes, folded paper tents, simple sculpture pieces, and so on. Virtually anything will work.

- One or more strong flashlights.

- Sturdy cardboard for the platform and paper support walls.

➤ *Name That Shadow*

What You'll Investigate: Dorothy Hodgkin fired X-rays at molecules and photographed the shadows created by individual atoms. By taking a series of these pictures at different angles, she was able to reconstruct the three-dimensional shape of the molecule and identify each atom in it.

You will use the same general procedure. However, you'll use visible light from a flashlight instead of X-rays because X-ray wavelengths are so small, they would sail straight through many of the objects you will use and not record them at all. Also, rather than recording your images on photographic film, you will draw your shadows on paper. Still, the process of using these images to reconstruct a three-dimensional scene will be virtually the same.

The Setup: Draw a 16-inch diameter circle (8-inch radius) on a piece of cardboard. Build two vertical, perpendicular cardboard support walls 18 inches high and 30 inches wide, each placed three inches behind this circle as shown in figure 12.2, page 218. These walls will be used to support the pieces of paper on which students will trace their shadow drawings. Draw lines extending out from the circle, as shown ("Light Aiming Lines"), to indicate the lines along which the flashlight must be aimed.

From *Great Moments in Science: Experiments and Readers Theatre.* © 1996. Teacher Ideas Press. (800) 237-6124.

Figure 12.2. Setup for creating shadow images.

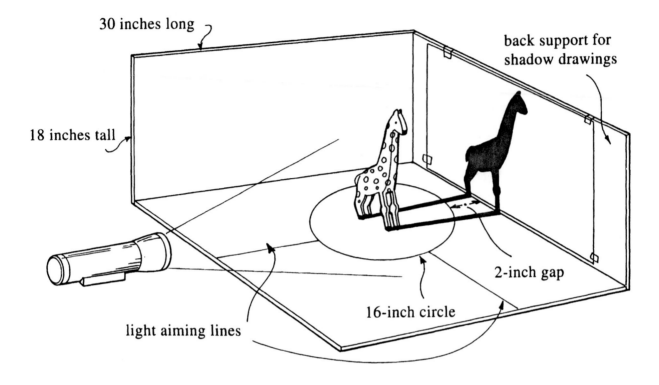

What to Do:

(This experiment should be conducted in small groups. However, when one group is running the experiment, other groups should not watch.)

1. A group selects between five and eight objects. After placing the square piece of paper over the cardboard base circle, they place their chosen objects anywhere within that circle. Try to pick as difficult a setup to decipher as possible, but no stacking!

2. The group tapes their two pieces of paper over the cardboard support walls and labels them "Left" and "Right."

3. With other lights out, the group shines a flashlight at the objects in the circle along one of the Light Aiming Lines. The flashlight should be held level with the base circle and just far enough away from it to shine light across the entire circle.

4. The group traces the outline of the shadows projected from their selected objects on the paper perpendicular to the line of the flashlight. Finally, shade in the shadow areas.

5. Once all shadow lines have been drawn and shaded, the group moves the flashlight ninety degrees and shines it along the second Light Aiming Line, tracing the shadows

From *Great Moments in Science: Experiments and Readers Theatre.* © 1996. Teacher Ideas Press. (800) 237-6124.

of these same objects on this second piece of paper. Remember that it is important to neither touch nor move any of the objects between making these two shadow drawings.

6. Finally, with overhead lights on, the group must trace the actual position of their objects on the paper they placed under the objects and over the cardboard base circle.

7. After all groups have had their turn for the preceding steps, the instructor should collect the maps of actual object placement and have groups exchange complete sets of shadow drawings, with no mixing of drawings.

8. From these two shadow drawings, each group must now figure out the identity and location within the base circle of each object the other group selected.

9. Use the following hints if you are having difficulty:

   a. Each object should appear on both shadow drawings unless a second, larger object is right in line with it along one of the Light Aiming Lines.

   b. The two drawings are at right angles to each other.

   c. Place each shadow drawing in the same relative position it was in when it was drawn. Then put a dot at about where the flashlight had to be for each drawing and draw lines back from the edge of each shadow to that dot.

   d. Where the lines from each shadow drawing for each separate object intersect marks the location of that object in the original circle.

What's Going On?—Sources of Error: This exercise requires slow, careful, and well-planned work, both drawing the shadows, and in recreating a three-dimensional image from those shadows. However, even when the work is performed with care, errors are possible. With only two views to work from, it is possible for some objects to remain hidden behind or in front of others. It is also difficult to differentiate all objects from other, similar ones from only two shadow images. Finally, by having to guess at the original flashlight location, it is possible to err in placing all objects in your solution.

What to Observe: If you know what you are looking for, seemingly meaningless shadow blobs can contain a great amount of information. There were only a dozen different shapes for you to choose. It was probably pretty easy for you to decide which shadows represented which shapes. You can imagine that it would be considerably harder if any shadow could represent any of almost a hundred different kinds of atoms, all of which had the same basic shape and produced shadows that differed in only subtle ways.

Try to imagine the maximum number of shapes you could differentiate in this way. What would make your job easier?

Questions to Ask Yourself: What kind of shapes were easy to decipher? Which were difficult? How many views do you think you would need to unravel a complex molecule of 90 close-packed atoms? How would you decide which views you needed?

From *Great Moments in Science: Experiments and Readers Theatre.* © 1996. Teacher Ideas Press. (800) 237-6124.

Bridges to Books

This story deals with one aspect of our understanding of the physical world around us. You can learn much more about these concepts in your library. The following list gives you key words, concepts, and questions to begin your exploration in a school or public library.

Dorothy Hodgkin was only one of many researchers exploring the properties and uses of crystals in the early twentieth century. See what references you can find on her in the library, but also search for references to other crystallographers (those who study **crystallography**).

What is a **crystal**? How do we use them today? Have you ever seen a crystal? Is there any difference between the crystal glasses used at formal dinners, the crystals you buy for several dollars and hang in windows, and the crystals Dorothy and others use in research? See what your library can tell you about crystals.

Dorothy Hodgkin used **X-rays** in a technique called **X-ray diffraction**. What is an X-ray? Who named them? Who discovered them? Are they naturally occurring rays or are they man-made? What do we use X-rays for today? How different are X-rays from visible light waves or from sound waves?

References for Further Reading

The following references deal with the major characters, concepts, and processes in this chapter.

Balibar, Francoise. *The Science of Crystals*. New York: McGraw-Hill, 1993.

Berry, James. *Exploring Crystals*. New York: Crowell-Collier Press, 1976.

Burke, John. *Origins of the Science of Crystals*. Berkeley, CA: University of California Press, 1966.

Carona, Philip. *Crystals*. New York: Follett, 1971.

Haber, Louis. *Women Pioneers of Science*. New York: Harcourt, Brace, Jovanovich, 1979.

Hammond, C. *Introduction to Crystallography*. New York: Oxford University Press, 1990.

Holden, Alan. *Crystals and Crystallography*. Cambridge, MA: Harvard University Press, 1990

Mercer, Ian. *Crystals*. Cambridge, MA: Harvard University Press, 1990.

Sanders, Lenore. *The Curious World of Crystals*. Englewood Cliffs, NJ: Prentice-Hall, 1974.

Shiels, Barbara. *Winners: Women and the Nobel Prize*. Minneapolis, MN: Dillon Press, 1985.

Stangl, Jean. *Crystals and Crystal Gardens You Can Grow*. New York: Franklin Watts, 1990.

Symes, R.F. *Crystals and Gems*. New York: Alfred A. Knopf, 1991.

Consult your librarian for additional titles.

Index

About the Author

The only West Point graduate ever to become a professional storyteller, Kendall Haven also holds a master's degree in oceanography and spent six years as a senior research scientist for the United States Department of Energy before finding his true passion for storytelling and a different kind of "truth." He now has performed for more than 2 million children and adults in 38 states, and has presented workshops to more than 20,000 teachers on the practical, in-class teaching power of storytelling. Haven has won numerous awards both for his story-writing and for his storytelling. He has become one of the nation's leading advocates for the educational value of storytelling, is director of the National Whole Language Umbrella Storytelling Action Group, and is on the board of directors of the National Storytelling Association.

Haven has published five audiotapes and two picture books of his original stories; created a three-hour high-adventure radio drama for National Public Radio on the effects of watching television that has won five major national awards; and is the author of the extremely popular *Marvels of Science: 50 Fascinating 5-Minute Reads* (Libraries Unlimited, 1994) and *Amazing American Women: 40 Fascinating 5-Minute Reads* (Libraries Unlimited, 1995).

Haven has used his writing talent to create stories for many nonprofit organizations including the American Cancer Society, the Institute for Mental Health Initiatives, several California crisis centers, the Children's Television Resource and Education Center, a regional hospital, and the Child Abuse Prevention Training Center of California.

He lives with his wife and nephew in the rolling Sonoma County grape vineyards of rural northern California.

More to Explore!

From # Teacher Ideas Press

BLAST OFF! Rocketry for Elementary and Middle School Students
Leona Brattland Nielsen

You'll launch excitement in the classroom with this complete teaching package on rocketry. It's packed with fascinating facts and motivational activities! **Grades 4–8.**
viii, 109p. 8½x11 paper ISBN 1-56308-438-4

FRANTIC FROGS AND OTHER FRANKLY FRACTURED FOLKTALES FOR READERS THEATRE
Anthony D. Fredericks

Use these wacky stories to encourage reading or as a showcase for students to learn how to write their own scripts. More than 20 reproducible satirical scripts grab the attention of even the most restless or reluctant learner. Learning sneaks up on them while they're laughing! **Grades 4–8.**
xiii, 123p. 8½x11 paper ISBN 1-56308-174-1

MARVELS OF SCIENCE: 50 Fascinating 5-Minute Reads
Kendall Haven

Ideal for both read-alouds and reading assignments, these 50 short stories take just minutes to read but amply illustrate scientific principles and the evolution of science through history. **Grades 3** _and up._
xxii, 238p. paper ISBN 1-56308-159-8

STAGINGS: Short Scripts for Middle and High School Students
Joan Garner

These original, skill-specific scripts were designed around the guidelines for the theatre discipline of the National Standards for Arts Education. Simple and affordable to produce, the nine plays make up this resource that _Booklist_ calls "A must purchase for drama and literature studies." **Grades 6–12.**
xiii, 233p. 8½x11 paper ISBN 1-56308-343-4

STEPPING STONES TO SCIENCE: True Tales and Awesome Activities
Kendall Haven

Science comes to life for young students in these 13 action-packed stories! Historically accurate accounts combine with extension activities to teach young learners the basic skills and procedures of science. **Grades 2–5.**
xi, 155p. 8½x11 paper ISBN 1-56308-516-X

¡TEATRO! Hispanic Plays for Young People
Angel Vigil

Actors and audience members experience and learn more about Hispanic culture and traditions of the American Southwest with these 14 reproducible scripts. **Grades 3–9.**
xviii, 169p. 8½x11 paper ISBN 1-56308-371-X

For a FREE catalog or to place an order, please contact:

Teacher Ideas Press
Dept. B58 · P.O. Box 6633 · Englewood, CO 80155-6633
1-800-237-6124, ext. 1 · Fax: 303-220-8843 · E-mail: lu-books@lu.com

Check out the TIP Web site!
www.lu.com/tip